Sarastro GmbH

Technischer Betriebswirt - Formelsammlung
Betriebswirtschaftliche Prüfungsteile

Sarastro

Sarastro GmbH (Hrsg.)

Technischer Betriebswirt - Formelsammlung
Betriebswirtschaftliche Prüfungsteile

1. Auflage | ISBN: 978-3-86471-323-1

Erscheinungsort: Paderborn, Deutschland

Erscheinungsjahr: 2015

Formelsammlung für die Vorbereitung der betriebswirtschaftlichen Teile auf den Abschluss des Technischen Betriebswirts.

Vorwort

Die vorliegende Formelsammlung dient dem Einsatz in der Erwachsenenbildung. Es dient Kursteilnehmern bei der Prüfungsvorbereitung und - nach Absprache mit dem jeweils zuständigen Prüfungsamt - auch während der Prüfung.

Das betriebswirtschaftliche Geschehen ist vielfach geprägt von Formeln und Kennzahlen. Ähnlich wie in den Naturwissenschaften erscheint dadurch der Einstieg in das Fachgebiet Außenstehenden aber häufig als kompliziert und kryptisch. Auch später haben viele Lernende das Problem, sich Formeln und Kennzahlen zu merken und die Definition der Kennzahlen im Gedächtnis zu behalten. Genau hier setzt die Formelsammlung an: In diesem Buch werden die wichtigsten betriebswirtschaftlichen Formeln und Kennzahlen gebündelt und leicht verständlich dargestellt. Nach Absprache mit dem örtlichen Prüfungsamt eignet sich die Formelsammlung auch als Nachschlagewerk während der Prüfung. Seitens des Herausgebers, der selbst jahrelang in Prüfungsausschüssen diverser IHK und des DIHK verantwortlich war, bestehen hier keine Bedenken. Leider kann aufgrund unterschiedlicher regionaler Anwendung keine Garantie gegeben werden, dass alle Aufsichten die Formelsammlung zulassen.
Bitte vergewissern Sie sich deswegen vorab darüber.
Für konstruktive Kritik und Anregungen sind das Autorenteam, der Herausgeber sowie der Verlag stets dankbar. Bitte schreiben Sie uns an carsten.padberg@sarastro-verlag.de

Paderborn, 2015
Prof. Dr. Carsten Padberg (Herausgeber)

Inhalt

Allgemeine Erfolgskennzahlen

Die **Produktivität** betrachtet in Mengen- oder physikalischen Einheiten das Produktionsergebnis des Unternehmens.

$$Produktivität = \frac{Outputmenge}{Inputmenge}$$

Arbeitsproduktivität:

$$Arbeitsproduktivität = \frac{Produktionsergebnis}{Arbeitsstunden}$$

oder

$$Arbeitsproduktivität = \frac{Produktionsergebnis}{Arbeitskräfte}$$

Die **Wirtschaftlichkeit** gibt an, wie hoch der Ertrag im Verhältnis zum Aufwand ist. Ist die Wirtschaftlichkeit genau 1, sind gerade die Kosten gedeckt, bleibt die Wirtschaftlichkeit kleiner als 1, arbeitet das Unternehmen defizitär.

$$Wirtschaftlichkeit = \frac{wertmäßiger\ Output}{wertmäßiger\ Input} = \frac{Ertrag}{Aufwand}$$

Bei der **Rentabilität** wird der erzielte Gewinn in Relation zum eingesetzten Kapital gesetzt. Die zwei wichtigsten Kennzahlen sind:

Mit der **Eigenkapitalrentabilität** gibt man die Verzinsung des Eigenkapitals an.

$$Eigenkapitalrentabilität = \frac{Gewinn}{Eigenkapital} * 100$$

Die **Umsatzrentabilität:** gibt das Verhältnis zwischen dem erzielten Gewinn und der Höhe des Gesamtumsatzes. Sie zeigt, wieviel Gewinn mit jedem umgesetzten Euro erwirtschaftet wird.

$$Umsatzrentabilität = \frac{Gewinn}{Umsatz} * 100$$

Vorsicht bei den Rentabilitäten ist bei der Gewinndefinition angebracht. Üblicherweise werden hier bilanzielle Werte herangezogen (Der Jahresüberschuss als Nachsteuergewinn).

Betriebsleistung:

Auf Basis der Betriebsleistung lassen sich nachfolgend weitere Erfolgskennzahlen berechnen. Die Betriebsleistung errechnet sich folgendermaßen:

Umsatzerlöse
± Bestandsveränderungen an Halb- und Fertigfabrikaten bzw. unfertigen Arbeiten
+ Skontoerträge
+ sonstige ordentliche Erträge
+ aktivierte Eigenleistungen
=Betriebsleistung

Material bzw. Warenintensität:

$$Material - bzw.\ Warenintensität =$$

$$\frac{Wareneinsatz\ bzw.\ Materialeinsatz}{Betriebsleistung} * 100$$

$$Wareneinsatz = Anfangsbestand + Zukäufe - Endbestand$$

Personalintensität:

$$Personalintensität = \frac{Personalkosten}{Betriebsleistung} * 100$$

Fremdkapitalzinsen in der Betriebsleistung:

$$Fremdkapitalzinsen\ in\ der\ Betriebsleistung =$$

$$\frac{Fremdkapitalzinsen}{Betriebsleistung} * 100$$

Abschreibungen in der Betriebsleistung:

$$Abschreibungen\ in\ der\ Betriebsleistung =$$

$$\frac{Abschreibungen}{Betriebsleistung} * 100$$

Nutzwertanalyse:

$$Teilwertnutzen = Gewicht * Bewertung$$

$$Gesamtnutzenwert = \Sigma\ Teilnutzwerte$$

Finanzierung

Berechnung des **Kapitalumschlags** und dem daraus folgenden **Kapitalbedarf** eines Unternehmens

$Kapitalumschlagshäufigkeit\ pro\ Jahr\ bei\ Vorräten =$

$$\frac{360\ Tage}{durchschnittliche\ Lagerdauer}$$

$Kapitalumschlagshäufigkeit\ pro\ Jahr\ bei\ Forderungen =$

$$\frac{360\ Tage}{durchschnittliche\ Forderungsdauer}$$

$$Kapitalbedarf\ bei\ Vorräten = \frac{Umsatz\ p.\,a.}{Lagerumschlagshäufigkeit}$$

$Kapitalbedarf\ bei\ Forderungen =$

$$\frac{Umsatz\ p.\,a.}{Forderungsumschlagshäufigkeit}$$

$Kapitalbedarf =$

$kumulierte\ Ausgaben - kumulierte\ Einnahmen$

$$Kapitalbedarf =$$

$$\emptyset\ Wochenausgaben * Zahl\ der\ Wochen\ bis\ Produktionsbeginn$$

$$Kapitalbedarf =$$

$$\emptyset\ Monatsausgaben * Zahl\ der\ Monate\ bis\ Produktionsbeginn$$

$$Gesamtkapitalbedarf =$$

$$Anlagenkapitalbedarf + Umlaufkapitalbedarf$$

$$Umlaufkapitalbedarf =$$

$$(Kapitalbindungsdauer - Lieferantenziel)$$
$$* \emptyset\ Auszahlungen\ pro\ Tag$$

Zur **Effektivzinsberechnung** wird folgende Formel genutzt:

$$Effektiver\ Jahreszins =$$

$$\frac{Kredtikosten}{Nettodarlehensbetrag} * \frac{24}{Laufzeit\ in\ Monaten + 1} * 100$$

Lieferantenkredit

$$Effektiver\ Jahreszins\ in\ \% = \frac{Skontosatz * 360}{Zahlungsziel - Skontofrist}$$

Langfristige Kreditfinanzierung

Zur Berechnung der durchschnittlichen jährlichen Finanzierungskosten eines Schuldners wird folgende Formel benötigt:

$$K = \frac{j\ddot{a}hrliche\ Auszahlungen}{erhaltene\ Kapitalbetrag} * 100$$

Zur Berechnung der durchschnittlichen jährlichen Finanzierungskosten eines Gläubigers wird folgende Formel benötigt:

$$K = \frac{j\ddot{a}hrliche\ Einzahlungen}{Auszahlungsbetrag} * 100$$

effektive Finanzierungskosten des Schuldners:

lineare Interpolation:

$$(K_o - K_E) - \sum_{t=1}^{n} \frac{Z_{N_t} + K_t}{\left(1 + i_{eff}\right)^t} - \frac{T_n}{\left(1 + i_{eff}\right)^n} = 0$$

effektive Finanzierungskosten des Gläubigers:

lineare Interpolation:

$$-K_0 + \sum_{t=1}^{n} \frac{Z_{N_t} + T_t}{(1 + i_{eff})^t} = 0$$

Gesamtkapitalkosten

$$Eigenkapitalrendite = \frac{Gewinn}{Eigenkapital} * 100$$

$$Fremdkapitalkosten = r_{FK} * (1 - s)$$

r_{FK}: Fremdkapitalrendite
S: Gewinnsteuersatz

Die **Kapitalstrukturanalyse** eines Unternehmens, also das Verhältnis zwischen Eigenkapital und Fremdkapital wird folgendermaßen berechnet.

$$Eigenkapitalquote = \frac{Eigenkapital}{Gesamtkapital}$$

$$Fremdkapitalquote = \frac{Fremdkapital}{Gesamtkapital}$$

Gewichtete Gesamtkapitalkosten - Weighted Average Cost of Capital (WACC):

$$WACC = r_{FK} * (1 - s) * \frac{FK}{GK} + r_{EK} * \frac{EK}{GK}$$

mit

r_{FK}: Fremdkapitalzinssatz
S: Gewinnsteuersatz
r_{EK}: Eigenkapitalrendite

Discounted Free Cash Flow:

$$DFCF = EK + \sum_{t=1}^{T} \frac{FCF_t}{(1 + WACC)^t} - FK$$

Leverage Effekt

$$r_{EK} = r + \frac{Fremdkapital}{Eigenkapital} * (r - r_{FK})$$

r = Gesamtrendite
r_{FK} = Fremdkapitalzinsssatz

Aktienbewertung

Um den **Gewinn** einer Aktie zu berechnen wird folgende Formel genutzt:

$$GewinnPro\ Aktie = \frac{Jahresüberschuss}{Anzahl\ der\ Aktien}$$

Um den aktuellen Aktienkurs in Relation zur Ausschüttung der Aktiengesellschaft (Rendite) zu setzen, berechnet man die **Dividendenrendite**:

$$Dividendenrendite = \frac{Dividende}{Kurs\ pro\ Aktie} * 100$$

Um Auskunft darüber geben zu können, ob eine Aktie im Verhältnis zum Unternehmensgewinn ausreichend Gewinn abwirft nutzt man das

Kurs-Gewinn-Verhältnis (KGV):

$$KGV = \frac{Aktienkurs}{Gewinn\ pro\ Aktie}$$

Erstemission von Nennwertaktien:

$$Grundkapital = Nennwert * Anzahl\ der\ Aktien$$

$$Kaptialrücklage =$$

$$(Emissionskurs - Nennwert) * Anzahl\ der\ Aktien$$

$$Eigenkaptial = Grundkapital + Kapitalrücklage$$

Kapitalerhöhung bei Nennwertaktien:

$$Anzahl\ der\ neuen\ Aktien = \frac{\Delta Grundkapital}{Nennwert}$$

$$Mischkurs = \frac{m_{alt} * K_{alt} + n * K_{neu}}{m + n}$$

$$Wert\ des\ Bezugsrechts = alter\ Kurs - Mischkurs$$

$$Bezugsrecht = \frac{K_a - K_n}{\frac{m}{n} \mid 1}$$

Bei in Inanspruchnahme des Bezugsrechts kann die Anzahl der neuen Aktien folgendermaßen ermittelt werden:

$$BV = \frac{m}{n}$$

$$BV = \frac{Grundkapital\ der\ Erhöhung}{\Delta Grundkapital}$$

Der Aktionär kann nach der Kapitalerhöhung neue Aktien zu diesem Kurs (Anzahl alte Aktien durch das Bezugsverhältnis) kaufen. Für die neuen Aktien muss er den Mischkurs bezahlen.

Erstemission von Stückaktien:

$$Wert\ je\ Aktie = \frac{Grundkapital}{Anzahl\ der\ Aktien}$$

Im Rahmen der **kurzfristigen Finanzplanung** wird der Liquiditätsstatus für kurze Zeiträume bestimmt.

$$Anfangsbestand + geplante\ Einzahlungen$$
$$-\ geplante\ Auszahlungen$$

Entscheidungskriterium: > 0 freie monetäre Mittel,
Unternehmen ist zahlungsfähig
< 0 liquide Mittel fehlen,
Zahlungsunfähigkeit und
Unterdeckung

Zur Ermittlung der Einzahlungen von Kunden für einzelne Wochen durch Dispositionsziffernverfahren wird folgende Formel verwendet. Dabei kann aber für jeden Kunden nur eine Dispositionsziffer vergeben werden:

$$\bar{t} = \frac{\sum_{i=1}^{n} K_i * t_i}{\sum_{i=1}^{n} K_i}$$

Bilanzkurs einer Aktie:

$Bilanzkurs\ einer\ Aktie =$

$$\frac{Eigenkapital}{gezeichnetes\ Kapital} * Aktiennennbetrag$$

Investitionsrechnung

Die Verwendung der monetären Mittel wird als **Investition** bezeichnet. Sie beginnt mit der Auszahlung in Erwartung späterer monetärer Rückflüsse.

Investitionsformen:
- Sachinvestitionen z.B. Grundstücke, Anlagen
- Finanzinvestitionen z.B. Beteiligungen, Aktien, Forderungen
- Immaterielle Investitionen z.B. Werbung, Ausbildung, F&E, Sozialleistungen

Merkmale von Investitionen
allgemein:
- hoher Anschaffungswert
- häufig zunächst Projektcharakter, deswegen notwendige Planung
- beeinflusst strukturelle Liquidität
- einmalige, zeitpunktgenaue Belastung der Liquidität
- lange Nutzungsdauer
- Auseinanderfallen von Einzahlungen und Auszahlungen
- Fixkosten beeinflussen Gewinn über die Abschreibungen
- Grundlage des technischen Fortschritts

speziell:
- Beitrag zur Gewinnerwirtschaftung und Rentabilität
- Risikounterschiede
- Umkehrbarkeit

Statistische Verfahren

Kostenvergleichsrechnung

Entscheidungskriterium: minimale gesamte durchschnittliche
jährliche Kosten = minimale $\emptyset K_G$

$$\emptyset K_G \ ohne \ Liquidit\ddot{a}tserl\ddot{o}s = \frac{I_0}{n} + \frac{I_0}{2} * i \ + weitere \ \emptyset K_f + \emptyset K_v$$

$$\emptyset K_G \ = \ \emptyset K_f + \emptyset K_v$$

$$\emptyset K_f = \ \emptyset AfA + \ \emptyset Zinsen + \ weitere \ \emptyset K_f$$

$$\emptyset AfA = \frac{I_0}{n}$$

$$\emptyset Zinsen = \frac{I_0}{2} * i$$

$$\emptyset K_G \ mit \ Liquidationserl\ddot{o}s =$$

$$\frac{I_o - L_E}{n} + \frac{I_0 + L_E}{2} * i \ + weitere \ \emptyset K_f + \emptyset K_v$$

$$\emptyset AfA = \frac{I_o - L_E}{n}$$

$$\emptyset Zinsen = \frac{I_0 + L_E}{2} * i$$

Die Kostenvergleichsrechnung eignet sich besonders für eine schnelle und einfache Entscheidungsfindung bezüglich der Kosten. Allerdings werden Erlöse und Gewinne sowie der Zeitfaktor nicht erfasst. Weiterhin werden nur durchschnittliche Kosten berücksichtigt.

Rentabilitätsvergleichsrechnung

Entscheidungskriterium: ØR_{max}
$\text{ØR}_{alt} < \text{ØR}_{neu}$

$$\text{ØRentabilität} = \frac{\text{ØGewinn}}{\text{ØKapitalbindung}} * 100$$

$$\text{ØKapitalbindung} = \frac{I_0 + L_E}{2}$$

$$\text{ØGewinn} = \text{ØErlöse} - \text{ØKosten}$$

Statische Amortisationsrechnung

Entscheidungskriterium:
eine Investition = $\quad \text{AD}_{Investition} <$ vorgegebene AD_{min}
mehrere Investitionen=
AD_{min} UND $\text{AD}_{Investition} <$ vorgegebene AD_{min}

Kumulationsmethode

Jahr	kumulierte Einzahlungen	kumulierte Auszahlungen	Differenz
1 2 3			kum. Einz. < kum. Ausz. kum. Einz. < kum. Ausz. kum. Einz. > kum. Ausz.

$AD =$

Jahr, in dem letztmalig eine negative Differenz erzielt wurde

$$+ \frac{Betrag \; bis \; zu \; 0 \; in \; zweiten \; Jahr}{gesamte \; Erwirtschaftungen \; des \; 2. und \; 3. Jahres}$$

Durchschnittsmethode

- nur anwendbar, wenn E_t - A_t in jedem Jahr gleich sind, d.h. die Nettozahlungsüberschüsse gleich sind

ODER

- nur anwendbar, wenn Einzahlungen - AfA in jedem Jahr gleich sind, d.h. die Gewinne gleich sind

$$AD = \frac{Anschaffungswert}{\emptyset jährlicher \; Rückfluss}$$

$$AD = \frac{I_0}{\emptyset Einzahlungen - \emptyset Auszahlungen} \quad und$$

$$AD = \frac{I_0}{\text{ØGewinn} - \text{ØAfa}}$$

Die dargestellten Formeln eignen sich nicht für eine Wirtschaftlichkeitsberechnung, da keine Aussagen über die gesamte Wirtschaftlichkeit des Unternehmens möglich sind. Ebenso wird die Zeit nach der Wiedererwirtschaftung von I_0 nicht weiter berücksichtigt. Daher sollte die Berechnung der Amortisation nur ergänzend hinzugezogen werden.

Grundsätzlich sind die statistischen Verfahren nicht ganz fehlerfrei, da die Inputgrößen in ihrer zeitlichen Struktur nicht berücksichtigt werden und nur durchschnittlich einbezogen werden. Weiterhin ist es bei einem hohen I_0 Wert nicht möglich, eine solide Entscheidung zu treffen.

Dynamische Verfahren

Durch **Aufzinsen** wird der Endwert (EW) bestimmt. Dabei werden alle geplanten E auf das Ende der Nutzungsdauer (n) aufgezinst und aufsummiert.

$$EW = \sum_{t=1}^{n} E_t (1 + i)^{n-t}$$

Oder

| K_n: Endwert des eingesetzten Kapitals inkl. Zinsen |
| K_0: eingesetztes Kapital vor Verzinsung |

$$K_n = K_0 * (1 + i)^n$$

Durch **Abzinsen** wird der Barwert BW_0 für den Zeitpunkt t_0 bestimmt. Dabei werden alle geplanten E auf den Anfang der Nutzungsdauer abgezinst und aufsummiert.

$$BW = \sum_{t=1}^{n} \frac{E_t}{(1+i)^t}$$

Oder

$$K_0 = K_n * (1+i)^n$$

Die **Kapitalwertmethode** ist auf alle Investitionen anwendbar. Dabei gilt:

- E_0 bis E_n sind geplante Einzahlungen über die Nutzungsdauer n
- A_0 bis A_0 sind geplante Auszahlungen über die Nutzungsdauer n

Der grundlegende Wert ist E_0. Alle Einzahlungen müssen auf diesen Wert diskontiert werden

Entscheidungskriterium: KW > 0
                          Alternative mit KW_{max}

Kapitalwert ohne Liquiditätserlös

in t_0 sind die Einzahlungen = 0
in t_0 sind die Auszahlungen und damit auch die Investionen = 0

$$i = \frac{r}{100} = \frac{Verwertungsgrad\ \%}{100}$$

Der Koeffizient i bzw. der Kalkulationszinssatz r ist die vom Investor subjektiv festgelegte Mindestverwertung. Hierdurch fließt die Risikoberwertung mit in die Berechnung ein. Je höher i gewählt wird, desto risikoscheuer ist das Verhalten. Je niedriger i gewählt wird, desto risikofreudiger verhält man sich. Es handelt sich hierbei auch um den expliziten Kapitalkostensatz für Beschaffung von EK und FK.

$$KW_{ohne\ Liquiditionserlös} = -I_0 + \sum_{t=1}^{n} \frac{E_t - A_t}{(1+i)^t}$$

Kapitalwert mit Liquiditätserlös

- L_E wirkt wie Einzahlung und muss über die komplette Laufzeit auf E_0 diskontiert werden
- $L_E n$ = Liquidationserlös am Ende der Laufzeit

$$KW_{mit\ Liquiditionserlös} = -I_0 + \sum_{t=1}^{n} \frac{E_t - A_t}{(1+i)^t} + \frac{L_E n}{(1+i)^n}$$

Annuitätenmethode

Entscheidungskriterium: AN> 0
Alternative mit AN_{max}

$$AN = KW * WK = KW * \frac{(1+i)^n * i}{(1+i)^n - 1}$$

mit
WF:Wiedergewinnungsfaktor
n: geplante Nutzungsdauer
i: vorgegebener Verwertungsanspruch

Dynamische Amortisierungsdauer

Entscheidungskriterium: $AD < AD_{min}$
$AD_1 < AD_2$ und $AD_1 < AD_{min}$

AD_{min} ist vom Investor vorgegeben

$$-I_o + \sum_{t=1}^{n} \frac{E_t - A_t}{(1+i)^t} = KW_t \quad und \quad KW_t = 0$$

Zunächst muss hier der Kapitalwert berechnet werden. Dieser wird dann gleich 0 gesetzt, sodass t zu AD wird.

Lineare Interpolation: $AD = \frac{|KW_t negativ|}{|KW_t\ negativ| + KW_{t+1}\ positiv} + t$

Methode des internen Zinssatzes

Ziel der Berechnung ist es, die interne Verwertung des eingesetzten Kapitals (I_o) zu ermitteln.
Bestimmung nur für **Normalinvestitionen**: KW-Funktion hat nur eine Schnittpunkt mit der x-Achse

Entscheidungskriterium: $i_{Investition}$ (i_i) > $i_{min.}$ = vorteilhaft
$i_{Investition}$ (i_i) < $i_{min.}$ = unvorteilhaft

$$i_i = \frac{r_i}{100}$$

r_{min} vom Investor vorgegeben

$$KW(i) = 0 = -I_o + \sum_{t=1}^{n} \frac{E_t - A_t}{(1+i)^t}$$

Lineare Interpolation:

$$i_i = \frac{KW_1 * (i_2 - i_1)}{|KW_1| \pm |KW_2|} + i$$

Barwertgewinnungsfaktor

$$Barwertgewinnungsfaktor = \frac{(1+i)^n - 1}{i * (1+i)^n}$$

| i: Zinssatz |
| n: Jahre |

Bewertung von Unternehmen

Zur **Vermögensstrukturanalyse** dienen besonders die folgenden Kennzahlen:

$$Anlageintensität = \frac{Anlagevermögen}{Gesamtvermögen} * 100$$

$$Umlaufintensität = \frac{Umlaufvermögen}{Gesamtvermögen} * 100$$

$$Vermögenskonstitution = \frac{Anlagevermögen}{Umlaufvermögen} * 100$$

$$Vorratsintenisät = \frac{Vorräte}{Geamtvermögen} * 100$$

$$Investitionsquote =$$

$$\frac{Nettoinvestitionen\ bei\ Sachanlagen}{Sachlagenbestand\ am\ Jahresanfang} * 100$$

$$Anlagendeckungsgrad\ A = \frac{Eigenkapital}{Anlagevermögen} * 100$$

$$Anlagendeckungsgrad\ B =$$

$$\frac{Eigenkapital + langfristiges\ Fremdkapital}{Anlagevermögen} * 100$$

$$Anlagenabnutzungsgrad =$$

$$\frac{kummulierte\ Abschreibungen\ auf\ Sachanlagevermögen}{Anschaffungskosten\ Sachanlagevermögen} * 100$$

Umsatzrelationen

$$Sachanlagenbindung = \frac{Sachanlagevermögen}{Umsatzerlöse} * 100$$

$$Anlagennutzung = \frac{Umsatz}{Sachanlagevermögen} * 100$$

$$Vorratshaltung = \frac{Vorräte}{Umsatz} * 100$$

$$Umschlagsdauer\ des\ Vorratsvermögen =$$

$$\frac{\emptyset Lagerbestand\ des\ Umlaufvermögens}{Umsatz} * 360\ Tage$$

$$Umschlagshäufigkeit =$$

$$\frac{Umsatzerlöse}{\emptyset Lagerbestand\ des\ Umlaufvermögens} * 360\ Tage$$

Die **Goldene Finanzierungsregel** wird genutzt, um die Fristenkongruenz zu analysieren. Es wird untersucht, ob das Unternehmen die investierten Vermögensgegenstände mit Kapital gleicher Laufzeit refinanziert. Langfristige Investitionen sollten mit langfristigem Kapital finanziert werden. Kurzfristige Investitionen mit kurzfristiger Kapitalbindungsdauer:

$$\frac{langfristiges\ Vermögen}{langfristiges\ Kapital} \leq 1 \quad \text{und} \quad \frac{kurzfristiges\ Vermögen}{kurzfristiges\ Kapital} \geq 1$$

Die **Goldene Bilanzregel** bildet ab, inwiefern langfristig gebundenes Vermögen langfristig finanziert wird.

Goldene Bilanzregel im engeren Sinne:
$$\frac{Eigenkapital + langfristiges\ Fremkapital}{Anlagevermögen} \geq 1$$

Goldene Bilanzregel im weiteren Sinne:
$$\frac{Eigenkapital + langfristiges\ Fremkapital}{Anlagevermögen + langfristiges\ Umlaufvermögen} \geq 1$$

Um die kurzfristige Liquidität eines Unternehmens zu berechnen, gibt es die **Liquiditätsgrade**. Dabei handelt es sich um Kennzahlen, die in Prozent angeben, inwiefern das Unternehmen fähig ist, kurzfristige Verbindlichkeiten mit flüssigen Mitteln zu begleichen.

Die flüssigen Mittel bestehen vornehmlich aus den Positionen Kassenbestand, Bankguthaben und Schecks. Das kurzfristige Fremdkapital beinhaltet Verbindlichkeiten gegenüber Kreditinstituten, Verbindlichkeiten aus Lieferung und Leistung, sonstige Verbindlichkeiten (alle mit einer Laufzeit < 1 Jahr), kurzfristige Rückstellungen sowie die passive Rechnungsabgrenzung. Kapitalgesellschaften ordnen manchmal auch den Bilanzgewinn den kurzfristigen Verbindlichkeiten zu, wenn dieser an die Aktionäre ausgeschüttet werden soll.

Liquidität 1. Grades

$$Liquidität\ 1.\ Grades =$$

$$\frac{flüssige\ Mittel}{Kurzfristige\ Verbindlichkeiten + Steuerrückstellungen + sonst.\ Rückstellungen + passiver\ Rechnungsabgrenzungsposten}$$

Die Liquidität 1. Grades gibt an, wie hoch der Anteil der flüssigen Mittel an dem kurzfristigen Fremdkapital ist. Eine Liquidität 1. Grades in Höhe von 20% sagt aus, dass lediglich 20% der kurzfristigen Verbindlichkeiten mit den flüssigen Mitteln beglichen werden können.

Liquidität 2. Grades

Bei der Liquidität 2. Grades werden die flüssigen Mittel (aus der Liquiditätskennziffer 1. Grades) um die kurzfristigen Forderungen ergänzt und zum kurzfristigen Fremdkapital ins Verhältnis gesetzt. Die Liquiditätskennzahl 2. Grades wird häufig bei der Kreditwürdigkeitsprüfung hinzugezogen.

$$Liquidität\ 2.\ Grades =$$

$$\frac{flüssige\ Mittel + langfristige\ Forderungen}{Kurzfristige\ Verbindlichkeiten\ +\ Steuerrückstellungen\ +\ sonst.\ Rückstellungen\ +\ passiver\ Rechnungsabgrenzungsposten}$$

Die Liquidität 2.Grades gibt an, inwieweit die flüssigen Mittel und die Forderungen das kurzfristige Fremdkapital decken. Als Faustregel gilt, dass die Liquidität 2. Grades mindestens 100 % betragen soll. Liegt sie unter 100 %, so könnte dies ein Hinweis auf einen zu hohen Lagerbestand sein. Eine Liquidität 2. Grades in Höhe von 80 % sagt beispielsweise aus, dass 80 % des kurzfristigen Fremdkapitals durch flüssige Mittel und kurzfristige Forderungen gedeckt sind.

Liquidität 3. Grades

Bei der Liquidität 3. Grades werden die flüssigen Mittel (aus der Liquiditätskennziffer 1. Grades) um die übrigen Bilanzpositionen des Umlaufvermögens ergänzt und zum kurzfristigen Fremdkapital ins Verhältnis gesetzt (komplettes Umlaufvermögen).

$$Liquidität\ 3.\ Grades =$$

$$\frac{Umlaufvermögen}{Kurzfristige\ Verbindlichkeiten\ +\ Steuerrückstellungen\ +\ sonst.\ Rückstellungen\ +\ passiver\ Rechnungsabgrenzungsposten}$$

In der Praxis nicht immer zutreffende Grobempfehlung: Die Liquidität 3. Grades sollte mindestens 200 % betragen. Liegt sie unter 200 %, kann es beim Absatz bzw. bei der Preisgestaltung Probleme geben. Sollte die sie unter 100% liegen, würde das bedeuten, dass eine Existenzgefährdung vorliegen könnte.

Das **Working Capital** zeigt, ob ein Unternehmen sein Umlaufvermögen mit langfristig zur Verfügung stehendem Kapital finanziert.
Ist das Ergebnis positiv, bedeutet dies, dass ein Teil des Umlaufvermögens mit langfristig zur Verfügung stehendem Kapital finanziert wird. Wenn das Umlaufvermögen nicht ausreicht, um die gesamten kurzfristigen Verbindlichkeiten zu decken, ist das Ergebnis negativ.
Unternehmen sollten ein möglichst positives Ergebnis anstreben, da ein negativer Wert gegen die Goldene Bilanzregel verstößt, da langfristige Investitionen mit kurzfristigem Kapital finanziert werden müssen. Das stimmt in der Praxis nicht immer, wie große Handelsunternehmen eindrucksvoll zeigen, die sich zu einem Großteil durch Lieferantenkredite finanzieren.

$$Working\ Capital$$
$$= Umlaufvermögen$$
$$- kurzfristige\ Verbindlichkeiten$$

Bei dieser Berechnungsformel gibt das Ergebnis keinen prozentualen Anteil an, sondern eine absolute Kennzahl.
Working Capital Management nutzen viele Unternehmen um das Working Capital zu optimieren. Die Unternehmen möchten erreichen, dass die Kennzahl weder zu hoch noch zu gering ist. Es gibt einige Regeln, die Ansätze für das optimale Working Capital vorgeben. Die „bankers rule" besagt, dass das Umlaufvermögen mindestens doppelt so hoch sein soll, wie das kurzfristige Fremdkapital, um Liquiditätsengpässe zu vermeiden.

Umschlagshäufigkeiten messen, wie häufig sich bestimmte Bilanzpositionen in einer bestimmten Periode „umschlagen", wobei die jeweiligen Kehrwerte die Umschlagsdauer dieser Positionen zeigen.[1]

$$Umschlagshäufigkeit = \frac{Umsatz}{Durchschnittsbestand\ der\ Vorräte}$$

Beim **Debitorenumschlag** geht es darum, wie zeitnah die Debitoren die Rechnungen des Unternehmens begleichen. Ist der Debitorenumschlagswert hoch, kommen die Kunden ihren Forderungen schnell nach. Ein niedriger Debitorenumschlag weist darauf hin, dass die Debitoren bei einem Kauf auf Ziel erst sehr spät die Rechnung bezahlen. Der Debitorenumschlag eines Unternehmens sollte daher hoch sein.

$$Debitorenumschlag = \frac{Umsatz}{durchschnittlicher\ Forderungsbestand}$$

Um die Dauer bestimmen zu können wie lang die Debitoren durchschnittlich brauchen, um ihre Forderungen zu begleichen, nutzt man das **Debitorenziel**. Diese Kennzahl gibt die durchschnittliche Anzahl an Tagen an.

$$Debitorenziel = \frac{durchschnittlicher\ Forderungsbestand}{Umsatzerlöse} * 360$$

---

[1] Vgl. Coenenberg (2003a), S. 951.

Umgekehrt kann man ebenso berechnen, wie lange das Unternehmen braucht, die Forderungen der Kreditoren zu begleichen. Dafür nutzt man das **Kreditorenziel**:

$$Kreditorenziel =$$

$$\frac{durchschn.\,Verb.\,aus\,Lieferungen\,und\,Leistungen}{Umsatzkosten} * 360$$

Return on Investment (ROI):

$$Return\,on\,Investment =$$

$$Umsatzrentabilität * Kapitalumschlagshäufigkeit$$

Return on Stock Investment (ROSTI):

$$ROSTI = Spanne\,in\,\%\,vom\,Wareneinsatz$$
$$* Umschlagshäufigkeit\,des\,Lagers$$

Cashflow

Der Cashflow ist eine absolute Kennzahl und wird in Euro ausgedrückt. Über mehrere Jahre betrachtet können Aussagen über die vergangene Jahre gemacht werden und zukünftige Jahre können prognostiziert werden. Des Weiteren kann aufgrund des finanzwirtschaftlichen Überschusses die Innenfinanzierungskraft eines Unternehmens bestimmt werden. Wegen der Eliminierung der Abschreibungsmethoden ist der Cashflow aussagefähiger als der Jahresüberschuss.

$Cashflow =$
Jahresüberschuss
+ Abschreibungen
– Zuschreibungen
+ Erhöhung langfristiger Rückstellungen
–Verminderung langfristiger Rückstellungen

Beim **ertragswirtschaftlichen Cashflow** wird das operative Ergebnis vor Finanz- und Beteiligungsergebnis sowie unter Eliminierung der Abschreibungen berechnet.

Ertragswirtschaftliche, Cashflow (GKV) =
Umsatz
+ Bestandsveränderungen
+ andere aktivierte Eigenleistungen
+ sonstige betriebliche Erträge
– Materialaufwand
– Personalaufwand
– sonstige betriebliche Aufwendungen
+ Erträge aus Wertpapieren und Ausleihungen
+ Sonstige Zinserträge und ähnliche Erträge
– Zinsaufwendungen und ähnliche Aufwendungen

Die **Cashflow-Marge** gibt an, wie viel Prozent der Umsatzerlöse dem Unternehmen zur Investitionsfinanzierung, Schuldentilgung und Dividendenzahlung frei zur Verfügung stehen. Mit der Cashflow-Marge kann die operative Unternehmensrentabilität gemessen werden. Sie ist ein Indikator für die Ertrags- und Selbstfinanzierungskraft eines Unternehmens. Je höher die Cashflow-Marge, desto besser ist die Liquidität zu beurteilen. Verglichen mit der Umsatzrentabilität hat die Cashflow-Marge den Vorteil, dass die international divergierenden Bilanzierungsrichtlinien aufgrund der Vorteile des Cashflows weitgehend neutralisiert werden können und somit eine objektivere Vergleichbarkeit von verschiedenen Unternehmen hergestellt werden kann.

$$Cashflow\text{-}Marge = \frac{Ertragswirtschaftlicher\ Cashflow}{Umsatz}$$

$$Cashflow\ Umsatzrendite = \frac{Cashflow}{Umsatz} * 100$$

$$Cashflow - Rentabilität = \frac{Cashflow}{Gesamtkapital} * 100$$

Die **Kapitalstruktur** eines Unternehmens beschreibt das Verhältnis zwischen Eigen- und Fremdkapital. Die Kapitalstruktur wird mit verschiedenen Kennzahlen analysiert:

Der **Verschuldungskoeffizient** gibt den Umfang der Verschuldung an. Mit weiteren Analysen kann das Fremdkapital in kurz-, mittel- und langfristige Tranchen unterteilt werden. Durch eine Aufnahme von Fremdkapital kann bei einer bestimmten Eigenkapitalrentabilität die Eigenkapitalverzinsung optimiert werden.

$$Verschuldungskoeffizient = \frac{Eigenkapital}{Fremdkapital}$$

Die **Eigenkapitalquote** gibt Auskunft über den Anteil von Eigenkapital am Gesamtkapital. Je höher die Eigenkapitalquote, umso höher ist die finanzielle Stabilität des Unternehmens und umso geringer ist die Abhängigkeit von Fremdkapitalgebern.

$$Eigenkapitalquote = \frac{Eigenkapital}{Gesamtkapital} * 100$$

Synonyme: Eigenkapitalintensität, Eigenkapitalausstattung

Parallel dazu gibt es ebenfalls die **Fremdkapitalquote** eines Unternehmens. Bei einer hohen Fremdkapitalquote ist das Unternehmen sehr abhängig von den Kreditgebern und hat daher eine unsicher finanzielle Basis. Dementsprechend wir die Fremdkapitalquote auch Anspannungsgrad genannt.

$$Fremdkapitalquote = \frac{Framdkapital}{Gesamtkapital} * 100$$

Um das Fremdkapital zu analysieren kann man die Kennzahl **Fremdkapitalstruktur** anwenden. Sie gibt Auskunft über die Zusammensetzung des Fremdkapitals:

$$Fremdkapitalstruktur = \frac{kurzfristiges\ Fremdkapital}{gesamtes\ Fremdkapital} * 100$$

Der Anteil des kurzfristigen Fremdkapital sollte möglichst gering sein, um dauerhaft liquide und wirtschaftlich stabil zu sein.

$$Vermögensentwicklung = \frac{Vermögensanteil}{Betriebsleistung} * 100$$

$$Rücklagenquote = \frac{Rücklagen}{Eigenkapital} * 100$$

$$Selbstfinazierungsgrad = \frac{Gewinnrücklagen}{Gesamtkapital} * 100$$

Der **dynamische Verschuldungsgrad** ist eine Kennzahl zur Beurteilung der Schuldentilgungsfähigkeit eines Unternehmens und wird insbesondere bei Kreditwürdigkeitsprüfungen angewandt.

$$Dyn.Verschuldungsgrad =$$

$$\frac{Fremdkapital - liquide\ Mittel - Wertpapiere - kfr.Forderungen}{Cashflow}$$

Der dynamische Verschuldungsgrad gibt an, in wie viel Jahren ein Unternehmen die Verbindlichkeiten mit dem Cashflow zurückzahlen kann. Je kleiner der Wert dieser Kennzahl ist, desto schneller kann ein Unternehmen seine Verbindlichkeiten aus eigenen Mitteln tilgen. Hat die Kennziffer einen Wert von < 5 Jahren, so gilt dieses in der Regel als zufrieden stellend. Ein geringer Wert des dynamischen Verschuldungsgrades gilt als ein Nachweis für die finanzielle Stabilität eines Unternehmens. Der Vorteil ist, dass ein Unternehmen mit kleinem dynamischen Verschuldungsgrad relativ unabhängiger von seinen Gläubigern ist. Ein dynamischer Verschuldungsgrad mit einem Wert von > 7 Jahren gilt grundsätzlich als grenzwertig.

Für eine genauere Interpretation ist das Ergebnis des dynamischen Verschuldungsgrads beispielsweise von der Branche abhängig, in dem das Unternehmen tätig ist. Die vorliegende Kennzahl kann zwar in den einzelnen Jahren Schwankungen unterliegen, hat aber den Vorteil, dass sie relativ resistent gegen Bilanzpolitik ist.

Bei der **Rentabilität** wird der erzielte Gewinn in Relation zum eingesetzten Kapital gesetzt. Die zwei wichtigsten Kennzahlen sind:

Mit **Eigenkapitalrentabilität** gibt man die Verzinsung des Eigenkapitals an.

$$Eigenkapitalrentabilität = \frac{Gewinn}{Eigenkapital} * 100$$

Die Kennzahl **Gesamtkapitalrentabilität** zeigt die Verzinsung des gesamten Kapitals, bestehend aus Eigenkapital und Fremdkapital.

$$Gesamtkapitalrentabilität =$$

$$\frac{Jahresüberschuss\ v.St. + Fremdkapitalzinsen}{Gesamtkapital} * 100$$

Die **Umsatzrentabilität**: gibt das Verhältnis zwischen dem erzielten Gewinn und der Höhe des Gesamtumsatzes. Sie zeigt, wieviel Gewinn mit jedem umgesetzten Euro erwirtschaftet wird.

$$Umsatzrentabilität = \frac{Gewinn}{Umsatz} * 100$$

Gesamtkapitalumschlag

$$Gesamtkapitalumschlag = \frac{Umsatzerlöse}{Gesamtkapital}$$

Umsatzrendite:

$$Umsatzrendite = \frac{Gewinn}{Nettoumsatz} * 100$$

Relativer Marktanteil

$$relativer\ Marktanteil = \frac{eigener\ Marktanteil}{Martanteil\ des\ stärksten\ Konkurrenten}$$

Marktanteil (%)

$$Marktanteil\ (\%) = \frac{Umsatz\ des\ Unternehmens}{Marktvolumen} * 100$$

Analyse der Aufwands- und Ertragsstruktur

$$Personalintensität = \frac{Personalaufwand}{Umsatz} * 100$$

$$Materialintensität = \frac{Materialaufwand}{Umsatz} * 100$$

$$Abschreibungsintensität =$$

$$\frac{planmäßige\ Jahresabschreibung\ auf\ Sachanlagen}{Umsatz} * 100$$

$$Herstellintensität = \frac{Herstellungskosten}{Umsatz} * 100$$

$$Vertriebsintensität = \frac{Vertriebskosten}{Umstaz} * 100$$

$$FuE - Intensität = \frac{FuE - Kosten}{Umsatz} * 100$$

$$\text{Verwaltungsintensität} = \frac{\text{Verwaltungskosten}}{\text{Umsatz}} * 100$$

$$\text{Leistung pro Kopf} = \frac{\text{Gesamtleistung}(\text{€})}{\text{Mitarbeiteranzahl}}$$

$$\text{Leistung pro Stunde} = \frac{\text{Gesamtleistung}}{\text{produktive Stunden}}$$

$$\text{Wertschöpfung} =$$

$$\text{Umsatzerlöse} - \text{Materialeinzelkosten} - \text{Fremdleistungen}$$

$$\text{Wertschöpfung bezogen auf die Personalkosten} =$$

$$\frac{\text{Wertschöpfung}}{\text{Personalkosten}} * 100$$

$$\text{Wertschöpfung pro Kopf} = \frac{\text{Wertschöpfung}}{\text{Mitarbeiteranzahl}}$$

$$Wertschöpfung\ pro\ Stunde = \frac{Wertschöpfung}{produktive\ Stunden}$$

$$Personalaufwandsquote = \frac{Personalaufwand}{Gesamtleistung} * 100$$

Personalbedarfsplanung

Nettopersonalbedarf=

Sollpersonalbedarf am Periodenende

– vorhandener Personalbestand am Periodenanfang

+ geplante Personalabgänge während der Periode

– geplante Personalzugänge während der Periode

Personalbeschaffung

$$Ausbildungsplatzattraktivität = \frac{Anzahl\ Bewerber}{Anzahl\ Ausbildungsplätze}$$

$$Vorstellungsquote = \frac{Vorstellungsgespräche}{Anzahl\ der\ Bewerbungen} * 100$$

$$Einstellungsquote = \frac{abgeschlossene\ Arbeitsverträge}{Anzahl\ der\ Bewerbungen} * 100$$

$$durchschnittliche\ Personalbeschaffungskosten =$$

$$\frac{Gesamtkosten\ der\ Personalbeschaffung}{Anzahl\ der\ Einstellungen} * 100$$

$$Personalentwicklungskostenanteil =$$

$$\frac{Personalentwicklungskosten}{Gesamtpersonalkosten} * 100$$

$$Effizienz\ der\ Personalbeschaffung =$$

$$\frac{Bewerbungen}{Beschaffungsmaßnahme}$$

$$Grad\ der\ Personaldeckung =$$

$$\frac{tatsächliche\ Einstellungen}{Anzahl\ benötigter\ Mitarbeiter} * 100$$

$$Produktivität\ der\ Personalbeschaffung =$$

$$\frac{Bewerbungen, bzw\ Einstellungen}{Beschaffungsmitarbeiter}$$

$$Personalbeschaffungskosten\ pro\ Einstellung =$$

$$\frac{Gesamtkosten\ der\ Personalbeschaffung}{Gesamtleistungszahl\ der\ Einstellungen}$$

$$Frühfluktuationsrate =$$

$$\frac{aufgelöste\ Arbeitsverträge\ in\ der\ Probezeit}{Anzahl\ der\ Einstellungen} * 100$$

Lohnformen

Zeitlohn

$$Zeitlohn = Lohn\ pro\ Zeiteinheit * Zeiteinheiten$$

Leistungslohn

Akkordlohn

Zeitakkord

$$Zeitakkord = Leistungsmenge * Vorgabezeit * Minutenfaktor$$

Leistungsmenge: Istleistung in Stück pro Stunde
Vorgabezeit: Sollarbeitszeit pro Stück
Minutenfaktor: $\dfrac{Akkordrichtsatz}{60\ Minuten}$
Akkordrichtsatz: tariflicher Mindestlohn pro Stunde + Akkordzuschlag

Geldakkord

$$Geldakkord = Leistungsmenge * Geldsatz\ pro\ Stück$$

Geldsatz pro Stück: Vorgabezeit * Minutenfaktor

Prämienlohn

$$Prämienlohn = Grundlohn + Prämie$$

Personalcontrolling

$$Personalintensität = \frac{Personalaufwand}{gesamte\ Aufwendungen} * 100$$

$$Umsatz\ pro\ Mitarbeiter = \frac{Umsatzerlöse}{Anzahl\ der\ Mitarbeiter}$$

$$Cashflow\ pro\ Mitarbeiter =$$

$$\frac{Cashflow}{durchschnittliche\ Anzahl\ der\ Mitarbeiter}$$

$$Personalkosten\ der\ Mitarbeiter =$$

$$\frac{Gesamtaufwendungen\ für\ Personal}{durchschnittliche\ Anzahl\ der\ Mitarbeiter}$$

$$durchschnittliche\ Personalkosten\ pro\ Stunde =$$

$$\frac{Gesamtaufwendungen\ für\ Personal}{Anzahl\ der\ geleisteten\ Arbeitsstunden}$$

$$\text{Überstundenquote} = \frac{\text{Überstunden}}{\text{Normalstunden}} * 100$$

$$\text{Krankenstandsquote} = \frac{\text{Anzahl der Krankentage}}{\text{Sollarbeitszeit}} * 100$$

$$\text{Fluktuationsquote} =$$

$$\frac{\text{Anzahl der Personalabgänge}}{\text{durchschnittliche Anzahl der Beschäftigten}} * 100$$

$$\text{Fluktuationquote nach Schlüter} =$$

$$\frac{\text{Anzahl der Personalabgänge}}{\text{Personalbestand am Anfang} + \text{Zugänge}} * 100$$

$$\text{Fehlzeitenquote} = \frac{\text{Fehlzeiten}}{\text{Sollarbeitszeit}} * 100$$

$$\text{Durchschnittsalter} =$$

$$\frac{\text{Lebensalter aller Beschäftigten in Jahren}}{\text{durchschnittliche Anzahl der Beschäftigten}}$$

$$durchschnittliche\ Betriebszugehörigkeit =$$

$$\frac{Betriebszugehörigkeit\ aller\ Beschäftigten\ in\ Jahren}{durchschnittliche\ Anzahl\ der\ Beschäftigen}$$

$$Behindertenanteil =$$

$$\frac{Anzahl\ der\ Beschäftigten\ mit\ Behinderung}{durchschnittliche\ Anzahl\ der\ Beschäftigten} * 100$$

$$Frauenanteil =$$

$$\frac{Anzahl\ der\ beschäftigten\ Frauen}{durchschnittliche\ Anzahl\ der\ Beschäftigten} * 100$$

$$Ausbildungquote =$$

$$\frac{Anzahl\ der\ Auszubildenden}{durchschnittliche\ Anzahl\ der\ Beschäftigten} * 100$$

$$\ddot{U}bernahmequote =$$

$$\frac{Anzahl\ \ddot{u}bernommer\ Auszubildender}{Anzahl\ der\ Auszubildenden\ mit\ beendeter\ Ausbildung} * 100$$

$$Qualifikationsstruktur =$$

$$\frac{Anzahl\ der\ Besch\ddot{a}ftigten\ mit\ bestimmter\ Qualifikation}{Anzahl\ der\ Besch\ddot{a}ftigten} * 100$$

$$Weiterbildungzeit\ pro\ Mitarbeiter =$$

$$\frac{Gesamtanzahl\ der\ Weiterbildungstage}{Anzahl\ der\ Mitarbeiter}$$

$$Weiterbildungskosten\ pro\ Mitarbeiter =$$

$$\frac{Weiterbildungskosten}{Anzahl\ der\ Besch\ddot{a}ftigten}$$

$$Kapazit\ddot{a}tsbedarf\ (in\ Stunden) = \frac{St\ddot{u}ckzahl * Vorgabezeit}{60}$$

$$Kapazitätsbestand\ (in\ Stunden) =$$

$$Mitarbeiter * Tage * Stunden\ pro\ Tag * Planungsfaktor$$

$$Kapazitätsauslastung\ (in\ \%) = \frac{Bedarf}{Bestand} * 100$$

$$Zusatzbedarf\ (in\ Stunden) = Bedarf - Bestand$$

$$Durchschnittlicher\ Verdienst =$$

$$(€/h)\frac{\Sigma(€/Periode)}{Ist - Auftragszeit\ (€/Periode)}$$

$$Personalkostenintensität = \frac{Personalaufwand}{Umsatz} * 100$$

$$Personalkostenquote = \frac{Personalaufwand}{Gesamtleistung} * 100$$

$$Wirkungsgrad = \frac{Arbeitsergebnis}{Arbeitsgegenstand} * 100$$

$$Zeitgrad = \frac{Soll - Auftragszeit}{Ist - Auftragszeit} * 100$$

Oder

$$Zeitgrad = \frac{\Sigma\,Vorgabezeiten/Periode}{\Sigma\,Istzeiten/Periode} * 100$$

$$Personalleistung\ in\ Umsatz\ je\ Person = \frac{Umsatz}{Anzahl\ der\ Personen}$$

$$Personalleistung\ in\ Umsatz\ je\ Stunde = \frac{Umsatz}{Anzahl\ der\ Stunden}$$

Lohn- und Gehaltsabrechnung

Bruttolohn
- Steuerabzüge
- Abzüge in der Sozialversicherung
= Nettolohn
- Abzüge vom Nettolohn
=Auszahlungsbetrag

Einkauf

Einfache Ermittlung der Beschaffungsmenge

Bedarf an Materialien anhand der geplanten Produktionsmenge
+Mehrbedarf an Ausschuss, Schwund, Reparatur und Wartung
−Lagerbestand
−Bestellbestand
+Vormerkbestand
−Werkstattbestand
=Beschaffungsmenge

Optimale Bestellmenge:

Andlersche Formel zur optimalen Bestellmenge =

$$\sqrt{\frac{200 * Jahresbedarf\ in\ Stück * bestellfixe\ Kosten\ proBestellung}{Bestellpreis\ pro\ Stück * (Zinskostensatz\ pro\ Jahr + Lagerkostensatz\ pro\ Jahr)}}$$

Berücksichtigung von Preissteigerungen

optimale Beschaffungsmenge =

$$\left(\frac{neuer\ Preis}{alter\ Preis} - 1\right) * \frac{100 * Monatsbedarf}{Lagerungskostensatz\ im\ Monat}$$

Berücksichtigung von Mengenrabatten

$$R_{min} = \frac{L * X_{opt}}{2 * n} * \left(\frac{X_{opt}}{X_{min}} + \frac{X_{min}}{X_{opt}} - 2 \right)$$

mit

R_{min}: Mindestrabattsatz
L: Lagerungskostensatz
X_{min}: Mindestmenge, ab der Rabatt gewährt wird
X_{opt}: optimale Beschaffungsmenge

Einstandspreis

Listenpreis
−Rabatte (Mengenrabatte, Treuerabatte)
=Zieleinkaufspreis
−Skonti
=Bareinkaufspreis
+Bezugskosten
=Einstandspreis

Angebotskalkulation

Bezugspreis
+Handlungskosten
=Selbstkosten
+Gewinn
=Barverkaufspreis
+Kundenskonto
+Vertreterprovision
=Zielverkaufspreis
+Kundenrabatte
=Listenpreis

Rückwärtskalkulation

Listenpreis
−Kundenrabatte
=Zielverkaufspreis
−Vertreterprovision
−Kundenskonto
=Barverkaufspreis
−Gewinn
=Selbstkosten
−Handlungskosten
=Bezugspreis

Differenzkalkulation

Listenpreis
−Rabatt
=Zielverkaufspreis
−Skonto
=Barverkaufspreis
−Gewinn
=Selbstkosten

Kalkulation mit Handelsspannen

$$Kalkulationszuschlag = Listenpreis - Bezugspreis$$

$$Handelsspanne = \frac{Kalkulationszuschlag}{Listenpreis} * 100$$

$$Umsatzerlös - Wareneinsatz = Rohertrag$$

$$Kalkulationszuschlagssatz = \frac{Rohertrag}{Umsatzerlöse} * 100$$

$$Verkaufspreis\ mit\ Mwst. =$$

$$Einstandspreis\ ohne\ Mwst. + Aufschlag$$

$$Spanne = Mwst.\ vom\ Verkaufspreis + Rohertrag\ netto$$

$$Aufschlag = \frac{Spanne\ (€)}{Einstandspreis\ (€)} * 100$$

Oder

$$Aufschlag = \frac{Abschlag\ (\%)}{100\% - Abschlag\ (\%)} * 100$$

$$Abschlag = \frac{Spanne\ (\text{€})}{Verkaufspreis\ (\text{€})} * 100$$

Oder

$$Abschlag = \frac{Aufschlag\ (\%)}{Aufschlag\ (\%) + 100\%} * 100$$

Beschaffungskosten

$$Beschaffungskosten =$$

$$Fixkosten\ pro\ Bestellung * \frac{Bedarf\ pro\ Periode}{Bestellmenge}$$

Preisklausel

$$P_{neu} = \frac{P_0}{100} * (F + M * \frac{M_{neu}}{M_{alt}} + L * \frac{L_{neu}}{L_{alt}}$$

P_{neu}: Preis am Tag der Lieferung
P_0: Angebotspreis
F: Fixkosten und Gewinnanteil in % von P
M: Materialkosten in % von P
M_{neu}: Materialpreis am Tag der Lieferung in €
M_{alt}: Materialpreis bei Vertragsschluss in €
L: Lohnkostenanteil in % von P
L_{neu}: tariflicher Ecklohn am Tag der Lieferung in €
L_{alt}: Tariflicher Ecklohn bei Vertragsschluss in €

Lagerkennzahlen

ABC-Analyse

Als erstes erfolgt die Berechnung des Werts eines Produkts/Kumulierter Wert aller Produkte:

$$Wertanteil\ in\ Prozent = \frac{Wertanteil\ des\ Produkts}{kumulierter\ Wert\ aller\ Produkte}$$

$$Mengenanteil\ in\ Prozent = \frac{Menge\ des\ Produkts}{kumulierte\ Menge\ aller\ Produkte}$$

Hat man alle Wertanteile ermittelt, werden diese nach dem Wertanteil in Reihenfolge gebracht. Nach der Sortierung legt man die Klassen fest: Die Klasse A sollte ungefähr 80% der Wertanteile, aber nur 10% der Mengenanteile ausmachen, die Klasse B 15% des Wertanteils bei 20% der Menge und die Klasse C 5% der Wertanteile, aber dafür ca. 70% der Mengenanteile.

XYZ-Analyse

Bei der XYZ-Analyse teilt man die Güter zusätzlich nach der Regelmäßigkeit des Bedarfsanfalls in drei Klassen ein:
X-Produkte haben einen regelmäßigen und schwankungsfreien Bedarf, den man gut planen kann.
Y-Produkte unterliegen regelmäßigen Schwankungen, lassen sich aber aufgrund bspw. saisonaler Schwankungen ungenau planen.

Z-Produkte werden nur unregelmäßig benötigt, daher ist die Planbarkeit der Beschaffung kaum gegeben.

Zur **Lagerbestandsüberwachung** gibt es verschieden Kennzahlen:

Lieferbereitschaftsgrad:

$$Lieferbereitschaftsgrad = \frac{Anzahl\ der\ bedienten\ Bedarfspositionen}{Anzahl\ aller\ Bedarfspositionen} * 100$$

Lagerumschlagshäufigkeit:

$$Lagerumschlagshäufigkeit = \frac{Materialeinsatz\ pro\ Jahr}{durchschnittlicher\ Lagerbestand}$$

Lagerdauer:

$$Lagerdauer = \frac{Vorräte}{Materialeinsatz\ pro\ Jahr} * 360$$

Durchschnittliche Lagerdauer:

$$Durchschnittliche\ Lagerdauer = \frac{360\ Tage}{Lagerumschlagshäufigkeit}$$

Lagerbestand in % des Umsatzes:

$$Lagerbestand\ in\ \%\ des\ Umsatzes = \frac{Lagerbestand}{Umsatz} * 100$$

Bestandsveränderungen:

$$Bestandsmehrung = Produktionsmenge > Absatzmenge$$

$$Bestandsmehrung = Schlussbestand > Anfangsbestand$$

$$Bestandsminderung = Produktionsmenge < Absatzmenge$$

$$Bestandsminderung = Schlussbestand < Anfangsbestand$$

Materialintensität:

$$Materialintnsität = \frac{Materialaufwand}{Umsatz} * 100$$

Lagerungskosten

$$Lagerungskosten =$$

$$\emptyset Lagermenge * Einstandspreis * Zinsfaktor\ für\ Lagerung$$

Lagerzinssatz

$$Lagerzinssatz = \frac{Zinssatz\ pro\ Jahr * \emptyset Lagerdauer}{360\ Tage}$$

Flächennutzungsgrad

$$Flächennutzungsgrad = \frac{belegte\ Lagerflächen}{vorhandene\ Lagerflächen} * 100$$

Raumnutzungsgrad

$$Raumnutzungsgrad = \frac{belegtes\ Lagervolumen}{vorhandenes\ Lagervolumen} * 100$$

Bestände

Sollbestand

$$Sollbestand = Anfangsbestand + Zugänge - Abgänge$$

Durchschnittlicher Lagerbestand

$$\emptyset Lagerbestand = \frac{Anfangsbestand + Endbestand}{2}$$

Verfügbarer Bestand

$Verfügbarer\ Bestand =$

$Aktueller\ Lagerbestand - Vormerkbestand + Bestellbestand$

Meldebestände

Bestellpunktverfahren

$Meldebestand =$

$$Verbrauch$$
$$* (Wiederbeschaffungszeit$$
$$+ Überprüfungszeitraum) + Sicherheitsbestand$$

Bestellrhythmusverfahren

$Meldebestand =$

$$\frac{Verbrauch * (Wiederbeschaffungszeit + Überprüfungszeitraum}{Vorhersageperiode}$$

Sicherheitsbestand nach Verbrauchswerten

$$SB = \emptyset Verbrauch\ pro\ Periode * Beschaffungsdauer$$

Oder

$$SB =$$

$$ermittlerter\ Verbrauch\ in\ der\ Beschaffungszeit$$
$$+\ Zuschlag\ für\ Verbrauchsschwankungen\ und\ Zuverlässigkeit$$
$$der\ Lieferanten\ bzw.\ Produktion$$

Oder

$$SB =$$

$$mengemäßiger\ Umsatz\ pro\ Monat$$
$$*\ Reichweite\ des\ Meldebestands$$

Sicherheitsbestand nach Fehlerfortpflanzungsgesetz

$$SB = \sqrt{V^2 + L^2 + M^2 + B^2}$$

mit

V^2: Verbrauchsabweichung in Mengeneinheiten
L^2: Lieferzeitabweichungen in Mengeneinheiten
M^2: Minderlieferungen in Mengeneinheiten
B^2: Bestandsabweichungen in Mengeneinheiten

Sicherheitsbestand nach statistischer Bestimmung

$$SB = Sicherheitsfaktor * mittlere\ absolute\ Abweichung$$

Sicherheitsbestand nach Sicherheitszeit

$$SB =$$

$$\emptyset Verbrauch\ pro\ Tag * (Wiederbeschaffungszeit + Sicherheitszeit)$$

$$SZ = \sqrt{V^2 + L^2 + M^2 + B^2}$$

mit

V²: Sicherheitszeit zum Ausgleich von Verbrauchsabweichungen
L²: Sicherheitszeit zum Ausgleich von Lieferfristüberschreitungen
M²: Sicherheitszeit zum Ausgleich von Minderlieferungen
B²: Sicherheitszeit zum Ausgleich von Fehlern in der Bestandsführung

Produktion

Bei der **optimalen Losgröße** wird die Fertigungsmenge ermittelt, bei der die Lagerkosten und die Lagerkosten minimal sind.

$Optimale\ Losgröße =$

$$\sqrt{\frac{200 * Jahresbedarf\ in\ Stück * fixe\ Rüstkosten}{Herstellkosten\ pro\ Stück * (Zinskostensatz\ in\ \% + Lagerkostensatz\ in\ \%)}}$$

Der **Break-even-Point** ist an dem Punkt erreicht, an dem die Verkaufserlöse genau die fixen und variablen Kosten decken. Dieser Punkt wird auch Gewinnschwelle genannt.

$$Break\text{-}even\text{-}Menge = \frac{Fixkosten}{Preis\ pro\ Stück - variable\ Stückkosten}$$

Produktionsprogrammplanung:

$Gewinn\ /\ Verlust =$

$Summe\ aller\ Deckungsbeiträge - Fixkosten$

Zur **Produktionsprozesssteuerung** werden folgende Kennzahlen genutzt:

Der **Beschäftigungsgrad** vergleicht die tatsächliche Produktionsmenge mit der geplanten Produktionsmenge.

$$Beschäftigungsgrad = \frac{Istbeschäftigung}{Planbeschäftigung} * 100$$

Der **Kapazitätsauslastungsgrad** veranschaulicht die Auslastung der Kapazitäten, z. B. die Auslastung der Maschinen in der Produktion.

$$Kapazitätsauslastungsgrad = \frac{Istauslastung}{Maximalauslastung} * 100$$

Die **Ausschussquote** gibt den prozentualen Anteil der Produktionsmenge eines Produktes wieder, der nicht weiterverwendet werden kann.

$$Ausschussquote = \frac{Ausschussmenge}{Produktionsmenge} * 100$$

Kapazitätserweiterungsfaktor (Lohmann-Ruchti-Effekt):

$$Kapazitätserweiterungsfaktor = 2 * \frac{Nutzungsdauer}{Nutzungdauer + 1}$$

Kapazitätsbedarf und Kapazitätsbestand in Stunden:

$$Kapazitätsbedarf = Zeit\ pro\ Vorgang * Anzahl\ der\ Vorgänge$$

$$Kapzitätsbestand = Arbeitszeit\ pro\ Tag * Anzahl\ der\ Personen * Anzahl\ der\ Tage$$

$$Kapazitätsbestand\ real =$$

$$Kapazitätsbestand\ theoretisch - nicht\ nutzbare\ Kapazität$$

Deckungsbetrag:

$$Deckunsbetrag = Kapazitätsbestand\ real - Kapazitätsbedarf$$

Deckungsbetrag > 0 → Überdeckung = Unterbelegung
Deckungsbetrag = 0 → Deckung = 100% Belegung
Deckungsbetrag < 0 → Unterdeckung = Überbelegung

Make or Buy-Entscheidung

$$k_V \leq Einstandpreis\ bei\ Fremdfertigung \rightarrow Eigenfertigung$$

$$k_V = K_{gr} = Grenzkosten$$

Materialbedarfsermittlung

Nettomaterialbedarf:

Bruttobedarf
+ Zusatzbedarf (Ausschuss, Schwund)
= Gesamtbruttobedarf
- Lagerbestand
- Bestellbestand
- Werkstattbestand
+ Reservierungsbestand
+ Sicherheitsbestand
= Nettobedarf

$$Wertevolumen\ \left[\frac{€}{Artikel}\right] =$$

$$Jahresbedarf\ \left[\frac{Mengeneinheit}{Artikel}\right] * Preis\ \left[\frac{€}{Mengeneinheit}\right]$$

deterministische Materialbedarfsermittlung

$$Sekundärbedarf\ der\ Komponente$$
$$= Bedarf\ des\ Erzeugnisses$$
$$* Stücklistenmenge\ der\ Komponente$$

stochastische Materialbedarfsermittlung

arithmetischer Mittelwert:

$$V = \frac{T_1 + T_2 + T_3 + \ldots + T_n}{n}$$

mit

V: Vorhersagewert
T_1 bis T_n: tatsächlicher Verbrauch der   Perioden 1 bis n
n: Anzahl der Peridoden

gleitender Mittelwert:

$$V = \frac{T_7 + T_8 + T_9 + T_{10} + T_{11}}{n}$$

Die am weitesten zurückliegenden Werte werden eliminiert und durch neue ersetzt.

gewogener gleitender Mittelwert:

$$V = \frac{T_1 * G_1 + T_2 * G_2 + T_3 * G_3}{n}$$

mit $\boxed{G_1 \text{ bis } G_4 \text{: Gewichtungsfaktoren}}$

Die Summe der Gewichtungsfaktoren muss 100% sein

exponentielle Glättung erster Ordnung:

$$V = AV + \alpha(T - AV)$$

mit $\boxed{\begin{array}{l} \text{AV: alter Vorhersagewert} \\ \alpha \text{: Glättungsfaktor} \\ \text{T: Tatsächlicher Verbrauch} \end{array}}$

Fehlerberechnung:

Standardabweichung:

$$\sigma = \frac{1}{n} * \sum_{K=i+1-n}^{i} (T_K - M_k)^2$$

σ: Standardabweichung
   Sigma = hoher Wert $\rightarrow$ ungenaue Vorhersage, flache Glockenkurve
   Sigma = niedriger Wert $\rightarrow$ geringe Abweichung vom tatsächlichen Bedarf (Verbrauch)
                steile Glockenkurve

T_K: tatsächlicher Verbrauch
M_k: Vorhersagewert als gleitender Mittelwert über n Perioden
n: konstante Anzahl von Perioden, die als gleitender Zeitraum gewählt wurden
i: laufende Periode
K: Periode

$$Standardabweichung = 1{,}25 * MAD$$

Mittlere absolute Abweichung:

$$MAD_{i+1} = \frac{1}{n} * \sum_{K=i+1-n}^{i} |T_K - M_k|$$

mit MAD_{i+1}: mittlere absolute Abweichung

Marketing/Vertrieb

In diesem Kapitel geht es vor allem um die Kennzahlen, mit denen man den Markt und den Absatz steuern und kontrollieren kann.

Umsatz

$$Umsatz = Menge * Zielpreis$$

Zielkosten

$$Zielkosten = Zielpreis - Zielgewin$$

Die **Marktposition** des Unternehmens kann durch folgenden Kennzahlen wiedergegeben werden:

$$absoluter\ Marktanteil = \frac{Absatzvolumen}{Marktvolumen} * 100$$

$$relativer\ Marktanteil =$$

$$\frac{eigener\ absoluter\ Marktanteil}{absoluter\ Marktanteil\ des\ größten\ Konkurrenten} * 100$$

$$Sättigungsgrad\ des\ Marktes = \frac{Martkvolumen}{Marktpotenzial} * 100$$

$$Marktwachstum =$$

$$\frac{aktuelles\ Marktvolumen - Marktvolumen\ der\ Vorperiode}{Marktvolumen\ der\ Vorperiode} * 100$$

Bedeutende **Vertriebskennzahlen** sind:

$$Angebotserfolg = \frac{erhaltene\ Aufträge}{abgegebene\ Aufträge} * 100$$

$$Auftragsreichweite = \frac{Auftragsbestand}{Umsatz\ der\ letzten\ 12\ Monate} * 100$$

$$durchschn.\ Umsatz\ pro\ Kunde = \frac{Umsatzerlöse}{Kundenzahl} * 100$$

$$Exportquote = \frac{Umsatzerlöse\ im\ Ausland}{Gesamte\ Umsatzerlöse} * 100$$

$$Flächenleistung\ in\ Umsatz\ je\ m^2\ Verkaufsfläche =$$

$$\frac{Umsatz}{Verkaufsfläche}$$

Die **Preiselastizität** der Nachfrage beschreibt die prozentuale Veränderung der Nachfragemenge bei einer Preiserhöhung oder Preissenkung.

$$Preiselastizität = \frac{relative\ Mengenänderung}{relative\ Preisänderung}$$

Ökonomen nutzen die **Preis-Absatz-Funktion**, um das Verhältnis zwischen dem Preis und der Absatzmenge darzustellen.

$$P(x) = a - b * x$$

mit

P: Preis pro Stück
a: Prohibitivpreis
b: Verhältnis der proportionalen Veränderung von Preis und Absatzmenge
x: Absatzmenge in Stück

Um den maximalen Gewinn zu errechnen, benutzt man die
Gewinnfunktion.

$$Gewinn = Erlös - Kosten$$

Der Erlös wird berechnet, indem man die Preis-Absatz-Funktion
mit der abgesetzten Menge x multipliziert.

$$E(x) = P(x) * x$$

Die **Kostenfunktion** ergibt sich aus den variablen und fixen
Kosten.

$$K = K_{fix} + K_{variabel} * (x)$$

Im Rahmen der **Preiskalkulationen** unterscheidet man zwischen Industrie und Handel:

Preiskalkulation in der Industrie	Preiskalkulation im Handel
Materialkosten	Einkaufspreis
+Fertigungskosten	-Rabatt, Bonus, Skonto
=Herstellungskosten	+Bezugskosten
+Verwaltungsgemeinkosten	**=Einstandspreis (auch**
+Vertriebskosten	**Bezugspreis)**
=Selbstkosten	+Handlungskosten
+Gewinnzuschlag	**=Selbstkosten**
=Zielverkaufspreis (netto)	+Gewinnzuschlag
+Umsatzsteuer	**=Zielverkaufspreis (netto)**
=Zielverkaufspreis (brutto)	+Umsatzsteuer
	=Zielverkaufspreis (brutto)
ggf.+Kundenrabatte	
	ggf.+Kundenrabatte

$$Kaufpreisminderung =$$

$$\frac{Wert\ der\ mangelhaften\ Sache * vereinbarter\ Kaufpreis}{objektiver\ Wert\ der\ fehlerfreien\ Sache}$$

Ausgleich einer Preissenkung durch Umsatzerhöhung

$$U+= \frac{p(\%)}{AB-p(\%)-K_V-Mwst.-Inkasso} * 100$$

mit

AB: Abschlag
K_V: Variable Kosten
p: Zinssatz in %
U+: Umsatzerhöhung in %

Ausgleich einer Preissenkung bei Mischkalkulation

$$AN = \frac{(AFn * 100\%) - (AFs * S)}{N}$$

mit

AN: Ausgleichsaufschlag Normalware bei Mischkalkulation in %
AFn: bisheriger Aufschlag in %
AFs: Aufschlag Sonderangebote in %
S: Anteil Sonderangebote am Sortiment in %
N: Anteil Normalware am Sortiment in %

Marktpotenzial

$Marktpotenzial =$

$Einwohner\ des\ Einzugsgebiets$
$* \emptyset\ pro\ Kopf\ Ausgaben\ in\ der\ Branche$
$* Kaufkraft\ des\ Einzugsgebiets$
$+ Zuflüsse\ aus\ Kaufkraft\ aus\ anderen\ Einzugsgebieten$
$- Abflüsse\ an\ Kaufkraf\ in\ andere\ Einzugsgebiete$

Controlling

Bilanz

Aktiva	Passiva
Mittelverwendung	Mittelherkunft
Vermögen	Kapital

Es werden verschiedene **Kostenbegriffe** verwendet. Die wichtigsten sind:

Produktionskosten

Variable Kosten
Kosten, die von der Produktionsmenge abhängig sind
Bsp.: Kosten für Roh-, Hilfs- und Betriebsstoffe

Fixe Kosten
Kosten, die von der Produktionsmenge unabhängig sind
Bsp.: Abschreibungen auf Gebäude

Sprungfixe Kosten
Kosten, die in bestimmten Intervalle fix sind
Bsp.: Abschreibungen auf Maschinen bei Erweiterung des Maschinenparks

Gesamtkosten
Kosten aller produzierten Stücke in einer bestimmten Periode

Stückkosten	Kosten pro Stück
Grenzkosten	Kosten für ein zusätzlich produziertes Stück

Kostenträgerrechnung

Einzelkosten	Kosten, die einem Kostenträger, z B. einem Produkt direkt zugeordnet werden können *Bsp.: Fertigungslohnkosten, Materialkosten*
Echte Gemeinkosten	Kosten, die einem Kostenträger nicht direkt zugeordnet werden können *Bsp.: Energiekosten, Abschreibungen, Versicherungen*
Unechte Gemeinkosten	Kosten, die im Sinne der Wirtschaftlichkeit nicht elne Kostenträger zugeordnet werden sollen *Bsp.: Hilfsstoffe*

Kosten mit Zeitbezug

Normalkosten
Durchschnittliche Kosten in der Vergangenheit
Bsp.: Durchschnittliche Kosten der letzten fünf Jahre

Istkosten
Vergangenheitskosten
Bsp.: Kosten der vergangenen Periode

Plankosten
Voraussichtliche Kosten in der Zukunft
Bsp.: Kostenschätzungen für das nächste Jahr

Relevanz der Kosten

Relevante Kosten   Kosten, die durch eine Entscheidung, z.B. Entscheidung zu einer Investition, beeinflusst werden. Die Kosten fallen nur an, wenn diese ausgeführt wird

Irrelevante Kosten   Kosten, die durch eine Entscheidung (z.B. Investition) nicht beeinflusst werden, da diese Kosten auch anfallen, wenn die Investition nicht durchgeführt wird

Kostenarten

Grundkosten   Zweckaufwendungen, die dem
Betriebszweck dienen, aufwandsgleich
Kosten
Bsp.: handelsrechtliche
Abschreibungen

Kalkulatorische Kosten   Zum einen Anderskosten
Bsp.: Kalkulatorische Abschreibungen
Zum anderen Zusatzkosten durch die
Annahme von Opportunitätskosten
Bsp.: Kalkulatorischer
Unternehmerlohn, kalkulatorische
Miete, kalkulatorische Zinsen

Zahlungswirksamkeit

Pagatorische Kosten
Zahlungsgleiche Kosten, Zahlungen, die wirklich getätigt
werden
Bsp.: Miete, Gehälter, Materialkosten

Kalkulatorische Kosten
Kosten, die der Kostenrechnung dienen, die aber nicht zur
reellen Auszahlung führen
Bsp.: Kalkulatorische Zinsen, kalkulatorische Miete

Kostenrechnungssystem

Vollkostenrechnung
Den Kostenträgern werden alle Kosten zugerechnet
Bsp.: Klassische Kostenrechnung

Teilkostenrechnung
Den Kostenträgern werden nur verursachte Kosten
zugerechnet
Bsp.: Deckungsbeitragsrechnung

Gesamtkosten	$K = K_V + K_F$	Summe aus fixen und variablen Kosten
Fixe Kosten	$K_F = \dfrac{K_F}{x}$	Von der Produktionsmenge x unabhängige Kosten
Variable Kosten	$K_V = \dfrac{K_V}{x}$	Von der Produktionsmenge x abhängige Kosten
Stückkosten	$k = \dfrac{K}{x}$	Gesamtkosten pro produziertem Stück
Fixe Stückkosten	$K_F = \dfrac{K_F}{x}$	Von der Produktionsmenge x unabhängige Stückkosten
Variable Stückkosten	$K_V = \dfrac{K_V}{x}$	Von der Produktionsmenge x abhängige Stückkosten
Grenzkosten	$K' = \dfrac{dK}{dx}$	Kosten pro zusätzlich produzierter Produkteinheit

Die Kosten werden in der **Kostenfunktion K=f(x)** dargestellt.
Die Funktion zeigt den Zusammenhang zwischen
Gesamtkosten K und der Produktionsmenge x.

Bei **Proportional steigenden Kosten** erhöhen sich die
Gesamtkosten pro mehr produzierte Einheit um den gleichen
Betrag.

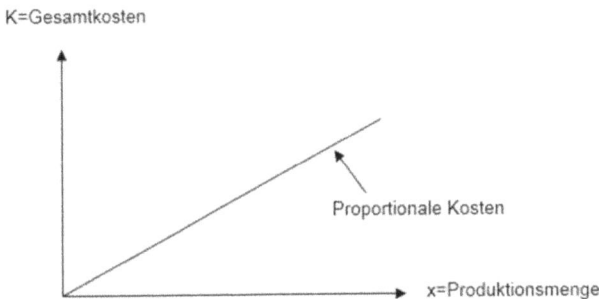

K=Gesamtkosten

Proportionale Kosten

x=Produktionsmenge

Bei **Degressiv steigenden Kosten** erhöhen sich die
Gesamtkosten pro mehr produzierte Einheit um einen immer
kleiner werdenden Betrag. Diesen Kostenverlauf findet man bei
sinkenden Materialkosten durch zum Beispiel Mengenrabatt.

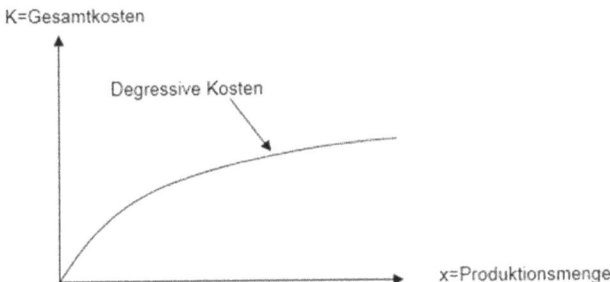

K=Gesamtkosten

Degressive Kosten

x=Produktionsmenge

Weiterhin gibt es **Progressiv steigende Kosten** bei denen sich
die Gesamtkosten pro zusätzlich produziertem Stück immer
stärker erhöhen. Eine mögliche Ursache für diesen
Kostenverlauf können zum Beispiel zu leistende
Überstundenzuschläge und dadurch höhere Personalkosten
sein.

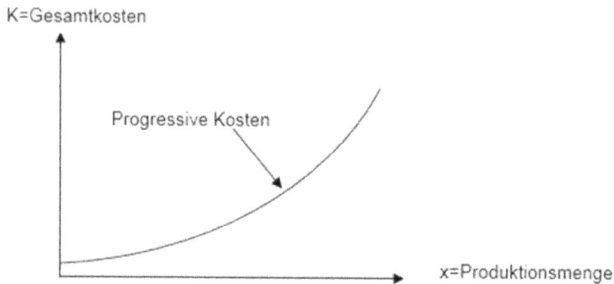

K=Gesamtkosten

Progressive Kosten

x=Produktionsmenge

Die **Fixen Kosten** bleiben auch bei steigender
Produktionsmenge. Ein Beispiel dafür sind Mietkosten für eine
Produktionshalle.

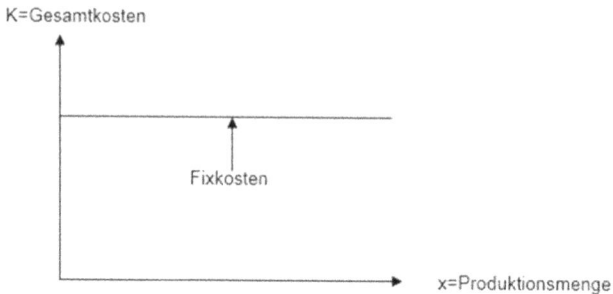

K=Gesamtkosten

Fixkosten

x=Produktionsmenge

Bei **Sprungfixen Kosten** sind die Gesamtkosten nur in bestimmten Produktionsintervallen fix. Sobald die Produktionsmenge ein bestimmtes Niveau überschreitet steigen die Gesamtkosten sprungartig an. Die sprungfixen Kosten werden daher auch intervallfixe Kosten genannt.
Ursachen sind dafür beispielsweise steigende Abschreibungen durch die Erweiterung des Maschinenparks.

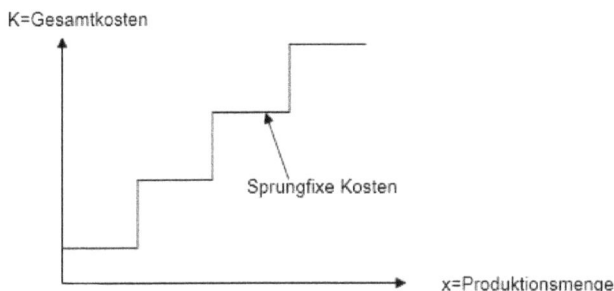

K=Gesamtkosten

Sprungfixe Kosten

x=Produktionsmenge

Bei der **Fixkostendegression** gelingt es Unternehmen, dass die Fixkosten mit steigender Produktionsmenge gleichzeitig sinken.
Die ist zum Beispiel der Fall, wenn die Miete für eine Produktionshalle nicht auf 100, sondern auf 200 Produkte umzulegen ist.

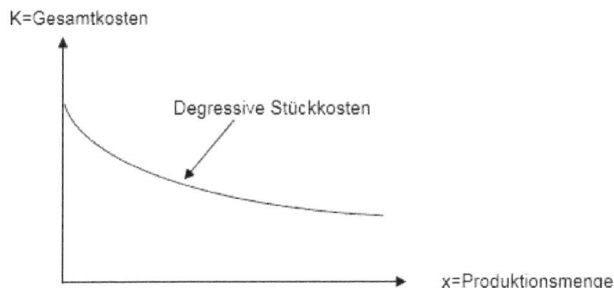

K=Gesamtkosten

Degressive Stückkosten

x=Produktionsmenge

Mischkosten

$$Reagibilti\ddot{a}tsgrad = \frac{prozentuale\ Kosten\ddot{a}nderung}{prozentuale\ Besch\ddot{a}ftigungs\ddot{a}nderung} * 100$$

$$Grenzkosten = \frac{Ver\ddot{a}nderung\ der\ Gesamtkosten}{Ver\ddot{a}nderung\ der\ Besch\ddot{a}ftigung}$$

$$Grenzkosten = \frac{neue\ Gesamtkosten - alte\ Gesamtkosten}{neue\ Besch\ddot{a}ftigung - alte\ Besch\ddot{a}ftigung}$$

Zur **Ermittlung des Materialverbrauchs** werden verschiedene Methoden genutzt. Drei bekannte und gängige werden im Folgenden dargestellt:

Mit der **Inventurmethode** sind die Inventurzählungen am Ende einer Periode maßgeblich.

Materialverbrauch =

Lageranfangsbestand (lt. Inventur am Periodenanfang
+ Lagerzugänge (lt. System, bzw. Lieferscheine)
− Lagerendbestand (lt. Inventur am Periodenende)

Bei der **Skontrationsmethode** wird der Materialverbrauch anhand der Bücher geprüft. Die Ermittlung erfolgt mit Materialentnahmescheinen. Diese Methode wird auch Fortschreibungsmethode genannt.

$Materialverbrauch =$

$$Lagerabgänge\ (lt.\ Materialentnahmescheine)$$

Eine weitere Methode ist die **Rückrechnungsmethode**, bei der der Verbrauch anhand der Produktionsmengen der Produkte mithilfe von Stücklisten oder Prozessbeschreibungen berechnet wird.

$Materialverbrauch =$

$$Menge\ an\ Endprodukten\ in\ Stück$$
$$*\ Sollmaterialverbrauch\ pro\ Stück\ des\ Endprodukts$$

Durchschnittwertermittlung

$\emptyset - Wert =$

$$\frac{Anfangsbestand\ [€] + \sum aller\ Zugänge\ [€]}{(Anfangsbestand\ [Stück] \sum Summe\ aller\ Zugänge\ [Stück]}$$

Auch bei der **Bewertung des Materialverbrauchs** hat man verschiedene Verfahren zur Verfügung.

Beim **Durchschnittswertverfahren** werden aus den gezahlten Ist-Preisen in der Vergangenheit Durchschnittspreise ermittelt. Mit diesen Durchschnittpreisen wird der Materialbedarf bewertet.

$Durchschnittlicher\ Einkaufspreis =$

$$\frac{p_1 * x_1 + p_2 * x_2 + ... + p_n * x_n}{x_1 + x_2 + ... + x_n}$$

p: Einkaufspreis einer Materialart für eine bestimmte Lieferung 1,2,...,n
x: gelieferte Menge der Materialart bei der Lieferung 1,2,...,n

$Standardwert = Planmenge * Verrechnungspreis$

$Wareneinzelkosten = Einstandspreis * Menge\ des\ Auftrags$

Bei den **Verbrauchsfolgeverfahren** wird angenommen, dass die Materialien immer in einer bestimmten Reihenfolge entnommen werden. Die bezeichnet man als Verbrauchsfolgefiktion. Die gezahlten Preise für die entnommenen Preise bilden die Basis für die Bewertung des Materialverbrauchs.

Es gibt vier verschiedene Verbrauchsfolgefiktionen.

Verbrauchsfolgeverfahren	Verbrauchsfolgefiktion
FIFO = First In, First Out	Die *zuerst* eingekauften Materialien werden auch als Erstes verbraucht
LIFO = Last In, First Out	Die *zuletzt* eingekauften Materialien werden als Erstes verbraucht
HIFO = Highest In, First Out	Die Materialien mit dem *höchsten* Einkaufspreis pro Stück werden als Erstes entnommen
LOFO = Lowest In, First Out	Die Materialien mit dem *niedrigsten* Einkaufspreis pro Stück werden als Erstes entnommen

Bei **Festpreisverfahren** nimmt man einen konstanten Materialpreis, um Preisschwankungen zu vermeiden und die Berechnung zu vereinfachen. Zur Bestimmung des Festpreises kann man sich orientieren an

- Durchschnittspreisen der Vergangenheit
- Wiederbeschaffungspreisen
- Planpreisen

Anschaffungs- und Herstellkosten

Anschaffungskosten:

Anschaffungspreis
- Anschaffungsminderungen (Rabatt, Bonus, Skonti)
+ Anschaffungsnebenkosten (Transportkosten, Installationskosten)
+ nachträgliche Anschaffungskosten
=Anschaffungskosten

Herstellungskosten im Handelsrecht:

Fertigungsmaterial
+ Fertigungslöhne
+ Sondereinzelkosten der Fertigung
+ Materialgemeinkosten
+ Fertigungsgemeinkosten
= Mindest-Herstellungskosten
+ Verwaltungsgemeinkosten
= Höchst-Herstellungskosten

Herstellkosten im Steuerrecht:

Fertigungsmaterial
+ Fertigungslöhne
+ Sondereinzelkosten der Fertigung
+ Materialgemeinkosten
+ Fertigungsgemeinkosten
= Mindest-Herstellkosten
+ Verwaltungsgemeinkosten
= Höchst-Herstellkosten

Kostenstellenrechnung

Die **Ist-Gemeinkostenzuschläge** werden mittels Kalkulationssätzen aus dem Betriebsabrechnungsbogen (BAB) gebildet:

$$MGKZ = \frac{MGK}{MEK} * 100$$

$$FGKZ = \frac{FGK}{FLK} * 100$$

$$EKGKZ = \frac{EKGK}{HK\ des\ Umsatz} * 100$$

mit

MGKZ: Materialgemeinkostenzuschlagssatz
MGK: Materialgemeinkosten
MEK: Materialeinzelkosten
FGKZ: Fertigungsgemeinkostenzuschlagssatz
FGK: Fertigungsgemeinkosten
FLK: Stundenverrechnungssatz/Fertigungslöhne
EKGKZ: Entwicklungs- und Konstruktionsgemeinkostenzuschlagssatz
EKGK: Entwicklungs- und Konstruktionsgemeinkosten

$$VVGKZ = VwGKZ + VtGKZ$$

$$VwGKZ = \frac{VwGK}{HK\ des\ Umsatz} * 100$$

$$VtGKZ = \frac{VtGK}{HK\ des\ Umsatz} * 100$$

$$RFGKZ = \frac{RFGK}{FLK} * 100$$

$$HGKZ = \frac{HGK}{WK} * 100$$

mit

VVGKZ: Verwaltungs- und Vertriebsgemeinkostenzuschlagssatz
VwGKZ: Verwaltungsgemeinkostenzuschlagssatz
VwGK: Verwaltungsgemeinkosten
VtGKZ: Vertriebsgemeinkostenzuschlagssatz
VtGK: Vertriebsgemeinkosten
RFGKZ: Restfertigungsgemeinkostenzuschlagssatz bei Anwendung der Maschinenkostenverrechnung
RFGK: Restfertigungsgemeinkosten
HGKZ: Handelsgemeinkostenzuschlagssatz
HGK: Handelsgemeinkosten

$$Normalgemeinkosten =$$

$$Nomalgeimeinkostenzuschlagssatz * Bezugsgröße$$

Normalgemeinkosten > Ist-Gemeinkosten = Kostenüberdeckung
Normalgemeinkosten < Ist-Gemeinkosten = Kostenunterdeckung

Kalkulatorische Kosten

Die **Kalkulatorischen Abschreibungen** werden genutzt, um den tatsächlichen Wertverlust von zum Bespiel Maschinen im Anlagevermögen darzustellen. Die kalkulatorischen Abschreibungen sind unabhängig von der handelsrechtlichen Abschreibung. Es gibt verschiedene Methoden zur Berechnung von kalkulatorischen Abschreibungen:

Die **Lineare Abschreibung** ist eine einfache und gebräuchliche Methode bei der immer gleichhohe Beträge abzogen werden.

$$a = \frac{A - RW}{n}$$

a: Abschreibungsbetrag
A: Ausgangswert
RW: Restwert
n: Nutzungsdauer

$$Wiederbeschaffungswert = A * Preissteigerungsindex$$

$$Preissteigerungsindex =$$

$$\frac{Preisindex\ im\ aktuellen\ Jahr\ der\ Wiederbeschaffung}{Preisindex\ im\ Jahr\ der\ Anschaffung}$$

Bei der **arithmetisch-degressiven Abschreibungen** sinkt der abzuschreibende Betrag mit jedem weiteren Jahr um denselben Betrag.

$$a = \frac{A - RW}{N} * T$$

a: Abschreibungsbetrag
A: Ausgangswert
RW: Restwert
N: Summe der einzelnen Perioden
    der Abschreibung (1+2+3+...+n)
T: Restnutzungsdauer

Eine weitere Abschreibungsmethode ist die **Geometrisch-degressive Abschreibung**, bei stets der gleiche Prozentsatz vom Restbuchwert abgezogen wird.

$$a = RBW_{t-1} * \left[100 * \sqrt[n]{\frac{RW}{A}} \right]$$

RBW_{t-1}: Restbuchwert am Ende der Vorperiode

Bei der **Leistungsabschreibung** orientieren sich die Abschreibungsbeträge an der tatsächlich erbrachten Leistung des Anlagegegenstandes.

$$a_t = \frac{A - RW}{LE_G} * LE_t$$

a_t: Abschreibungsbetrag im Jahr t
LE_G: Summe der Leistungseinheiten, die ein Anlagegegenstand während der Nutzungsdauer leistet
LE_t: die im vergangenen Jahr t erbrachten Leistungseinheiten

Eine weitere Kennzahl im Bereich der kalkulatorischen Kosten sind die **Kalkulatorischen Zinsen**. Diese ergeben sich durch die Verzinsung des Eigenkapitals.

$Kalkulatorische\ Zinsen =$

$Kapitalkostenzinssatz * betriebsnotwendiges\ Kapital$

Das betriebsnotwendige Kapital setzt sich wie folgt zusammen:

Betriebsnotwendiges Kapital =   *Betriebsnotwendiges Anlagevermögen (z.B. Maschinen und Gebäude) +betriebsnotwendiges Umlaufvermögen (z.B. Roh- und Betriebsstoffe) – Abzugskapital*

Kalkulatorische Wagnisse werden berücksichtigt, um unternehmerische Wagnisse wie beispielweise Forderungsausfälle oder Diebstahl abzudecken.

$$Kalkulatorischer\ Wagniszuschlag =$$

$$Warenaufwendungen * Prozentsatz$$

$$Wagniszuschlag = \frac{geschätzer\ Verlust}{Bezugsgröße} * 100$$

Wagnis	Bezugsgröße
Anlagewagnis	Anschaffungskosten
Beständewagnis	Bezugskosten
Entwicklungswagnis	Entwicklungskosten
Vertriebswagnis	Umsatz zu Selbstkosten
Gewährleistungswagnis	Umsatz zu Selbstkosten
Fertigungswagnis	Herstellkosten

Der **Kalkulatorische Unternehmerlohn** ersetzt das fiktive Gehalt des Unternehmers. Auch wenn der Unternehmer in der Realität keine Gehaltszahlungen erhält, sollten diese in die allgemeine Preiskalkulation mit einfließen.

Man orientiert sich dabei an dem Gehalt, das ein Geschäftsführer in einem vergleichbaren Unternehmen erhalten würde.

Die **Kalkulatorische Miete** wird für Räume berechnet, die zwar betrieblich genutzt werden, für die aber keine Miete an Dritte gezahlt werden muss, da der Unternehmer Eigentümer ist. Die Höhe der kalkulatorischen Miete orientiert sich dabei an den regional üblichen Grundstückpreisen.

Kalkulation der Stückkosten

Kosten	Zwischensummen			
Materialeinzelkosten	= Material-kosten	= Herstell-kosten der Fertigung	= Herstell-kosten des Umsatz	= Selbst-kosten des Auftrags
+ Materialgemeinkosten				
+ Fertigungslohnkosten	= Fertigungs-kosten			
+ Fertigungsgemeinkosten				
+ Bestandsminderung				
- Bestandsmehrung				
+ Verwaltungsgemeinkosten				
+ Vertriebsgemeinkosten				

Divisionskalkulation

Einstufige Divisionskalkulation

$$Kosten\ pro\ Mengeneinheit = \frac{Gesamtkosten}{Mengeneinheit}$$

Zwei – oder mehrstufige Divisionskalkulation

$Kosten\ pro\ Mengeneinheit =$

$$\frac{Herstellkosten}{Produktionsmenge} + \frac{Verwaltungs - und\ Vertriebskosten}{Absatzemenge}$$

Äquivalenzziffernkalkulation

$Recheneinheiten\ (RE) =$

$$Mengeneinheit\ (ME) * Äquivalenzziffer$$

$$Kosten\ je\ Recheneinheit = \frac{Gesamtkosten}{\sum Recheneinheiten}$$

$$Selbstkosten\ \left[\frac{€}{ME}\right] =$$

$$Kosten\ je\ Recheneinheit * Äquivalenzziffer$$
$$Selbstkosten\ gesamt = Selbstkosten\ [€/ME] * Menge$$

mit
| RE: Recheneinheiten wie z.B. kg, Stück usw. |
| ME: Mengeneinheiten wie z.B. kg, Stück usw. |

Zuschlagskalkulation
Einstufige (summarische) Zuschlagskalkulation
Mehrstufige (differenzierende) Zuschlagskalkulation
Bezugsgrößenkalkulation

Kuppelkalkulation
Restwertmethode
Marktwertmethode

Deckungsbeitragsrechnung

$$DB = U - K_v$$

DB: Deckungsbeitrag einer Produktart
U: Umsatzerlöse eines Produktes
K_v: variable Gesamtkosten eines Produktes

$$db = p - k_v$$

db: Deckungsbeitrag pro Stück
p: Preis pro Stück
k_v: variable Stückkosten

Einstufige Deckungsbeitragsrechnung

Produkt	A	B	C
Umsatzerlöse			
– variable Kosten			
= **Deckungsbeitrag**			
Summe der Deckungsbeiträge			
– Fixkosten			
= **Betriebserfolg**			

Mehrstufige Deckungsbeitragsrechnung

z.B. Geschäftsbereich, Geschäftsart, Produktlinie etc.	z.B. Europa			z.B. Nordamerika		Gesamtwerte
Produktgruppen	I		II	III		
Produktarten	A	B	C	D	E	
Umsatzerlöse						
– variable Kosten Produktart						
Deckungsbeitrag I						
– fixe Kosten Produktart						
Deckungsbeitrag II						
– fixe Kosten Produktgruppe						
Deckungsbeitrag III						
– fixe Kosten Geschäftsbereich						
Deckungsbeitrag IV						
– fixe Kosten Gesamtunternehmen						
= Betriebserfolg						

Kurzfristige Preisuntergrenze p_{min}

$$p_{min} = k_V \, (€/St\ddot{u}ck)$$

Plankostenrechnung

Starre Plankostenrechnung auf Vollkostenbasis

$$K_P = x_P * p_P$$

K_P: Plankosten
x_P: Planmenge
p_P: Planpreis pro Stück

$$K_{ver} = \frac{K_P}{x_P} * x_I$$

K_{ver}: verrechnete Plankosten
K_P: Plankosten
x_P: Planmenge
x_I: Istbeschäftigung

$$K_I = x_I * p_I$$

K_I: Istkosten
x_I: Istbeschäftigung
p_I: Istpreis

$$Gesamtabweichung = K_I - K_{ver}$$

mit

K_I: Istkosten
K_{ver}: verrechnete Plankosten

Flexible Plankostenrechnung auf Teilkostenbasis (Grenzplankostenrechnung)

$$K_P = K_F * K_V$$

K_P: Plankosten
K_F: fixe Plankosten
K_V: variable Plankosten

$$K_S = \frac{K_V}{x_P} * x_I$$

K_S: verrechnete variable Sollkosten
K_V: variable Plankosten
x_P: Planmenge
x_I: Istbeschäftigung

$$K_{vI} = x_I * p_I - K_F$$

K_{vI}: variable Istkosten
x_I: Istbeschäftigung
p_I: Istpreis
K_F: fixe Plankosten

$$Gesamtabweichung = K_{vI} - K_S$$

mit

K_{vI}: variable Istkosten
K_S: verrechnete variable Sollkosten

$Umsatzabweichungen =$

$Ist\,Kosten\,des\,Umsatzes - Plankosten\,des\,Umsatzes$

$Beschäftigungsabweichung =$

$verrechnete\,Plankosten - Sollkosten$

$Preisabweichungen =$

$Ist\,Menge * Ist\,Preis - Ist\,Menge * Planpreis$

Bilanzierung des Umlaufvermögens

strenges Niederstwertprinzip

$$Bewertung\ zum\ Tageswert = Anschaffungskosten$$
$$> Tageswert$$

$$Bewertung\ zum\ Anschaffungswert = Anschaffungskosten$$
$$< Tageswert$$

Die Anschaffungskosten bilden bei der Bilanzierung des Umlaufvermögens immer die Obergrenze.

Wertpapierbewertung

Beim Kauf müssen Wertpapiere zu Anschaffungskosten aktiviert werden. Zum Bilanzstichtag müssen sie nach dem Niederstwertprinzip angesetzt werden. Es gelten folgende Bilanzierungsregeln:

$$Bewertung\ zum\ Tageswert = Anschaffungswert$$
$$> Tageswert$$

$$Bewertung\ zum\ Anschaffungswert = Anschaffungswert$$
$$< Tageswert$$

Auch hier bilden die Anschaffungskosten die Obergrenze, selbst wenn durch anschließende Werterhöhung ein höherer Wert erzielt wird. Nebenkosten sind anteilig zu berücksichtigen.

Für Wertpapiere des Umlaufvermögens muss das Niederstwertprinzip angewendet werden. Bei Wertanlagen des Analagevermögens gilt das gemilderte Niederstwertprinzip.

Gewinn und Verlustrechnung (GuV)

GuV nach Gesamtkostenverfahren:
Umsatzerlös
± Bestandsveränderung
+ Eigenleistung

= Gesamtleistung
+ sonstige Erträge
- Materialaufwand

= Rohergebnis
- Personalaufwand
- Anschreibungen
- sonstige betriebliche Aufwendungen
+ Zinserträge
- Zinsaufwendungen

= Ergebnis der gewöhnlichen Geschäftstätigkeit
± außerordentliche Erträge/ Aufwendungen

= Ergebnis vor Steuern
- Steuern vom Einkommen und Ertrag

= Jahresüberschuss/ Jahresfehlbetrag

GuV nach Umsatzkostenverfahren:
Umsatzerlös
- Herstellkosten

= Bruttoergebnis vom Umsatz
- Vertriebskosten
- allgemeine Verwaltungskosten
+ sonstige betriebliche Erträge
- sonstige betriebliche Aufwendungen
+ Zinserträge
- Zinsaufwendungen

= Ergebnis der gewöhnlichen Geschäftstätigkeit
± außerordentliche Erträge/ Aufwendungen

= Gewinn vor Steuer bzw. Verlust
- Steuern

= Gewinn nach Steuern bzw. Verlust

Finanzmathematik und Statistik

Mathematische Rechenregeln

Rechenregeln für Potenzen und Wurzeln

$$x^{-y} = \frac{1}{x^y}$$

$$x^{\frac{1}{y}} = \sqrt[y]{x}$$

$$x^y * x^z = x^{y+z}$$

$$x^z * y^z = (xy)^z$$

$$(x^y)^z = x^{y*z}$$

Rechenregeln für Logarithmen

$$\log(x * y) = \log(x) + \log(y)$$

$$\log\frac{x}{y} = \log(x) - \log(y)$$

$$\log(x^y) = y * \log(x)$$

Finanzmathematik

Zinsrechnung

$$Zinsen\ (€/Jahr) = \frac{K * p * T}{100\% * 360\ Tage}$$

K: Kapital
p: Zinssatz in €/Jahr
T: Tage

$$K_t = K_o * Zinsfaktor$$

Der Zinsfaktor ist von der Zinsberechnungsmethode abhängig.
Folgende Möglichkeiten gibt es zur Bestimmung des
Zinsfaktors:

einfach: $$ZF = 1 + rt$$

exponentiell: $$ZF = (1 + r)^t$$

K_t: Endkapital
K_o: Startkapital
r: Zinssatz
m: Anzahl der Zinsperioden p.a.

unterjährig exponentiell:
$$ZF = (1 + \frac{r}{m})^{mt}$$

stetig: $$ZF = e^{rt}$$

$$K_0 = K_t * Diskontfaktor$$

$$Diskontfaktor = \frac{1}{Zinsfaktor}$$

Rentenrechnung

Über einen Zeitraum von n Jahren werden periodisch Zahlungen der Höhe Z geleistet, die mit dem Zinssatz r verzinst werden. Dabei kann die Zahlung auch unterjährig stattfinden und entsprechend unterjährig verzinst werden. Mit den Barwertfaktoren und Endwertfaktoren ergibt sich der Barwert bzw. der Endwert einer solchen Zahlungsreihe.

$$Barwert = Barwertfaktor * Z$$

$$Endwert = Endwertfaktor * Z$$

		Barwertfaktor	Endwertfaktor
Nachschüssige Rente mit	Jährlichen Zahlungen	$\dfrac{(1+r)^n - 1}{r * (1+r)^n}$	$\dfrac{(1+r)^n - 1}{r}$
	m Zahlungen pro Jahr	$\dfrac{(1+\frac{r}{m})^{m*n} - 1}{\frac{r}{m} * (1+\frac{r}{m})^{m*n}}$	$\dfrac{(1+\frac{r}{m})^{m*n} - 1}{\frac{r}{m}}$
Vorschüssige Rente mit	Jährlichen Zahlungen	$\dfrac{(1+r)^n - 1}{r * (1+r)^{n-1}}$	$(1+r) * \dfrac{(1+r)^n - 1}{r}$
	m Zahlungen pro Jahr	$\dfrac{(1+\frac{r}{m})^{m*n} - 1}{\frac{r}{m} * (1+\frac{r}{m})^{m*n-1}}$	$\left(1+\dfrac{r}{m}\right) * \dfrac{(1+\frac{r}{m})^{m*n} - 1}{\frac{r}{m}}$

Renditerechnung

$$A = \sum_{i=1}^{n} DF_i * Z_i$$

Die Formel nach r auflösen

Praktikerformel zur näherungsweisen Berechnung:

$$r \approx \frac{Kupon + \dfrac{R\ddot{u}ckzahlung - Preis}{Restlaufzeit}}{Preis}$$

Duration und Konvexität

Duration

$$D = \frac{\sum_{i=1}^{n} t_i * Z_i * (r + 1)^{-t_i}}{\sum_{i=1}^{n} Z_i * (r + 1)^{-t_i}}$$

Modified Duration

$$MD = \frac{D}{1 + r}$$

Konvexität

$$K = \frac{\sum_{i=1}^{n} t_i * (t_i + 1) * Z_i * (r + 1)^{-t_i}}{(1 + r)^2 \sum_{i=1}^{n} Z_i * (r + 1)^{-t_i}}$$

	0	1	2	3	4	5	6	7	8	9
0,0	0,5	0,50399	0,50798	0,51197	0,51595	0,51994	0,52392	0,5279	0,53188	0,53586
0,1	0,53983	0,5438	0,54776	0,55172	0,55567	0,55962	0,56356	0,56749	0,57142	0,57535
0,2	0,57926	0,58317	0,58706	0,59095	0,59483	0,59871	0,60257	0,60642	0,61026	0,61409
0,3	0,61791	0,62172	0,62552	0,6293	0,63307	0,63683	0,64058	0,64431	0,64803	0,65173
0,4	0,65542	0,6591	0,66276	0,6664	0,67003	0,67364	0,67724	0,68082	0,68439	0,68793
0,5	0,69146	0,69497	0,69847	0,70194	0,7054	0,70884	0,71226	0,71566	0,71904	0,7224
0,6	0,72575	0,72907	0,73237	0,73565	0,73891	0,74215	0,74537	0,74857	0,75175	0,7549
0,7	0,75804	0,76115	0,76424	0,7673	0,77035	0,77337	0,77637	0,77935	0,7823	0,78524
0,8	0,78814	0,79103	0,79389	0,79673	0,79955	0,80234	0,80511	0,80785	0,81057	0,81327
0,9	0,81594	0,81859	0,82121	0,82381	0,82639	0,82894	0,83147	0,83398	0,83646	0,83891
1,0	0,84134	0,84375	0,84614	0,84849	0,85083	0,85314	0,85543	0,85769	0,85993	0,86214
1,1	0,86433	0,8665	0,86864	0,87076	0,87286	0,87493	0,87698	0,879	0,881	0,88298
1,2	0,88493	0,88686	0,88877	0,89065	0,89251	0,89435	0,89617	0,89796	0,89973	0,90147
1,3	0,9032	0,9049	0,90658	0,90824	0,90988	0,91149	0,91309	0,91466	0,91621	0,91774
1,4	0,91924	0,92073	0,9222	0,92364	0,92507	0,92647	0,92785	0,92922	0,93056	0,93189
1,5	0,93319	0,93448	0,93574	0,93699	0,93822	0,93943	0,94062	0,94179	0,94295	0,94408
1,6	0,9452	0,9463	0,94738	0,94845	0,9495	0,95053	0,95154	0,95254	0,95352	0,95449
1,7	0,95543	0,95637	0,95728	0,95818	0,95907	0,95994	0,9608	0,96164	0,96246	0,96327
1,8	0,96407	0,96485	0,96562	0,96638	0,96712	0,96784	0,96856	0,96926	0,96995	0,97062
1,9	0,97128	0,97193	0,97257	0,9732	0,97381	0,97441	0,975	0,97558	0,97615	0,9767
2,0	0,97725	0,97778	0,97831	0,97882	0,97932	0,97982	0,9803	0,98077	0,98124	0,98169
2,1	0,98214	0,98257	0,983	0,98341	0,98382	0,98422	0,98461	0,985	0,98537	0,98574
2,2	0,9861	0,98645	0,98679	0,98713	0,98745	0,98778	0,98809	0,9884	0,9887	0,98899
2,3	0,98928	0,98956	0,98983	0,9901	0,99036	0,99061	0,99086	0,99111	0,99134	0,99158
2,4	0,9918	0,99202	0,99224	0,99245	0,99266	0,99286	0,99305	0,99324	0,99343	0,99361
2,5	0,99379	0,99396	0,99413	0,9943	0,99446	0,99461	0,99477	0,99492	0,99506	0,9952
2,6	0,99534	0,99547	0,9956	0,99573	0,99585	0,99598	0,99609	0,99621	0,99632	0,99643
2,7	0,99653	0,99664	0,99674	0,99683	0,99693	0,99702	0,99711	0,9972	0,99728	0,99736
2,8	0,99744	0,99752	0,9976	0,99767	0,99774	0,99781	0,99788	0,99795	0,99801	0,99807
2,9	0,99813	0,99819	0,99825	0,99831	0,99836	0,99841	0,99846	0,99851	0,99856	0,99861
3,0	0,99865	0,99869	0,99874	0,99878	0,99882	0,99886	0,99889	0,99893	0,99896	0,999
3,1	0,99903	0,99906	0,9991	0,99913	0,99916	0,99918	0,99921	0,99924	0,99926	0,99929
3,2	0,99931	0,99934	0,99936	0,99938	0,9994	0,99942	0,99944	0,99946	0,99948	0,9995
3,3	0,99952	0,99953	0,99955	0,99957	0,99958	0,9996	0,99961	0,99962	0,99964	0,99965
3,4	0,99966	0,99968	0,99969	0,9997	0,99971	0,99972	0,99973	0,99974	0,99975	0,99976
3,5	0,99977	0,99978	0,99978	0,99979	0,9998	0,99981	0,99981	0,99982	0,99983	0,99983
3,6	0,99984	0,99985	0,99985	0,99986	0,99986	0,99987	0,99987	0,99988	0,99988	0,99989
3,7	0,99989	0,9999	0,9999	0,9999	0,99991	0,99991	0,99992	0,99992	0,99992	0,99992
3,8	0,99993	0,99993	0,99993	0,99994	0,99994	0,99994	0,99994	0,99995	0,99995	0,99995
3,9	0,99995	0,99995	0,99996	0,99996	0,99996	0,99996	0,99996	0,99996	0,99997	0,99997
4,0	0,99997	0,99997	0,99997	0,99997	0,99997	0,99997	0,99998	0,99998	0,99998	0,99998

Volkswirtschaft

Investitionen und Einkommen

$Nettoinvestitionen =$

$Bruttoinvestitionen - Ersatzinvestitionen$

Mit: Bruttoinvestitionen=Anschaffung von Anlagevermögen und
Veränderung von
Umlaufvermögen

Für private Haushalte:

$Y = C + S$ | Y: Zuflüsse durch Einkommen der Faktoren, wie z.B. Gehälter, Mieten, Zinsen, Pacht, Gewinne
C: Abflüsse, wie z.b. Konsumausgaben
S: Abflüsse, wie z.b. Sparen

Für Unternehmen:

$Y = C + I$ | Y: Abflüsse, wie z.B. Ausgaben für die Faktorleistungen (=Faktorkosten), bzw. der Wert der in dieser Periode zusätzlich erfolgten Produktion, bewertet zu Faktorkosten (= Nettowertschöpfung)
C: Zuflüsse, wie z.B. Umsatzerlöse aus Konsumgüterverkäufen
I: Zuflüsse, wie z.B. Wertezuwachs des Produktivkapitals im Unternehmenssektor

$Ex\ Post: S = I$

S: Abflüsse, wie z.B. Sparen
I: Zuflüsse, wie z.B. Wertzuwachs durch Investitionen

→ damit erreicht man ein
gesamtwirtschaftliches Gleichgewicht

$S_{geplant} > I_{geplant}$ → Ausgleich erfolgt über ein sinkendes
Zinsniveau

$S_{geplant} > I_{geplant}$ → Ausgleich erfolgt über ein steigendes
Zinsniveau

Volkswirtschaftliche Gesamtrechnung

Produktionskonto eines Unternehmens	
Soll (Aufwand)	Haben (Ertrag)
• Materialeinkäufe von anderen Unternehmen (Vorleistungen) • Abschreibungen auf Sachkapital • Indirekte Steuern abzüglich Subventionen • Kosten der Produktionsfaktoren, wie z.B. Löhne, Gehälter, Mieten, Pacht, Fremdkapitalzinsen, Gewinne	• Umsatzerlöse aus Güterverkäufen • Lagerveränderungen an eigenen Erzeugnissen • Selbst erstellte Anlagen

Bruttowertschöpfung =

   Bruttoproduktionswert − Vorleistungen

Nettowertschöpfung = Kosten der Produktionsfaktoren
     =Summe der entstandenen Einkommen
     =Bruttowertschöpfung-Abschreibungen

Einkommenskonto eines Haushalts	
Soll (Einkommensverwendung)	Haben (Einkommensbildung)
• Direkte Steuern und Sozialabgaben • Konsum • Sparen	• Bruttolohn, Bruttogehalt • Zins, Miete, Pacht (vor Steuern) • Gewinn (vor Steuern) • Sozialleistungen

Vermögensänderungskonto eines Unternehmens	
Soll (Vermögensverwendung)	Haben (Vermögensbildung)
• Bruttoinvestitionen	• Abschreibungen • Nicht entnommene Gewinne • Finanzierungsdefizit

Ergebnisgrößen in der Volkswirtschaft

Bruttoinlandsprodukt

BIP= Summe aller in einer Periode im Inland erbrachten Wertschöpfungen

BIP Entstehungsrechnung für das Jahr in Mrd. Euro:

Bruttowertschöpfung aller Unternehmen
+ Bruttowertschöpfung des Staates
+ Bruttowertschöpfung der privaten Haushalte
=Bruttowertschöpfung
+ Mehrwertsteuer und Einfuhrabgaben
= BIP zu Marktpreisen

BIP Verwendungsrechnung für das Jahr in Mrd. Euro:

Private Konsumausgaben
+ Konsumausgaben des Staates
+ Bruttoanlageinvestitionen (Ausrüstungen, Bauten, immaterielle Anlagen)
+ Vorratsveränderungen
=inländische Verwendung
+ Außenbeitrag (Export – Import)
= BIP zu Marktpreisen

Bruttonationaleinkommen

BNE = Summe aller in einer Periode von Inländern erbrachten Wertschöpfungen

BNE =   *BIP*
        + Erwerbs- und Vermögenseinkommen der Inländer aus dem Ausland (z.B. Zinseinkünfte, Auslandsgewinne, Miet- und Pachteinnahmen, Gehälter)
        – Erwerbs. Und Vermögenseinkommen der Nichtgebietsansässigen aus dem Inland (z.B. Zinszahlungen für Kapitalimporte des Auslands, Inlandsgewinne ausländischer Unternehmen)

BNE zu Marktpreisen =   *BIP zu Marktpreisen*
                        + Einkommen Einheimischer im Ausland
                        – Einkommen Ausländer im Inland

Gliederung des BNE

Nach der Entstehung:

$$BNE = Landwirtschaft + produzierte\ Waren \\ + Handel\ und\ Verkehr + Dienstleistungen + Staat$$

Nach der Verteilung:

$$BNE = \\ Einkommen\ aus\ unselbstständiger\ Arbeit \\ + Einkommen\ aus\ Unternehmertätigkeit\ und\ Vermögen \\ + indirekte\ Stuern + Abschreibungen - Subventionen$$

Nach der Verwendung:

$$BNE = privater\ Verbrauch + Staatsverbrauch + Investitionen \\ + Außenbeitrag$$

Volkseinkommen

VE = Summe aller von Inländern erwirtschafteten Einzeleinkommen

VE = Summe aller Arbeitnehmerentgelte + Summe aller Unternehmens- und
Vermögenseinkommen der Inländer

Verteilungsrechnung des BIP bis zum VE:

BIP
+ (Saldo) Einkommen der übrigen Welt
=BNE
− Abschreibung
=Nettonationaleinkommen
− indirekte Steuern
+ Subventionen
= Volkseinkommen (VE) = NNE zu Faktorpreisen

Zusammensetzung des VE bzw. Einkommensverteilung:

VE = Einkommen aus unselbstständiger Arbeit (=Einkommen
des Produktionsfaktors Arbeit)
    + Einkommen aus Unternehmertätigkeit und Vermögen
    (=Einkommen des Produktionsfaktors Boden und Kapital)

Lohnquote

$$Lohnquote = \frac{Bruttoeinkommen\ aus\ unselbstaändiger\ Arbeit}{Volkseinkommen} * 100$$

Gewinnquote

$$Gewinnquote = \frac{Einkommen\ aus\ Unternehmertätigkeit\ und\ Vermögen}{Volkseinkommen} * 100$$

Primäre und sekundäre Einkommensverteilung

Primäre Einkommensverteilung = auf dem Markt erzielte Bruttoeinkommen der Haushalte	
Umverteilungsprozess durch: 1. Abzüge vom Primäreinkommen 2. Transferzahlungen des Staates	Bruttoeinkommen −direkte Steuern u. Sozialabgaben + Sozialleistungen des Staates
Sekundäre Einkommensverteilung = verfügbare Einkommen der Haushalte	

Bilanzen

Leistungsbilanz

Leistungsbilanz = Saldo Handelsbilanz
+Saldo Dienstleistungsbilanz
+Saldo Einkommensbilanz
+Saldo laufende Übertragungsbilanz

Außenbeitrag zum BIP =
Saldo der Handeslbilanz
+ Saldo der Dienstleistungsbilanz

Bilanz der Erwerbs- und Vermögenseinkommen

Außenbeitrag zum BNE   = Saldo der Handelsbilanz
+Saldo der Dienstleistungsbilanz
+Saldo der Einkommensbilanz

Bilanz der laufenden Übertragungen=
empfangene laufende Übertragungen
– geleistete laufende Übertragungen

Devisenbilanz

Veränderung der Netto-Auslandsaktiva der Bundesbank =
+Saldo der Leistungsbilanz
+Saldo Vermögensübertragung
+Saldo Kapitalbilanz
+ Saldo statistisch nicht aufgegliederter
Transaktionen

Binnen- und Außenwert des Geldes

Geldarten

Geld= alle liquiden Mittel zu Kauf von Gütern und Leistungen

Bargeld= Banknoten und Münzen im Geldkreislauf
Buchgeld= alle Guthaben auf Bankkonten, die sofort oder in
absehbarer Zeit zum Güterverkauf bereitstehen

Buchgeldschöpfung der Banken/Kreditvergabe

$$Kreditvergabe =$$
$$Einzahlung \; (Einlage)$$
$$-Kassenreserve$$
$$-Mindestreserve$$

$$Gesamtreservesatz =$$
$$Kassenreserve \; (\%)$$
$$+Mindestreserve(\%)$$

$$gesamte \; Buchgeldschöpfung(€) =$$

$$\frac{erste \; Einlage(\%)}{Gesamtreservesatz \; (\%)} * 100$$

$$Buchgeldsch\ddot{o}pfungsmultiplikator =$$

$$\frac{1}{Reservesatz(\%)} * 100$$

$$aktive \; Buchgeldsch\ddot{o}pfung(\text{€}) =$$

$$\frac{erste \; Kredtivergabe \; (\text{€})}{Gesamtreservesatz \; (\%)} * 100$$

Lebenshaltungskostenindex = Verbraucherpreisindex (VPI)

$$VPI = \frac{Konsumsumme \; laufender \; Periode \; (\text{€})}{Konsumsumme \; Basisperiode} * 100$$

$$Preisindex = \frac{Preis \; im \; aktuellen \; Jahr}{Preis \; im \; Vorjahr} * 100$$

$$Kaufkraft \; der \; W\ddot{a}hrungseinheit =$$

$$\frac{W\ddot{a}hrungseinheit \; (\text{€})}{VPI(\%)} * 100$$

Geldwertänderung / Preisniveau

Fischer' sche Verkehrsgleichung=Qualitätsgleichung:

$$Gütervolumen = Geldvolumen$$

$$Gütermenge * Preisniveau =$$
$$Geldmenge * Umlaufgeschwindigkeit$$

$$Preisniveau = \frac{Geldmenge * Umlafgeschwindkeit}{Gütermenge}100$$

Geldwertstörungen:

Störung	Verhältnis von Geldvolumen und Gütermenge	Preisentwicklung	Geldwert-entwicklung
Inflation	Geldvolumen > Gütermenge	Preisniveau steigt	Geldwert sinkt
Deflation	Geldvolumen < Gütermenge	Preisniveau sinkt	Geldwert steigt

Inflation

$$Inflationsrate =$$

$$\frac{VPI\ lfd.\ Monat - VPI\ Vorjahresmonat}{VPI\ Vorjahresmonat} * 100$$

Außenwert des Geldes / Wechselkurs / Devisen

Devisen = ausländische Zahlungsmittel = Fremdwährung

Wechselkurs = Preis für 100 Einheiten ausländischer Währung, ausgedrückt in inländischer Währung (=Preisnotierung)

Devisenkurs = welche Menge an ausländischen Zahlungsmitteln in inländischer Währung gezahlt wird (=Mengennotierung)

Wirtschaftspolitik / Magisches Viereck

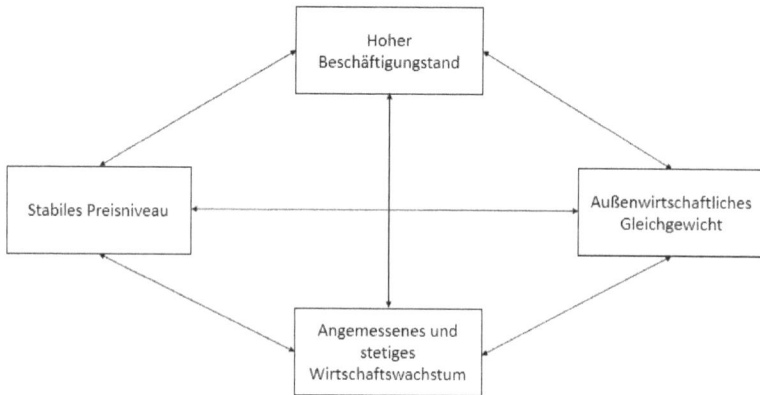

Beschäftigungsstand / Arbeitslosenquote

$$Arbeitslosenquote = \frac{registrierte\ Arbeitslose}{Gesamtzahl\ der\ Erwerbspersonen} * 100$$

Fiskalpolitik

Konjunkturlage	Aufgabe der Finanzpolitik des Staates	Art der Haushaltspolitik
Gleichgewicht	Ausgaben = Einnahmen	Neutrale Finanzpolitik
Konjunkturtief	Ausgaben > Einnahmen	Deficit Spending
Hochkonjunktur	Ausgaben < Einnahmen	Bildung von Rücklagen, Schuldenabbau

Märkte und Preisbildung

Angebotsfunktion

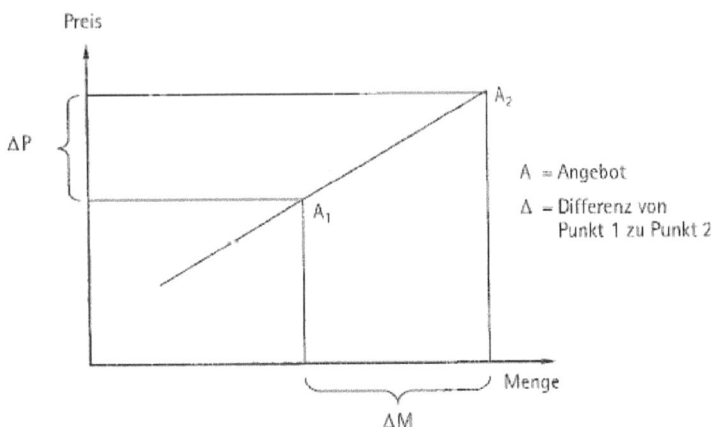

$$Preiselastizit\ddot{a}ten =$$

$$\frac{Mengen\ddot{a}nderung\ des\ Angebots\ (\%)}{Preis\ddot{a}nderung\ (\%)} = \frac{\Delta M}{\Delta P}$$

Nachfragefunktion

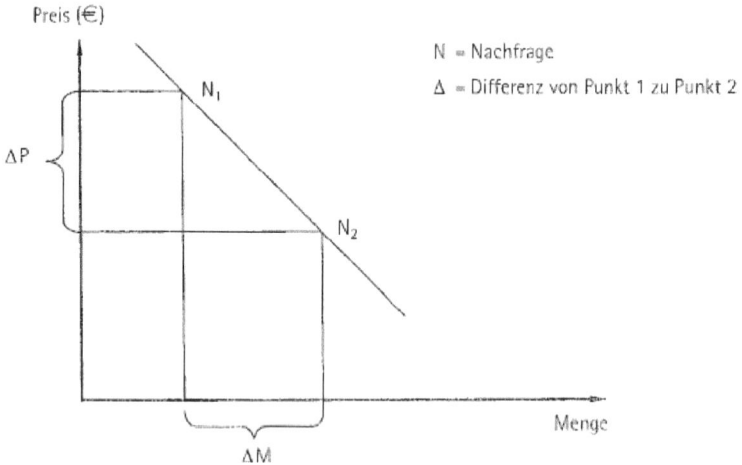

Preis (€)

N = Nachfrage
Δ = Differenz von Punkt 1 zu Punkt 2

ΔP

N₁ ... N₂ ... Menge ... ΔM

$Preiselastizität\ der\ Nachfrage =$

$$\frac{Mengen\ddot{a}nderung\ der\ Nachfrage(\%)}{Preis\ddot{a}nderung\ (\%)}$$

Elastische Nachfragereaktion: Preiselastizität der Nachfrage > 1
Unelastische Nachfragereaktion: Preiselastizität der Nachfrage < 1
Völlig unelastische Nachfragereaktion: Preiselastizität der Nachfrage = 1

$Einkommenselastizit\ddot{a}t\ der\ Nachfrage =$

$$Nachfrage\ddot{a}nderung\ (\%)$$
$$Einkommens\ddot{a}nderung\ (\%)$$

$$Marktanteil\ \% = \frac{Umsatz}{Marktvolumen} * 100$$

Marktgleichgewicht und Anpassungsprozess

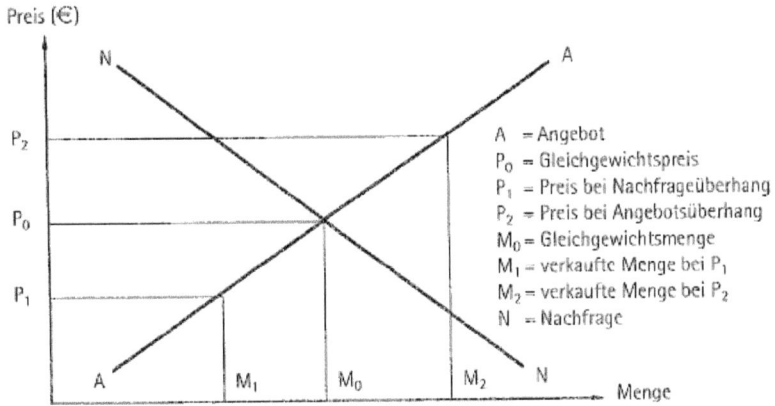

Preis (€)

$$A = \text{Angebot}$$
$$P_0 = \text{Gleichgewichtspreis}$$
$$P_1 = \text{Preis bei Nachfrageüberhang}$$
$$P_2 = \text{Preis bei Angebotsüberhang}$$
$$M_0 = \text{Gleichgewichtsmenge}$$
$$M_1 = \text{verkaufte Menge bei } P_1$$
$$M_2 = \text{verkaufte Menge bei } P_2$$
$$N = \text{Nachfrage}$$

Menge

9 783864 713231

This first separate publication of

Chip Crockett's Christmas Carol

is limited to 222 numbered copies

signed by the author and the artist.

CHIP ~ ~ ~ ~ ~
CROCKETT'S
CHRISTMAS
~ ~ ~ ~ CAROL

Elizabeth Hand

27 February 2013

The Argyle

For Lois,

I please to see you in the real world + not the virtual one! all but in (the real) London —

Beccon Publications
April 2006

Beccon Publications
75 Rosslyn Avenue
Harold Wood
Essex RM3 0RG, U.K.
beccon@dial.pipex.com

Printed and bound by
CPI Antony Rowe Ltd, Chippenham, England

To my children,
Callie and Tristan.

This is the story I told you on that long
drive home from Christmas House
in Vermont, long long ago.

With all my love.

CHIP~~~~~ CROCKETT'S CHRISTMAS ~~~~CAROL

"This day we shut out Nothing!"

"Pause," says a low voice. "Nothing? Think!"

"On Christmas Day, we will shut out from our fireside, Nothing."

"Not the shadow of a vast City where the withered leaves are lying deep?" the voice replies. "Not the shadow that darkens the whole globe? Not the shadow of the City of the Dead?"

Not even that ...

Charles Dickens -
"What Christmas Is as We Grow Older"

Tony was the one who called him.

"Brendan, man. I got some bad news."

Brendan felt a slight hitch in his stomach. He leaned back in his chair, nudging his office door closed so his secretary wouldn't hear. "Oh yes?"

"Chip Crockett died."

"Chip Crockett?" Brendan frowned, staring at his computer screen as though he was afraid Tony might materialize there. "You mean, like, *The Chip Crockett Show*?"

"Yeah, man." Tony sighed deeply. "My brother Jake, he just faxed me the obituary from the *Daily News*. He died over the weekend but they just announced it today."

There was a clunk through the phone receiver, a background clatter of shouting voices and footsteps. Tony was working as a substitute teacher at Saint Ignatius High School. Brendan was amazed he'd been able to hang onto the job at all, but he gathered that being a substitute at Saint Ignatius was way below being sanitation engineer in terms of salary, benefits, and respect. He heard a crackle of static as Tony ran into the corridor, shouting.

"Whoa! Nelson Crane, man! Slow down, okay? Okay. Yeah, I guess it was lung cancer. Did you know he smoked?"

"You're talking about Chip Crockett the kiddie show host. Right?" Brendan rubbed his forehead, feeling the beginning of a headache. "No, Tony, I didn't know he smoked, because I don't actually know Chip Crockett. Do you?"

"No. Remember Ogden Orff? That time he got the milk jug stuck on his nose? 'That's my boy, Ogden Orff!'" Tony intoned, then giggled. "And that puppet? Ooga Booga? The one with the nose?"

"Ogden Orff." Brendan leaned back in his chair. Despite himself, he smiled. "God, yeah, I remember. And the other one – that puppet who sang? He did 'Mister Bassman' and that witch doctor song. I loved him..."

"That wasn't a puppet. That was Captain Dingbat – you know, the D.J. character."

"Are you sure? I thought it was a puppet."

"No way, man. I mean, yes! I am ab-so-lute-ly sure – "

An earsplitting whistle echoed over the line. Brendan winced and held the phone at arm's-length, drew it back in time to hear Tony's voice fading.

"Hey man, that's the bell, I gotta go. I'll fax this to you before I leave, okay? Oh, and hey, we're still on for Thursday, right?"

Brendan nodded. "Right," he said, but Tony was already gone.

Late that afternoon the fax arrived. Brendan's secretary gave it to him, the curling cover sheet covered with Tony's nearly illegible scrawl.

Ogden Orff Lives!
See Ya Thurs.
At Childe Roland.
Tony

Brendan tossed this and turned to the Daily News obituary, two long columns complete with photo. The faxed image was fragmented but still recognizable – a boyishly handsome man in suit and skinny tie, grinning at a puppet with a huge nose. Above him was the headline:

AU REVOIR, OOGA BOOGA

Brendan shook his head. "Poor Ooga Booga," he murmured, then smoothed the paper on his desk.

> Iconic kiddie show host Chip Crockett died yesterday at his home in Manhasset, after a long and valiant battle with lung cancer. While never achieving the recognition accorded peers like Soupy Sales or Captain Kangaroo's Bob Keeshan, Chip Crockett's legend may be greater, because it lives solely in the memories of viewers. Like other shows from the late 1950s and early 1960s, The Chip Crockett Show was either performed live or videotaped; if the latter, the tapes were immediately erased so they could be reused. And, as though Fate conspired to leave no trace of Crockett's comic genius, a 1966 warehouse fire destroyed the few remaining traces of his work.
>
> For years, rumors of "lost" episodes raced among baby boomer fans, but alas, none have ever been found. The show's final episode, the last of the popular Chip Crockett Christmas specials, aired on December 23rd, 1965.
>
> The gentle Crockett was noted for a surreal sense of humor that rivaled Ernie Kovacs'. His cast consisted of a dozen puppets — all created by Crockett — and a rogue's gallery of over-the-top human characters, also given life by the versatile performer. Every weekday morning and again in the afternoon, Chip Crockett's jouncy theme would sound and the fun began, as potato-nosed Ooga Booga, sly Ratty Mouse, and the lovable knucklehead Ogden Orff appeared on WNEW-TV, reaching a broadcast audience of millions of children — and, occasionally, their unsuspecting parents.
>
> Chip Crockett was born in 1923 in Birdsboro, Pennsylvania. His broadcast career began in 1949 with a radio show…

Brendan sighed and looked up. Outside a sky the color of scorched nickel hung above Pennsylvania Avenue. In the very corner of his window, you could just make out the scaffolding that covered the Capitol building, a steel trellis overgrown with plywood and poured-concrete forms. When he and Robert Flaherty, his law partner, had first taken this office, Brendan had proudly pointed out the view to everyone, including the Capitol police officers who dropped in with paperwork and Congressional gossip during their breaks. Now Rob was dead, killed four years ago this Christmas Eve by a drunk driver, though Brendan still hadn't taken his name from the brass plate by the front door. The Capitol looked like an image from war-torn Sarajevo, and the officers Brendan had once known were unrecognizable behind bulletproof jackets and wraparound sunglasses.

"Mr. Keegan?" His secretary poked her head around the door. "Okay if I leave a little early today? It's Parent Conference week at Jessie's school –"

"Sure, sure, Ashley. You get that Labor Department stuff over to Phil Lancaster?"

"I did." Ashley already had her coat on, rummaging in a pocket for her farecard. "How's Peter these days?"

Peter was Brendan's son. "Oh, he's great, just great," he said, nodding. "Doing very well. Very, very well."

This wasn't true and, in fact, never really had been. Shortly after his second birthday, Peter Keegan had been diagnosed as having Pervasive Developmental Disorder, which as far as Brendan could figure was just a more socially acceptable term for his son's being (in the medical parlance) "somewhere within the autism continuum." Batteries of tests had followed – CAT scans, MRIs and PETs – and the upshot of it all was yet another string of letters: PDDNOS, or Pervasive Developmental Disorder Not Otherwise Specified. In other words, Peter Xavier Keegan, now four, had never spoken a word to anyone. If you touched him he moved away, deliberately but casually, with no more emotion than if he'd brushed up against a thorny hedge. If you tried to look him in the eye, he looked away; if anyone tried to hold him, however gently, he would scream, and hit, and bite, and eventually fall screaming to the floor.

He had not always been like that. Brendan had to remind himself every day, lest the fragmentary images of eighteen-month-old Peter smiling in his lap disappear forever. Once upon a time, Peter had been okay. Brendan had to believe that, despite the doctors who told him otherwise. That his son had been born with this condition; that Peter's neural wiring was defective; that the chances of reclaiming that other child – the one who clung to his father and babbled wordlessly but cheerfully, the one who gazed at Brendan with clear blue eyes and held his finger as he fell asleep – were slim or nil. Just last week Brendan's ex-wife, Teri, had begun a new regime of vitamin therapy for their son, the latest in an endless series of efforts to reclaim the toddler they had lost.

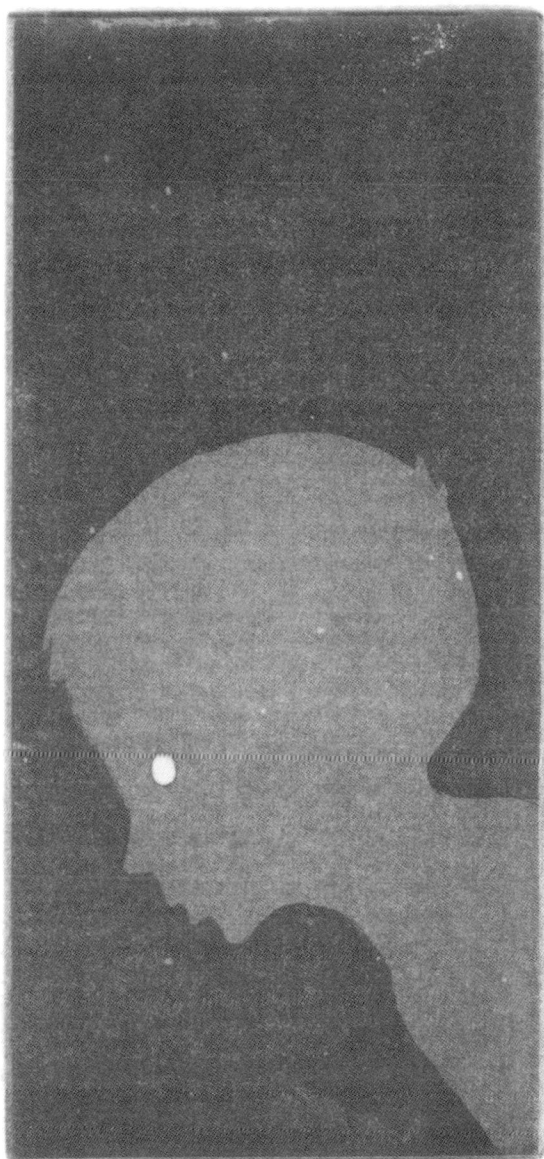

They were still waiting to see the results. And Brendan's secretary Ashley would have known all this because Teri had told her, during one of her daily phone calls to Brendan to discuss the million details of shared custody arrangements – pickup times, doctors' appointments, changes in Peter's medication, nightmares, biting incidents, bills for the expensive Birchwood School, missing shoes, and loose teeth. To his recollection, Brendan had never volunteered a single word about his son or his divorce to Ashley, but he had no doubt but that, if called upon, his secretary could testify in District Court about everything from his prior sexual relationship with his ex-wife (satisfactory if unremarkable) to his current attendance at AA meetings (occasional).

"Peter's very well," he repeated one last time. He made a tube of Tony's fax and eyed his secretary through one end. "Good luck at school, Ashley."

He walked home that evening, his briefcase nudging his leg as he made his way up Pennsylvania Avenue, keeping his bare head down against the chill night wind. Tony's fax stuck up out of his overcoat pocket, still curled into a tube. He ducked into the gourmet kitchen shop and bought some coffee beans, then headed down Fourth Street towards his apartment. He was thinking about the old *Chip Crockett Show*, and how his secretary was born a good ten years after it had gone off the air.

How did I get to be so old? he marveled, kicking at the pile of sodden leaves banked against his building's outer door. *"Mr. Keegan." When the hell did that happen?* And he went inside, to silence and *The Washington Post* still unread on the kitchen counter, the unblinking red eye of the answering machine signaling that no one had called.

~ ~ ~

Thursday night he met Tony Kemper at Childe Roland. The club had been a big hangout for them back when Brendan was in law school at Georgetown in the early 1980s. Tony was still playing with the Maronis in those days, and the Childe Roland was a popular after-hours spot for musicians on tour. Later, after Tony left the Maronis and moved back to D.C., he'd headlined with local bands, and he and Brendan and Brendan's cousin, Kevin, had gotten into the habit of meeting at the Childe Roland every Thursday after closing time, to drink and listen to whatever performers happened to drop by.

Now, years later, all three were veterans of Alcoholics Anonymous, although Kevin was the only one who still attended meetings regularly. But they still met once a week at the Childe Roland, sitting at a table in the shabby downstairs room with its brick walls and fading posters for Root Boy Slim and Tommy Keene and the Dale Williams Band. They'd eat hamburgers and drink coffee or Evian water, feed quarters to the vintage Wurlitzer jukeboxes, and argue politics and football over "96 Tears" and "Bastards of Young" and "Pretty Vacant."

Tonight Brendan was the first to arrive, as usual. He'd been divorced for nearly a year but still couldn't quite get the hang of being single. He didn't date, he didn't cook. He worked late when he could, but Flaherty, Keegan & Associates didn't generate enough of a caseload to merit more than two or three nights a week. He had Peter on alternate weekends and Tuesdays, but that still left a lot of downtime. He hated to admit it, but when Tony or Kevin had to cancel Thursdays at Childe Roland, Brendan was depressed – depressed enough that he'd come to Childe Roland by himself and sit at their usual place and feed the jukebox, playing the songs Kevin or Tony would have played, even the ones he hated.

But he wouldn't be alone tonight. He heard Tony before he saw him. Or rather, he heard everyone else seeing him –

"Tony, my man! What's shakin'?"

"Tony Maroni! 'Hooray, hello, whoa whoa whoa!' "

"Tony!"

"It's the Tonester!"

Brendan watched as his friend grinned and waved, crossing the room in that bizarre way he had, half-glide and half-slouch, resplendent in his ancient black leather jacket and decrepit Converse hightops, his long black hair streaked with grey, but otherwise pretty much unchanged from the lanky, goofy-faced nineteen-year-old who once upon a time had been the Great White Hope of Rock and Roll. On the Bowery, anyway, for a few years in the mid-1970s, which (according to Tony) was the last time rock had mattered.

That was when Tony founded The Maronis, the proto-punk band whose first, self-titled record had recently been cited by *The New York Times* as one of the ten most influential rock albums of the century. (The follow-up, *Maronis Get Detention*, came in at number 79.) The band's formula, equal parts three-chord rock and Three Stooges, won them a record contract with EMI, a national tour, and all the attendant problems as Tony, Mony, Pony, and Tesla (neé Tony Kemper, Marty Berenstein, Paul Schippa, and Dickie Stanton) played, fought, drank, dropped acid, shot up, and eventually OD'd.

Not all at the same time, of course, but that was it as far as EMI was concerned. The Maronis lost their only contract with a major label. Worse, they lost their catalog – they hadn't bothered with an attorney when they signed – and the ensuing decades had seen one failed lawsuit after another brought by band members, whenever one was flush enough to hire a lawyer.

Still, the band continued to tour and record, on the small New Jersey-based Millstone label. When Tesla died of a heroin overdose, he was replaced, first by Joni, the band's first female guitarist, and then by Sony, a Japanese fan who attached himself to the Maronis after their disastrous 1984 Tokyo appearance. That was when Tony left the band. Despite the rumors, he'd never gotten into heroin. Even as a kid in Yonkers he'd been terrified of needles; Kevin used to steal hypos from his doctor father and hide them in Tony's Deputy Dawg lunchbox, something Brendan would never have forgiven his cousin for, but Tony was incapable of anything resembling anger. Whatever demons he encountered, he fought them down with beer – preferably Budweiser, even when he (briefly) could have afforded Heineken. He'd finally lost it in Japan when, jet-lagged and suffering from food poisoning, he'd gotten the DTs and started screaming about Gojiro in the lobby of the Tokyo Hilton. Millstone had no money for an emergency medical evacuation, and so Brendan and Kevin arranged to have their childhood friend flown back to the States. Kevin had gone over to escort Tony – Kevin was raking it in at Merrill Lynch – and on their return he and Brendan checked their friend into detox.

He'd been sober ever since. Although, because he was Tony Maroni, this wasn't always readily apparent.

"Hey, Brenda Starr! How's it goin'?"

Brendan looked up, making a face at the boyhood nickname. "Tony. Good to see you –"

He reached across the table to shake his hand. Tony leaned forward and grabbed him in a hug. "Yeah, man, great to see you, too!" As though it had been a year instead of a week; as though they hadn't just talked on the phone, oh, about two hours ago. "Where's Kevo?"

Brendan shrugged. "He should be here soon."

"Right, right. The Family Man. Family matters. Family matters," Tony repeated, cocking his head and scrunching his face up. "Hey, get it? Like, it *matters* –"

"I get it, Tony."

"I never did. Not until just now."

Brendan sighed, glanced up to see a young woman in torn fishnets and polyester skirt, Mandelbrot tattoos and enough surgical steel piercings to arm an emerging nation. "Oh good. Here's the Bionic Waitress."

Tony whirled to grin at her. "Bethie! Hi! Hey, you look nice in that outfit –"

"It's my uniform, Tony," the waitress said, but smiled, displaying more gleaming metal and a tongue stud. "Where's your other partner in crime?"

"Kevo? He'll be here. He's got kids, you know –" Tony suddenly looked across the table, stricken. "Oh hey, man, I didn't mean – I mean, he's got kids too," he said, pointing at Brendan. "It's just –"

"Tony. It's okay," said Brendan.

"– just, uh, Kevin's got a lot of 'em. Well, two, anyway."

"Really?" The waitress looked down at Brendan curiously. "I never knew you were married."

"He's not," said Tony. "He's –"

"I'm divorced," Brendan broke in. He gave Tony an icy look. "I have a little boy."

"Yeah? You ought to bring him in some night. Okay, you want something now or you want to wait for your friend?"

They ordered, coffee for Brendan, club soda with lemon for Tony. When she brought the drinks back, Tony took the straw and blew its paper wrapper across the table at Brendan. "No offense, man," he said. "About–"

"None taken, Tony." Brendan lifted his coffee mug and smiled.

"Cheers."

"Cheers." Tony took a sip of his drink, then slid from his chair. "Gotta feed the jukebox, man. Right back."

Brendan watched as his friend sidled over to one of the club's vintage jukeboxes, spangled man-sized bijoux that glittered and bubbled and glowed along the brick walls. There was a Seeburg, a Rockola, and the Childe Roland's crown jewel: a 1946 Wurlitzer Model 1015, special edition "Rites of Spring" in mint condition, down to the 45s stacked on their glittering turntable spindle. Tony hunched over this now, drumming his fingers on the glass surface. The green-and-gold Bakelite pilasters and ruby lights made him look like one of his own adolescent daydreams, long hair touched with crimson, his Silly Putty face given a momentary semblance of gravity, as though he were gazing into some piece of sophisticated medical machinery instead of an old jukebox.

"Hey." Tony frowned. "What happened to 'Moulty?' And who the fuck put the Eagles on this thing?"

Brendan shook his head, marveling as he always did at how long it took Tony to make his selections. "You know," he said as Tony slouched back to the table, the opening drumbeats of "Be My Baby" echoing around them, "it took Phil Spector less time to record that than it did for you to punch it in."

Tony slid back into his seat. "Hey, you know what that is? That's the Big Bang, man! Bum, bum-bum! Bum, bum-bum! That's the noise God made when He made the universe! When I die, make sure they play that, okay?" He clapped a hand to his forehead. "Geez, I almost forgot! Check this out–"

He fumbled in a pocket of his leather jacket, withdrew a wad of folded-up paper. "There's, like, a Chip Crockett Web page. Listen –"

Tony smoothed out the paper, then cleared his throat. " 'Like a lot of other people, I grew up in the early 1960s watching *The Chip Crockett Show*,' " he read. " 'I was still pretty young when I watched it, though, and I don't really remember much, except that the puppets were sort of scary. But since starting this Web page I have had many other people write to me about their memories of the show, and I have come to realize that Chip Crockett has actually influenced me in ways that I am only beginning to understand.' "

Brendan shook his head. "Wow. That's some testimony."

"Yeah, man, but he's right. I mean, Chip Crockett had an amazing impact on me –"

"Yeah, but you're Tony Maroni. Chip Crockett could have invented you. Here, give me that –"

Brendan took the page and glanced down it. No pictures, just a web address, a brief introduction and listing of contents.

- *BROADCAST HISTORY*
- *ARTICLES & OBITUARIES (NEW)*
- *THEME SONG*
- *THE GREAT FIRE OF 1966*
- *CHIP CROCKETT'S CHRISTMAS SPECIAL*

"I didn't have time to print out the whole thing," Tony said apologetically. "I had duty in the computer lab but then there was a fire drill ..."

"I remember the Christmas Special." Brendan looked thoughtful. "It was *A Christmas Carol*, but with all the puppets playing the parts. Ooga Booga was Scrooge —"

"Scrooga Booga," Tony corrected him. "And Ogden Orff was Bob Cratchit—"

"Brendan." A gigantic hand suddenly descended to grip Brendan's shoulder. "Tony. Sorry I'm late." Kevin Donnelly's shadow fell across the table — a big shadow. "Eileen had to work late and I had to get the girls from dance and then dinner —"

Tony clasped Kevin's hand, moving his chair over to make room. Kevin sat and waved at their waitress.

"An O'Douls, please," he said, then turned to his cousin. "Brendan. How you doing?"

"Good, very good." Brendan smiled. "What's new with you?"

"Not much. What you got there?"

"The Chip Crockett Web page. Listen —" Brendan held the page up and gestured dramatically. " 'I have come to realize that Chip Crockett has actually influenced me in ways that I am only beginning to understand.' You know, I think Tony could start a religion based on this."

"Mmm. Eileen wouldn't like that. Let me see —"

In Kevin's hand the page looked insubstantial as tissue. He was a big man who in the course of two decades of steadfast bodybuilding had become absolutely huge, red-haired and ruddy-faced, his arms and shoulders so powerful they always looked as though they were about to burst through his hand-tailored suit jackets, like some demented Capitol Hill version of The Incredible Hulk. As a boy he'd terrorized not just Brendan and Tony but everyone within a five-block radius of Tuckahoe Road, and started dipping into the altar wine before his twelfth birthday. At Notre Dame on a football scholarship, he'd brought the team to the Nationals, then gone on to get an MBA from the Wharton School. He'd made his first million before he was thirty, gotten sober, bailed out of Merrill Lynch exactly one month before Black Monday, and taken a job as a lobbyist for Standard Oil.

"You read this, Brendan?" Kevin scowled. "Did you read this?"

"Yup. What do you think?"

Kevin continued to scan the printout, while Brendan flagged their waitress for more coffee. Whenever he saw his cousin, Brendan felt as though he were glimpsing himself in some alternate universe. Kevin looked like Brendan on steroids, Brendan's sandy hair turned to flame, Brendan's body pumped full of Vitamin B-12 and Proteinex. His cousin's career and domestic life were shiny perverse reflections of Brendan's own – immense financial success, gorgeous ex-model spouse, perfect children, perfect Potomac home, perfect perfect perfect. Whereas Brendan felt as though he were channeling his ex-wife through his secretary, and his only child seemed to live in that other universe as well, gazing into Brendan's world as though it were an empty expanse of sky.

"I think it's a capital offense if my taxes are paying Tony to print out this kind of stuff on school time." Kevin shook his head and handed the page back to Tony. "Tell me, Tony, how the hell do you keep that job? I mean, what do you tell those kids, as a teacher?"

"You know. Follow your bliss. Stay out of jail. I tell them to be really, really careful, otherwise they'll end up like me."

Brendan and Kevin laughed, but Tony only shrugged. "Well, it's true," he said. "The way I figure, I'm saving the school system thousands of dollars a year in anti-drug programs and stuff like that."

"But you never did drugs, Tony," said Kevin.

"Yeah, but they don't know that. I tell 'em: Stay in school, go to the college of your choice, learn a viable trade. Otherwise you'll spend the rest of your life giving practice SATs to dimbulbs like Nelson Crane."

The Bionic Waitress reappeared and refilled Brendan's coffee cup. As he moved the papers aside she glanced down at them curiously.

"Who died?"

"Chip Crockett," said Tony.

She wrinkled her nose. "Who's Chip Crockett?"

Tony rubbed his chin. "Well, he was this kiddie show host a long time ago. Kind of like Chuck McCann."

"Or Paul Winchell," said Kevin.

"Who're they?"

"Do you remember Uncle Floyd Vivino?" asked Brendan.

"Uh, no."

Tony frowned, thinking. Finally he brightened. "What about PeeWee Herman?"

The waitress scrunched her face up. "Mmm, maybe a little."

"Mister Rogers?"

"Sure!" She looked more closely at the obituary.

"Well, Chip Crockett was sort of like a cross between Mister Rogers and PeeWee Herman," explained Brendan.

"Or Adam Sandler," said Kevin. "Actually, he was more like a cross between Mister Rogers and Tony here."

The waitress laughed. "Wow. Sorry I missed out on that one."

She turned and headed back to the kitchen. Tony stared after her admiringly, then shoved his chair back. "'Scuse me, gotta hit the head."

His friends watched him go. "So," said Kevin, easing himself into the chair next to Brendan. "Tony's taking the news about Chip Crockett pretty hard. How 'bout you?"

"Aw, don't give him a hard time, Kev," said Brendan. He sometimes felt as though he'd spent his entire life defending Tony against Big Tough Guys like Kevin. "He gets on these kicks, he'll get over it."

Kevin looked hurt. "I wasn't giving him a hard time. I actually feel kind of bad about it myself."

"About Chip Crockett?"

"Sure. I liked Chip Crockett. Especially Ogden Orff ..." Kevin rapped his knuckles again his forehead and cried, "'No, Ogden, noooo!'" Then, in fonder tones, "'That's my boy – Ogden Orff!'"

Brendan smiled. "Good old Ogden Orff. But gee, Kev. I never figured you'd be all broken up about Chip Crockett."

"I dunno. I was thinking about how that fire just, like, wiped any evidence of him off the planet. Like if you're not on TV somewhere, or on the net, you just don't exist anymore. Freaks me out, all that stuff. You know, getting old. People dying. That kind of thing."

Brendan eyed his cousin suspiciously. "Is something wrong?" he asked, fighting the faintest, cruelest spasm of glee at the thought.

"No. That's the problem. Everything's perfect. Too perfect. I mean, the girls are gonna need braces in a year or two, and Eileen's a screaming banshee because of this remodeling job she's doing out in Warrenton, but – well, don't you ever feel like that? Like everything's just going too well?"

Brendan stared at his cousin. Kevin stared back, his bright blue eyes completely guileless. "No," Brendan said at last. He turned to grab his coffee from the waitress. "You know, I got to get going – I've got a case coming up, I need to go over some stuff before the weekend."

He took a gulp of coffee, pulled out a ten-dollar bill and slid it under the mug. Behind him Tony reappeared, grinning and singing along with the jukebox in that immediately recognizable, nasal just-north-of-the-Bronx voice. Brendan pulled on his overcoat, watching him. It was always disconcerting to him, the difference between Tony Kemper and Tony

Maroni. The latter's now-famous stage persona, a gangly stoop-shouldered goofus doing his trademarked knock-kneed dance – practically immobile from the waist up and looking as though he were swallowing the mike, his face hidden behind a curtain of lank black hair as he blurted out his customary greeting –"Hooray hello, whoa whoa whoa!" – followed by three-chord anthems like "ECT" and "Gonna Have a Bad Trip" and "Tibbets Park," the FM radio hit he'd dedicated to Brendan and Kevin –

> Come with me tonight
> Playin' in the dark
> We can have a great time
> Down at Tibbets Park ...

Tony Maroni was a goofball, a knucklehead, a refugee from all those kiddie shows they'd lived on back in Yonkers – Soupy Sales doing The Mouse, Chuck McCann sticking pennies on his eyes and pretending to be Little Orphan Annie, ventriloquist Paul Tripp arguing with his dummy sidekick Jerry Mahoney. Whereas the real Tony Kemper moved with an unconscious but intensely sexy, almost feminine grace: he was like someone feigning drunkenness, catching you off guard by catching himself just when you thought he was going to walk into the wall. And he was a great dancer. Back at Sacred Heart High School, Tony was the guy all the girls wanted to slow-dance with, while teenage guitarists struggled through the solos in "Southern Man" and "Nights in White Satin."

Now Tony blinked, staring at Brendan in dismay. "Brenda! You're not leaving already?"

"Sorry, Tony. I've got this case, we'd like to try and get a settlement before Christmas –"

"Wait." Kevin whistled and held a hand up, as though officiating a fight. "Before I forget: Eileen wants you both to come for Thanksgiving." He pointed at Brendan. "Do you have Peter that weekend? 'Cause the girls would love it if –"

"I think I do. I'm pretty sure Teri has him for Christmas."

"Great. What about you, Tony?"

Tony rubbed his chin. "Yeah, I think I can swing it. There's this girl I've been sort of seeing, but –"

"Well, bring her. Or dump her. Whatever. Just let Eileen know, okay?"

Tony nodded. He swung around to throw an arm over Brendan's shoulder. "See you here next week, then?"

"Righto." Brendan headed for the stairs, pausing to give his friends a salute. "Very, very good to see you guys."

"Call Eileen, okay? Let her know if you can come," Kevin called after him. "And hey, I really hope Peter can make it."

"I'll let you know," Brendan said with a wave. " 'Night –"

Kevin watched thoughtfully as his cousin disappeared up the steps. Beside him Tony sipped his club soda, tapping the table in counterpoint to the jukebox.

"You know," Tony said after a minute, "Peter's sort of like Tommy, isn't he?"

"Tommy?" Kevin started, shook his head. "Tommy who?"

"You know, Tommy – 'that deaf, dumb and blind kid sure plays a mean pinball.'"

Kevin swiveled to stare at him. His eyes narrowed as he drew his breath in. "You know what? You're an idiot, Tony," he said softly. "A total fucking idiot."

Tony put down his club soda. "I just meant –"

"And you ever say something like that to Brendan, I'll put your fucking lights out." He tossed a handful of bills on the table. "I'll see you at Thanksgiving."

"Yeah, sure." Tony waved meekly as Kevin left. "Thanksgiving. My favorite holiday. Damn, that's not what I meant, you know that's not what I meant." He ran a hand through his hair, fumbled around for a fistful of change and added it to the money on the table. Then he stood, rocking anxiously back and forth on his heels until he saw the waitress approaching. "Thanks Bethie," he said, grabbing the printout from Chip Crockett's Web page. "See you soon."

"Goodbye hello, Tony."

"Whoa whoa whoa," he said ruefully, and left.

~ ~ ~

As it turned out, Brendan saw Tony a lot sooner than Thanksgiving – the next day, in fact. Every other Friday Brendan had his son for the weekend, picking him up early from the Birchwood School, where fourteen caregivers exposed his son and seventeen other very young children to a rigorously ordered curriculum. The days were exquisitely maintained: children sat at table for meals, games were devised so that students learned cooperative behavior, objects were labeled and their names repeated consistently. Teachers taught parents to use the same specific words and phrases over and over again, to maintain consistency at home.

Brendan's ex-wife, Teri, had great faith in the Birchwood School and its intensive program of early intervention. Although the administration and teachers disliked labeling, most of their students had been diagnosed as having some form of Pervasive Developmental Disorder and, like Peter, their behavior placed them somewhere along the autism continuum. Whenever he visited the school Brendan found himself contemplating an adult correlation to this, something he called the Parental Anguish Continuum. Peter was verbally non-communicative and, like many of the other children, hypersensitive to touch and sensory stimulation. But his tantrums had grown less frequent in the last year, and he had done wonderfully well in the ordered environment at Birchwood. What would it be like to have a son like Sasha Petrowicz, whose sensitivity to the world was such that he spent much of the day screaming in pain? Or a daughter like Ivy Montrose, who had been adopted from an orphanage in Rumania and had a band of scar tissue across her forehead, from headbanging in an iron-sided crib? What would it be like to be Kurt and Donna Raymond, whose only child had died of pneumonia after surgery? Setting himself within that arc, Brendan with customary Irish Catholic stoicism (Teri called this denial) found himself counting his blessings. On one hand and with gritted teeth, to be sure; but Brendan knew better than to feel sorry for himself or his son, at least for more than an hour or two, and never when visiting the Birchwood School.

"Brendan! Hi!"

Peggy Storrs, Peter's teacher, waved to him from a corner. Brendan smiled and walked over. "Hi, Peggy. How's everyone doing?"

"He's having a pretty good day." Peggy sat cross-legged on the floor, a number of blocks scattered around her. She was in her late twenties, Brendan guessed, and completing her Masters in Education at G.W., a strong-featured young woman with thick chestnut hair (hidden beneath a brightly checked wool hat), wearing batiked cotton trousers and a fuzzy handknit sweater. Brendan figured her for a lesbian, because of the hat; she reminded him of certain nuns he'd had as teachers back at Sacred Heart, steely-eyed women who in another life might have become neurosurgeons, astrophysicists, attorneys specializing in medical malpractice. "Joni's got the flu, so I'm with Allen, too, which is making it a little difficult. We had a little outburst at snack time, but other than that Peter's doing great."

Peggy smiled at Brendan, then turned her attention back to work. Beside her, but a few feet apart from each other, knelt two little boys. They were stacking blocks, Allen in a distracted manner, placing two or three atop each other before knocking them down, Peter with intense concentration – stacking first a blue block, then a yellow one, then another blue, then yellow.

"Put in a green one, Peter," Peggy urged, and held out another block. "Here. Put in the green block."

Peter ignored her. He continued stacking, head tilted, his resolute gaze fixed not so much on the blocks as on some point just beyond. Watching his son made Brendan think of hummingbirds, how their metabolisms were supposedly so quick-working, their bodies and brains wired at a rate so much faster than humans, that they did not even perceive us. To a hummingbird, Brendan was only a massive grey-and-black blur, solid and unmoving as a boulder.

What was he to his son?

"Peter," he said gently. "Peter, hi. Hi, honey, hi Peter."

A smile flickered across Peter's face, so fast it was like one of those phantom looks that cross a dreamer's face in deep REM sleep. But Brendan recognized it. He smiled back, feeling a surge of joy so acute it was like grief. "Good, Peter! Take the green block from Peggy."

Peggy's hand hovered a few inches from the blue and yellow stack.

"Take the green block, Peter," she said.

Another flicker, annoyance this time; then only that unwavering concentration as Peter put another blue block on top of the pile. Brendan's stomach clenched. He knew his son wasn't being stubborn, but sometimes he found it impossible to keep from reading his behavior that way. If you saw these kids in an ordinary setting – and the Birchwood School was, in most ways, an ordinary setting – you might not know there was anything unusual about them. They were small, they wore rompers and Gap jeans and L.L. Bean sweaters, Teletubbies sweatshirts and Elmo sneakers, they toddled and ran around and cried like other kids. It was only after you'd been here for a while that you noticed the dreamily intent rocking in front of a window; the methodical ordering and reordering of blocks and cups and plastic forms; the boy whirling in a corner until reminded that it was time to go outside; the constant and insistently repeated statements from the teachers –

"Take the green block, Peter. I'm going to put it on top. I'm going to put the green block there, Peter –"

Peter's head was half-turned to pick up another yellow block from the floor. Peggy placed the green one on top of his tower, breaking its careful symmetry. Blue yellow blue yellow blue yellow blue –

Without a word Peter turned, smacking the pile. Blocks flew everywhere, one of them striking Allen on the leg. He began to cry, and Peggy moved quickly to comfort him.

"It's all right, Allen. That was an accident –"

"Right." Brendan let his breath out and clapped his hands on his knees. "We're going to the zoo now, Peter. This is the day when we go to the zoo."

The same flicker across the boy's face, water rushing over pale sand. Without looking at his father he shook his head. "Great," said Brendan. He pointed to the row of cubbies against one wall. "Let's go get your jacket and your knapsack. Have a good weekend, Peggy."

"You too, Brendan. Bye, Peter!"

Peter turned and walked to his cubby. On the way he paused to stare intently at the fish tank set in a small alcove by the kitchen. Peter was fascinated by the fish inside — obsessed, Brendan though in his bleaker moments — and, left to his own devices, the boy could stare fixedly at the aquarium for ten minutes at a time. Brendan followed him and started to gather his son's butterfly-colored paraphernalia, green and blue knapsack, yellow rubber boots in case it rained, yellow rubber duck. He went into the kitchen and retrieved Peter's medication, then caught up with Peter waiting by the door.

"Okay, Peter. You ready?"

They went to the zoo. Ever since his law school days Brendan had loved it, the illusion of order and safety and immense distance granted by carefully designed landscapes and cast-resin boulders.

He had learned, however, that all of this was too much for Peter; everything except the Reptile House. Peter was fascinated by the displays here, especially the iguanas as they slid with sinister intent from rock to sand, finally ending up in a great heap atop each other.

"Look at that lizard, Peter. How many lizards in that pile? One, two, three lizards ..."

Peter moved closer to the glass. Brendan stepped towards him, and bumped into someone.

"Excuse me, I'm sorry –"

"Hey, Brendan."

"Tony?" Brendan looked up into his friend's lopsided grin. Tony was wearing his work clothes, grey herringbone tweed jacket, skinny black tie. "Jeez, Tony, hi. What are you doing here?"

Tony shrugged. "Oh, I dunno. I like snakes, I guess."

"I know, but aren't you ..." Brendan stopped. "Oh no. Tony –"

Tony gave him a sheepish look. "Yeah. I, uh, actually, well – I got canned. That girl I was seeing –"

"Oh, Christ, Tony! Don't tell me, please don't tell me –"

"No! I mean, she's eighteen, anyway, but nothing happened, I just sort of hung out with her after school a couple of times, but someone said something, and –"

"Tony –"

"– and anyway, we didn't have all that much in common. As it turned out."

"'As it turned out.' 'As it turned out.' Tony, this is not a good thing. I mean, do you have an attorney –"

"No, man! Nothing happened. I'm not getting sued, or anything like that. I mean, I was only a substitute anyway. They just, uh, said it wasn't working out. Plus I already have another job, Russ Acton said he has a gig for me, working nights at Gigantor Records."

"Gigantor Records." Brendan shifted so he could keep an eye on Peter, still standing mesmerized by the iguanas. "Whoo boy. Tony ..."

"Hey, it's a good deal. Only three nights a week, plus I get the employee discount. But, uh, that's actually not why I was looking for you."

Brendan closed his eyes. Overhead a ceiling fan turned desultorily. He took a deep breath, and opened his eyes again. "Yes?"

"I, uh – well, you know, I only had this month-by-month lease after Kimberly split, and it turns out the lease wasn't even in her name but that guy she used to go out with, what's his name, you know, Roy, the bartender down at –"

"Tony."

"And I, uh, well – do you think I could crash at your place for a while? Just until I can get on my feet? Like a month or two, till the new year –"

Brendan shook his head. "I don't know if that would work, Tony. Like now – I have Peter every other weekend, and sometimes during the week, and –"

"It would be temporary. Very temporary. Say a week."

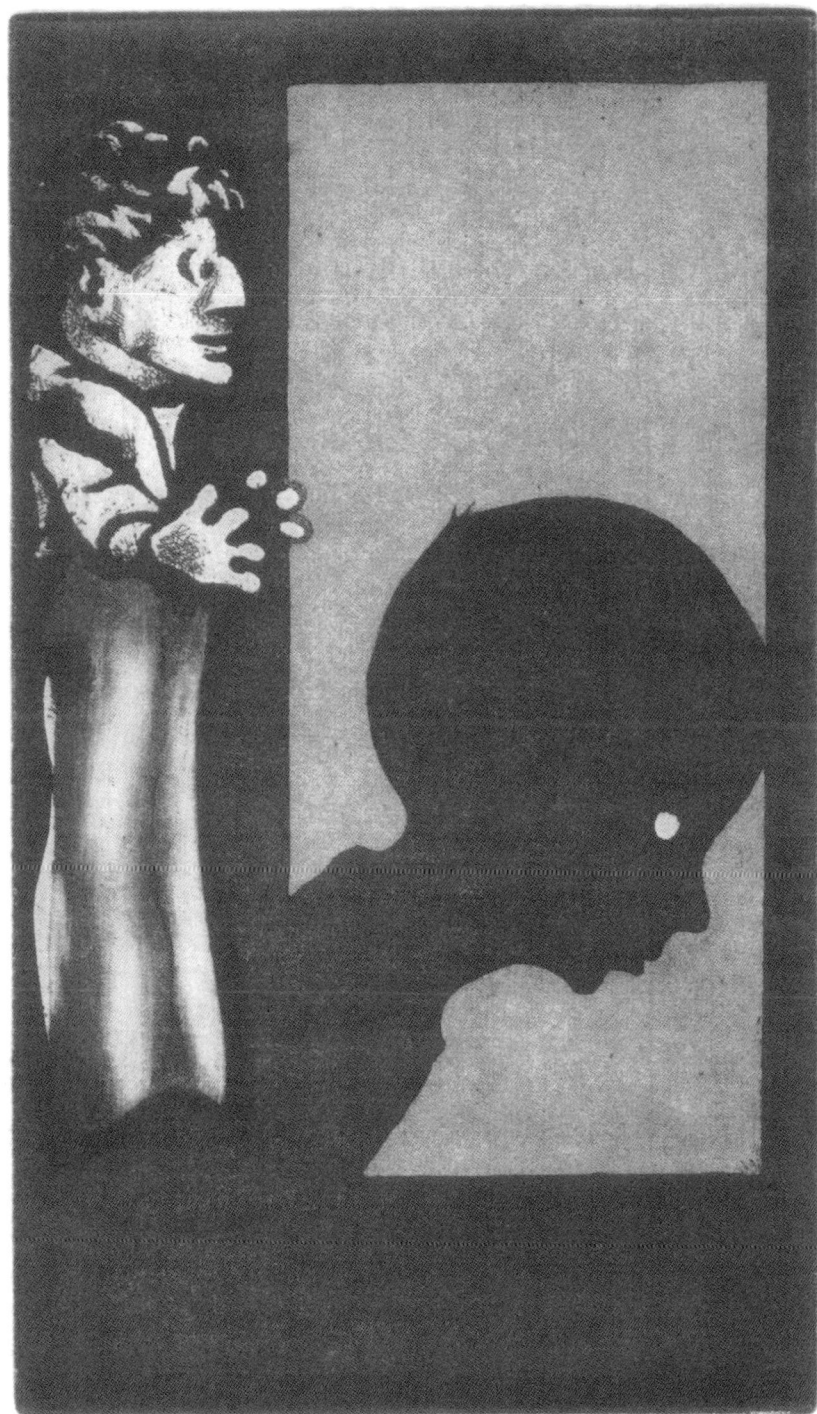

"You just said a month."

"Okay, fine, a month. And I promise, I promise it won't be any longer–"

Brendan rubbed his eyes, defeated. "Oh, Christ. All right. Yes. But only for –"

"– 'cause like, there's this place I'm guaranteed, I know I can get it, up by Nebraska Ave., but the guy isn't moving till right after New Year's. Plus that way I can, like, save up enough for the security deposit and stuff. And Christmas presents."

"It's okay, Tony. I mean, I guess it'll work out, if it's only for a while. Just – when Teri's over, maybe you better keep a low profile."

"Sure, man. I mean, I really appreciate it, I know it's a hassle and stuff –"

"It's no hassle."

"– but I really appreciate it." Tony tugged at the neck of his tweed jacket, then held out his hand. "Thanks, Brendan."

"No prob." Brendan gave his friend's hand a cursory shake, turned and walked over to the wall of glass cages. "Hey, Peter, look who's here. Uncle Tony."

"It's Crazy Uncle Tony!" Tony announced. He crossed to stand directly behind Peter. "Hey, look at all those lizards making a big pile. 'Dogpile on the rabbit! Dogpile on the rabbit!'"

Brendan frowned as Tony went on. "You remember – Bugs Bunny! Boy, check him out, that guy's huge." A flicker, and Peter tilted his head, looking where Tony pointed. "You know, I think I used to date his sister."

Brendan laughed. "How old was she?"

"Aw, man. I mean, you should've seen this girl, there's no way she looked under –"

"Uh-uh-uh. That's the first thing they teach you at law school: Never date anyone in high school. God, Tony. Do me a favor, do not mention this to Teri. Or anyone else."

"Absolutely, man." Tony's gaze didn't move from the cage. "I definitely dated that guy's sister."

"Come on, let's look at the crocodiles. Peter?" Brendan moved to take his son's hand. For a fraction of a second Peter's rested against his father's palm, warm and sticky, his fingernails rough where he'd bitten them. Then they slid away. Brendan felt that same small stab at his chest, familiar and painful as a pulled tendon; but he only looked at his son and smiled. "Remember the crocodiles? You liked them last time we were here ..."

They wandered through the rest of the reptile house, Tony expressing remorse over the remains of several white mice and a dead sparrow. After a quarter hour, Peter grew restive. He started grabbing at the railings in front of the glass cages and rocking back and forth, his cheeks flushed.

Brendan turned to Tony. "He's hungry," he said. "Okay Peter, time to go. It's time to leave the zoo now."

Peter said nothing, only rocked faster, back and forth on the rail.

"Time to go," repeated Brendan. "Come on, Peter. We have to leave now."

Peter closed his eyes and swung sideways.

"Peter," Brendan said again. He looked at Tony and took a deep breath. "All right, Peter – I'll have to pick you up, then –"

He stepped towards Peter, wrapped his arms firmly around him and started disentangling him from the rail. Peter kicked, grunting loudly; then began to scream. At the other end of the room a mother with two small girls stared at Brendan, frowning.

"Peter," Brendan said in a strained voice, prising his son's fingers from the railing. "Come on, Peter –"

Peter started crying. Brendan held him as tight as he could and carried him to the exit. When he saw the door, Peter's cries abruptly stopped, but he continued to push at his father, trying to get away. Tony bounced after them.

"I'm hungry too, Peter," Tony announced loudly. Peter narrowed his eyes and looked the other way. "Gentlemen? It's dinner time –"

Tony held the door for them as they stepped outside. "My treat," he said with a bow.

"Tony, you don't –"

"My treat. Come on, Peter, we're going to McDonald's."

Brendan shook his head. "That may not be a good idea, Tony." He bent and let Peter slide from his arms to the ground. "When he goes off like this..."

But Peter was already brightening. He took a few steps, stopped, and looked at the sky, shutting his eyes and letting that same half-smile flash across his face. Brendan watched him, then turned to Tony.

"Okay. We can try McDonald's," he said. "Just don't tell Teri, she'll hold you personally responsible for the extinction of the poison arrow frog."

Peter stared up at Tony, but looked away when the tall man gazed down at him.

"We can walk there," Tony said. "Right, Peter?" Peter turned, continuing to watch Tony from the corners of his eyes. Tony began to walk backwards down the sidewalk. "Plus, Brenda, this way you don't have to do the dishes afterwards ...

"– plus, I have one more favor to ask you," he added, sidling up alongside of Brendan as they approached Connecticut Avenue.

Brendan stopped, grabbing Peter as he ran towards the gate. "What?" he asked tersely. His son struck at his hands as he zipped up Peter's jacket and pulled a knit cap down over the boy's sleek hair.

"No biggie. Just, could you help me move my stuff? There's not a lot," Tony added, "it's just too much for one cab ride, you know, plus your car has so much more room."

Brendan sighed. "All right, Tony."

"And could you maybe do it tonight? 'Cause the landlady said she's, like, changing the locks tomor –"

"Yes, Tony."

Brendan's blue eyes glittered dangerously. Tony said nothing more; just nodded and walked with them up Connecticut Avenue, past the first crowds of commuters heading home in the early dusk.

They ate. Peter was quiet, repeatedly squeezing his chicken nuggets between his fingers and refusing to eat more than a few mouthfuls. But Brendan was relieved that it was nothing more than that, no screaming fits, no throwing food or trays or cups, nothing to make all the other parents and children turn from their Big Macs and Happy Meals to stare at an uncontrollable four-year-old and his ineffectual father. Afterwards they found Brendan's Volvo wagon and drove to Adams Morgan to retrieve Tony's stuff. This consisted of a stereo system, five large boxes of CDs and tapes, another six cartons containing records by Firesign Theater and dozens of one-hit wonders from the late '60s and early '70s; a small carton of paperbacks, heavy on the Illuminati and the Beats; a spatula; Tony's Mosrite electric guitar; and a single black trash bag holding Tony's wardrobe, which consisted entirely of black T-shirts and black jeans.

"That's it," Tony announced. He tossed the trash bag into the back of the car. In the middle seat, Peter sat quietly and stared out the side window. Brendan had remained behind the wheel – they were illegally parked, and he was also doing lookout duty for Roy, putative owner of both Tony's ex-girlfriend and her lease, a bartender known for his humorless attachment to World Wrestling Federation events.

"Good." Brendan leaned out the car window. "Now can we go?"

"Yeah, yeah, just hold on. One more thing –" Tony raced back upstairs, long hair flying. A moment later he returned and sprinted down the steps, his battered black leather jacket in his arms. "God, it feels so great getting out of that hellhole! I thought I'd never escape."

"You were only there for three months," said Brendan. The Volvo pulled away from the curb. Tony turned to look back.

"Yeah, well, it seemed like a lifetime," he said. "Hey, there's Roy!"

He rolled down the window, flapping his hands at a big bearded man in a Redskins windbreaker. "Yo, Roy! Your mother sews socks that smell!"

"Tony!" Brendan started to laugh. "You really are an idiot, you know that? That guy better not have your new address –"

"No way, man." He turned to grin at the boy in the back seat. "Pretty good, huh, Peter? Stick around with your old Uncle Tony, tomorrow I'll teach you how to meet girls." Peter smiled, so quickly that Brendan caught only the faintest shimmer of it in the rearview mirror. Tony beamed, pounding on the dashboard and nodding. "This is going to be great, Brenda, you know? Having the chance to hang out with you, spend some QT …"

"When do you start work?"

"Good question. You know, I think maybe I'm supposed to go in tonight, just to get acclimated. You got an extra key?"

"Tonight? What, like now? You want me to drop you –"

"No, man. I told you, I'm the graveyard shift, midnight to seven."

Brendan groaned. "You didn't tell me. And you better not wake me up or you'll be living in Stanton Square Park."

"No prob, man, no prob. Just give me an extra key, I'll kiss you guys good night and then bye-bye –"

Tony let his arm drape out the open window. As they rounded a corner he waved at a group of spike-haired kids hanging out in front of a 7-11. "Bye-bye," he repeated.

"Fuck you," one of the kids shouted. "Motherfucker, you fuck –"

A bottle exploded on the street just behind the car, broken glass spattering up against the rear window.

"Damn it!" Brendan swerved, then glanced at Tony. He was gazing at the dashboard, his expression unreadable. "Boy, talk about a lack of respect! If only they knew Tony Maroni was in this car."

"Good thing they don't." Tony's voice was flat. "Jello Biafra got the shit beat out of him in Berkeley by a bunch of kids like that. He was going to watch a gig at Gilman Street, they thought he'd sold out."

"Yeah, well, that won't happen to you," said Brendan dryly.

Tony turned back to staring out the window. In the seat behind them Peter began to snore softly, as the car turned down Mass. Ave. and they headed for Brendan's apartment.

It was nearly dark when they got there, the sulfur-yellow streetlights casting a Halloween glow over sidewalks and lawns and boxtree hedges. Brendan's place was a brick rowhouse, the second one from the corner on a street just a few blocks from the old riot corridor; a neighborhood that had spent the last fifteen years being gentrified without ever quite achieving its goal. He double-parked in front and gave Tony the keys, waiting in the car as Tony ran in and out with the stereo and guitar and boxes of records.

"Okay, that's everything except the clothes," Tony said breathlessly, hopping back into the front. "I stuck it all in the front closet, that okay?"

"Yeah." Brendan cocked a thumb at the backseat, where Peter lay slumped, his hand in his mouth. "But tonight you sleep on the couch – Peter'll be in his room."

"No prob."

He swung the car around the corner and parked in front of Big Mo's Liquor and Tobacco Plus. A few underdressed men stood in front, their breath staining the air as they cadged change from commuters hurrying home with shoulders hunched against the cold. Brendan glared at them as he stepped from the car.

"Damn winos, get a fucking job. All right, Peter," he said, and reaching into the back seat he hefted the boy in his arms. "Tony, can you get that stuff on your own?"

"Sure, man."

"The car alarm's set, don't mess with it once you close the door."

Brendan gave the street men a final scowl, then headed towards the corner. Tony hopped onto the sidewalk. He yanked out the black trash bag and his leather jacket, dropped them behind the car and slammed the door shut.

"Hey – you –" one of the men yelled hoarsely. "You – Whoa Whoa!" He lifted a malt liquor bottle in an unsteady toast.

Tony turned and smiled. "Dave. How you doin'?"

"Mmm fahn. Jus' fahn." Dave teetered on one foot, a wizened man in a filthy trench coat, wispy white hair sticking out from beneath a Microsoft gimme cap. At his feet a whippety mongrel wagged its tail frantically. "Uh-huh, uh-huh." Dave peered up at Tony with clouded eyes and stuck out one hand. "Whoa whoa whoa."

"Yeah, yeah. Here." Tony fished out a five-dollar bill and gave it to him, bent to scratch the dog's head. "Good doggie! Hold on –"

He peeled off his tweed jacket and held it up. "See if this fits, Dave."

"Thangs, thangs…" Dave smiled, showing a few ravaged teeth, and took the coat. Behind him the other men nodded approvingly. "Go' bless you…"

"No prob, man." Tony reached down for his leather jacket, grabbed the trash bag and started down the street. "See ya –"

Brendan met him at the door. "I'm getting Peter to bed. I pulled out the sofa for you, there's sheets and stuff in the bathroom." As Tony bounded past him into the living room he frowned.

"Where's your jacket?"

"I gave it to Dave the Grave."

"You gave it to Dave the Grave? I gave you that jacket!"

"Yeah, well now you can see it whenever you want," said Tony brightly. "I gotta fly, I've gotta be at work early tonight. Thanks again, man. Don't wait up for me."

"Right," Brendan said through clenched teeth. He watched as Tony raced back out the front door and down the steps to the sidewalk. "You have your keys?" he shouted after him.

"Keys to the city, man!" Tony yelled, punching the air with his fist as he started towards the Metro. "Later – !"

From the room behind him, Brendan heard his son banging impatiently on the door. "I'm coming, Peter." He gave Tony one last look, a gangly stoop-shouldered figure slouching its way downstream, past the overcoated men and women armed with briefcases and leather backpacks, the kids in their Timberland street gear and a single slight whitehaired man, weaving his way across Maryland Avenue in a white gimme cap and grey herringbone tweed jacket.

"Dave the fucking Grave," muttered Brendan, and he shut the door.

~ ~ ~

He and Peter were already up when Tony got home from work the next morning.

"You want breakfast?" Brendan pointed at the frying pan still on the stove. "There's some bacon left, I can make you eggs or something."

Tony shook his head. "No thanks. Got an Egg McMuffin on the way home. Check this out –"

He pulled a CD from his leather jacket. "Promo of the new Advent Moth. Wanna hear it?"

"No."

"Aw, c'mon –"

"No." Brendan slid back into his chair at the table beside Peter.

"Peter, here's Uncle Tony. Peter has to finish eating before he can leave the table," he said. "Okay, Peter. Pick up your fork, and eat this before it gets cold."

Tony stood watching them. "Hey, Peter," he said. "That looks like a good breakfast. Yum yum yum."

Peter sat at the table in a booster seat, a plastic bowl in front of him holding a small yellow heap of scrambled eggs. Around him the floor was smeared with more scrambled eggs and several pieces of toast. "Pick up the fork," repeated Brendan.

Peter reached for the cup. "That's the cup," said Brendan firmly. "Pick up the fork."

Peter put down the cup but did nothing. "This is the fork," said Brendan, pointing. "You eat your food with the fork." Peter picked it up stiffly, and began to eat.

"Listen," said Brendan. He looked up at Tony and patted the empty chair next to him. "We have to talk."

Tony sank obediently into the chair. "This isn't going to work, right?"

"Well, no, probably not. Or well, maybe for just a few days –" Brendan sighed and took a sip of coffee. "I was talking to Teri –"

"Oh, yeah, right. I thought we weren't supposed to tell Teri."

"I have to tell Teri, because of Peter." Brendan glanced at his son and smiled. "You're doing a good job with that fork, Peter." He turned back to his friend. "Look, Tony – you know what it's like. We're doing this intensive treatment, Peter's doing really well with it, and – well, we have to be consistent. Anything disruptive is just going to confuse him, and ..."

"Right," said Tony. He spread his hands out on the tabletop and began drumming them. Peter looked over, drew his own hand to his mouth, and bit it.

"Pick up your fork, Peter. Put down your hand and pick up your fork." Brendan reached over, took Peter's hand and brought it back to the table. Peter began to scream, but then abruptly stopped.

"See what I mean?" Brendan shot an exasperated look at Tony. "We're working on that kind of stim, him biting his hand –"

Tony nodded. "He's not doing it as much as he used to."

"He's not doing it at all. Hardly. That's one of the things you do – you don't let them indulge in any self-stimulation, not until after they've eaten their breakfast, or done computer time, or whatever. Then, instead of letting him bite his hand we give him something else –"

Brendan turned so the boy couldn't see him and went on *sotto voce*, "– we give him this rubber duck, he can soothe himself with that for a few minutes."

Tony rubbed his chin. "Uh-huh. Well, I can do that. I mean, I can remember to –"

"No, you can't. No offense, but just your being here is disruptive – not you personally, but anyone else beside me, or Teri. We have this all worked out and it's – well, it's pretty rigid, Tony, it's like this total one-on-one stuff and let me tell you, it's exhausting."

"But then maybe you can use me – I mean, I can help with something, right?" Tony asked, a little desperately.

"Well, maybe." Brendan gave his friend a doubtful look. "I guess we can try it and see."

"Why didn't you just tell me all this last night?"

"Jesus, Tony, you didn't really give me a chance, did you? I mean, you ambushed me at the zoo, saying how you're getting kicked out of your place and you've got twenty-four hours to live, and – use your fork, Peter."

"I didn't mean to put you out." Tony ran a hand through his long hair, his leather jacket squeaking. "Okay. Well, I guess I could, I can always find somewhere else to crash, just let me get on the horn and see who I can get in touch with, okay?"

"Wait. Let me finish – but hold on a minute." Brendan stood, got behind Peter's chair and put his hands firmly on the boy's shoulders. Peter wriggled, but paused as his father went on, "Peter – you did a good job eating your breakfast. You did a good job using your fork. Let's go in now, you can watch *Sesame Street*."

He pulled the chair out. Peter scrambled down and walked beside him into the living room. "See? Check this out –"

Brendan leaned down to pick up a videotape from a stack alongside the VCR. "We watch the same *Sesame Street* tape every day. It's close-captioned, and we read it out loud."

"He can read?"

Brendan slid the tape into the machine. Peter settled in the middle of the floor, staring straight ahead as his father walked past him and Big Bird filled the screen.

"Yes. No. I mean, I actually don't know what he can do," Brendan said, joining Tony back in the kitchen. "You know? They keep running all these tests, and – well, he tests above average for language comprehension, and he does well with all these learning games they play. And he's bonded really well with Peggy, his teacher, which is wonderful – at first he wouldn't even let her near him. But he's still not talking, obviously. And he's still doing the stims when he feels stressed out, though that's pretty normal."

Brendan drew a hand across his forehead, blinking as though the light were too bright. "But what's normal, right? God, I'm tired."

He looked at Tony and smiled wearily. Brendan had gained a few pounds when he quit drinking, and his light brown hair was thinner and flecked with grey, but otherwise he looked pretty much the same as he did back in law school. Same pale blue eyes behind tortoiseshell glasses, same faded freckles in a round boyish face, same faded rugby shirt and chinos and worn L.L. Bean topsiders. The kind of attorney a GS-3 receptionist might trust in a dispute over a rush-hour fender-bender, or a checkout clerk at Rite Aid who lost his job when his drinking became a problem; a guy who looked reliable and intelligent, but not dangerously so. Not like his ex-wife, a lawyer who represented a pharmaceutical corporation in federal lawsuits over the unanticipated side effects of designer drugs with names Tony couldn't even pronounce; a woman who wore Donna Karan clothes and contact lenses that tinted her hazel eyes an astonishing jade-green; a woman who before her divorce had taken a year off from her job, to stay home and work every single day with her autistic son.

"Well, you know, Brendan, maybe I could help out. I mean, if you told me how ..."

Brendan tilted back in his chair. "Thanks, Tony. But you know, it's like, complex. All this patterning stuff. The theory is, you just keep doing the same thing over and over and over again, and eventually you end up burning new neural pathways in the brain."

Tony raised an eyebrow. "Sounds weird. Actually, it sounds boring."

"Well, yeah, it is boring. Sort of. But it works. These kids – their brains are wired differently than ours. Someone like Peter, he goes into sensory overload at the slightest stimulation, the sort of thing maybe you or me wouldn't notice but he's incredibly sensitive to. The rest of us, our sensory levels are set at five or six; but his are cranked all the way up to nine, or ten."

"No – eleven!" Tony said, bopping up and down in excitement. "I get it! You know, like in Spinal Tap – the dials go all the way to eleven."

Brendan closed his eyes and took a deep breath. "You know, Tony – the best thing would probably be if – well, maybe you could kind of stay out of the way. It's fine your being here, I mean, I'd kind of even like it for a little while."

Tony looked hurt. "Oh. Thanks."

"Come on, Tony, you know what I mean. It's just incredibly stressful, that's all. Actually, it would be nice to have you around," Brendan went on a little wistfully. "Since Teri has commandeered Peter for most of the holidays. Not that he gets any of it," he ended, glancing into the living room.

How would you know what he gets? Tony thought. He leaned forward, leather-clad elbows nudging aside an empty glass of orange juice as he watched the little boy in the next room. On the floor in front of Peter, a huge plastic container of Legos had been spilled. Methodically, his brow furrowed, Peter was picking through the multicolored blocks, taking only the yellow and blue ones and being very careful not to even touch the others. On the TV behind him, a fuzzy red figure floated in a star-flecked ultramarine sky, silhouetted against a calm moon while a cat danced beneath. Tony blinked; letters scrolled across the bottom of the screen. On the floor, Peter tilted his head to one side, and his mouth moved silently.

"What's he saying?" said Tony. "Brendan? Is he, uh –"

Brendan turned, springing from his chair with such force that it skidded across the room. "Peter? Peter –"

Peter sat calmly and regarded the wall of yellow and blue that separated him from the remaining Legos. Above him Brendan stood, hands opened helplessly as he stared down at his son. "You okay, Peter? You okay?"

Peter said nothing, his mouth a straight line as he stretched out a hand and began to touch the blocks: yellow blue yellow blue yellow blue. After a moment Brendan turned and looked at Tony in the kitchen. "What happened?"

Tony opened his mouth, thought better of it. "Uh. Nothing. I mean –" He shook his head and shrugged. "Nothing, man. Sorry. I guess I'm just kinda beat, you know? I think I'll crash for awhile –"

He stood, chair scraping loudly. In the living room something flashed across Peter's face, unobserved by the grownups. A wince or perhaps a smile, the bright spark of a moth's wing in the dark. Brendan continued to stare at his friend.

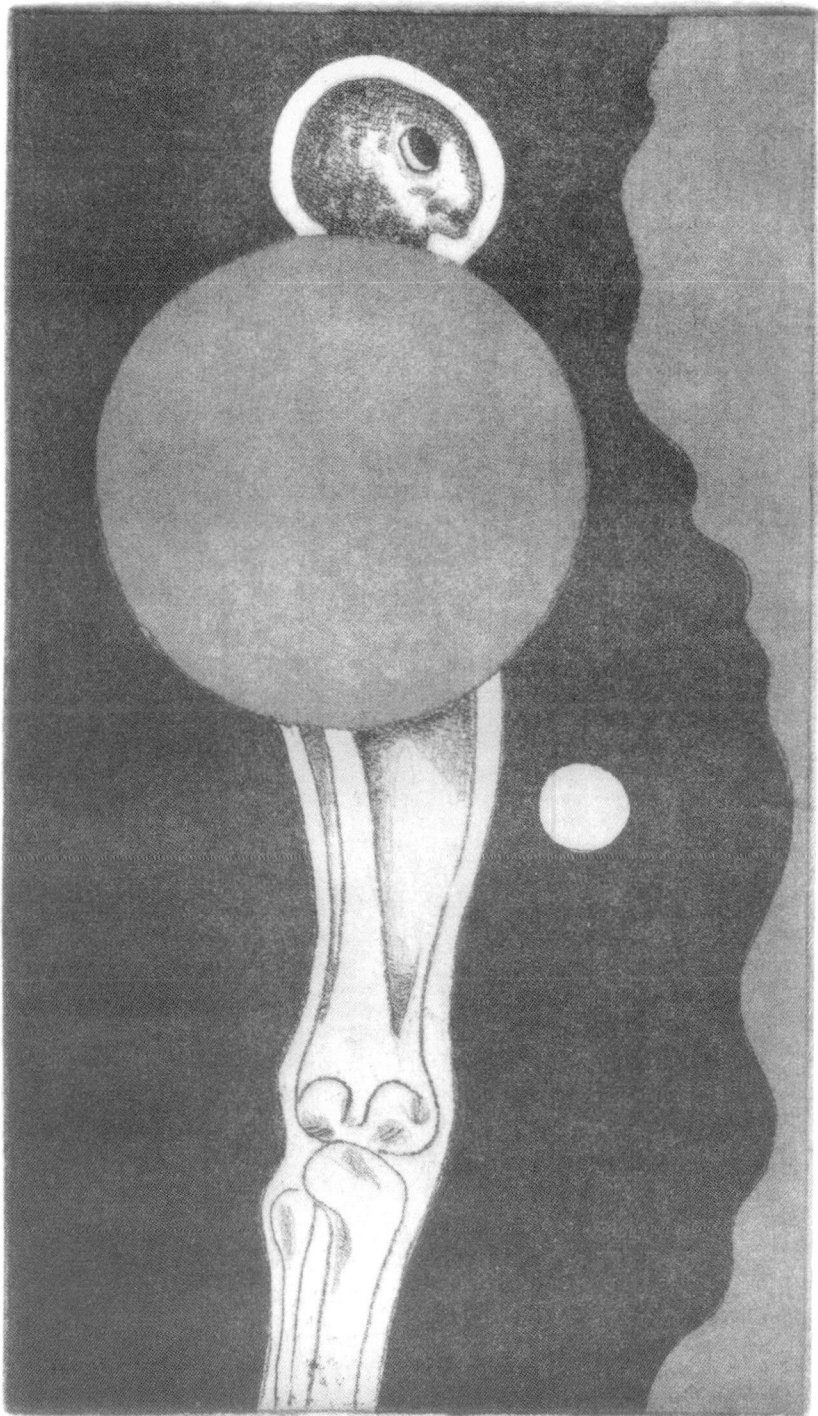

"Beat," he said at last. He nodded, pushed up the sleeve of his old rugby shirt to scratch his arm. "Right. Use my room – just sleep on top of the bed, there's a blanket in the closet. Teri's coming by at noon to pick up Peter. You can have his room then – okay, Peter? That okay if Uncle Tony uses your room?"

This time Peter did smile. Tony saw it. Brendan didn't; he had already turned to adjust the volume on the TV. For just an instant the two others locked eyes and for once Tony could really see him: Peter's gaze questioning, the blue eyes pale as his father's but green-flecked, the firmly-set mouth neither stubborn nor remote but merely intent, slightly distracted but also puzzled by all the to-do. Tony gazed back, and in that instant it was as though a thread were stretched taut between them, silvery and shimmering, ephemeral as Peter's smile, something else that only Tony could almost see –

"Hey," he murmured. "Hey ... !"

His heart surged as though on an explosive adrenaline rush, he had a flash of delight so intense and primal it was like one of those things you know you should never be able to remember but in a miraculous amphetamine moment you do: the first time you saw the moon, the first time you understood the color red; the first silver-grey flicker of a man's face on a small square screen, gentle and smiling, and other smaller faces dancing around him: a mouse, a beatnik, a gross-beaked clown. It was like that, seeing Peter smile, the echo of some emotional Big Bang – *bum, bum-bum!* –

And then it was gone. Without moving his head, Peter returned his attention to the blue and yellow wall of Legos. Tony was staring down at him open-mouthed, feeling at once bereft and exultant.

Fuckin' A, he thought. His hand closed on the back of his chair as he stood, dazed, love and sleeplessness and the rush of blood to his head all one solid revelation. He blinked, eyes aching as Brendan walked past him to gather dishes from the table.

"Tony. You go on," he said with a glance over his shoulder. "Peter and I'll be out for awhile, down at the park or something. If the phone rings just let the machine catch it, okay?"

Tony stared at him, then nodded. "Sure," he said. "Thanks, man."

He turned, stopped to look back. Peter was framed within the doorway, kneeling in front of his Legos. The TV hummed at his back, a fuzzy red figure twirled around the moon, words formed and changed on the screen.

"Bye Peter." Tony waited to see if the boy would look up, if that mad rush of feeling would overcome him again.

It didn't. Peter remained where he was, making his patterns: yellow blue yellow blue. Yellow.

"Bye bye," murmured Tony. He swiped a long strand of unwashed hair from his face; then turned and walked down the corridor to Brendan's room.

~ ~ ~

In the weeks that followed they fell into a surprisingly easy routine. Surprising because in all their years of knowing each other, Brendan and Tony had never actually lived together. Oh, there had been numerous occasions when one or the other had been bounced out by a girlfriend, or a group house had gotten just too crazy even for Tony's patience. And certainly there had been plenty of drunken evenings when Brendan had passed out on Tony's sofa or floor, or vice versa. And so Brendan had always assumed – extremely very wrongly, as Tony quickly pointed out with a hurt look – that Tony was a slob.

In fact Tony was exceedingly, even excessively, neat. He cleaned dishes immediately after washing them; he picked up damp towels and hung them over the shower rod to dry, and later folded them carefully, in three parts, and replaced them on the towel rack. If Brendan put his half-full coffee mug down somewhere and forgot about it, the next time he'd see it would be in the dishwasher, or back in the cupboard. Each section of The Washington Post was in the recycling bin as soon as it was read, and sometimes even sooner.

"You know, Tony, I was saving that Redskins article," Brendan said the Sunday before Thanksgiving, aggrieved to find the sports section gone a few hours before game time. "Christ, you're worse than my mother! Were you always like this?" Brendan gave his friend a suspicious look as Tony sorted through the CDs in the living room. "I thought you were a slob. Like me," he added, yanking the offending sports section from the recycling bin.

"No way, man."

"Yes, way – what about all those places you lived? What about your place with Kimberly? That was disgusting."

"Wasn't me, man." Tony shook his head. "That was her. That was all of them. I just like messy women," he said, shrugging. He held up a CD and struck a thoughtful pose: Marcus Welby, Punk Rocker. "I think they're better in bed. Haven't you ever noticed? Big Fat Slob Equals Great Head."

Brendan laughed. "Oh. That's what I've been doing wrong."

"Sure, man. Problem is, eventually, you just can't find 'em."

"You mean like, all the good ones are taken?"

"No, man – I mean, like, Kimberly's place was such a fucking pigsty, it took me a week to figure out she'd gone off with Roy." Tony turned back to the stack of CDs. "And you know, these days I'm so wired when I get home from work in the morning – it's like when I used to play. Takes me a while to wind down. It calms me, straightening stuff. And I mean, what's your fucking problem?" He glared over his shoulder at Brendan. "Cleaning up is a lot more productive than shooting smack."

Brendan hooted. "Is that what you told your students? 'This is Tony Maroni for a Drug-Free America. Clean your' – ouch!"

He ducked as a CD went skimming past his head. "Go watch your Foreskins game!" yelled Tony. "Let me clean in peace!"

They went out to dinner that night after the game, Tony's domestic abilities not extending as far as cooking food. Peter was at his mother's until Wednesday, when Brendan would pick him up for the long Thanksgiving weekend.

"How come you got the night off?" he asked Tony, dousing his salad with balsamic vinegar. "I thought Gigantor was open for all major holidays."

"They are. But I said I'd cover for Jason so he could go see his girlfriend in Charlottesville." Tony picked up a French fry, dabbed it in ketchup and drew a little heart; erased it and ate the fry. "Wish I had a girlfriend," he said. "We still on for Cousin Kevin's?"

"Far as I know. Kevin says Eileen's bought a five-hundred-pound turkey and upset the Chicago trading floor by sucking up cranberry futures. So I guess we're expected."

Tony laughed: he loved Eileen. "You think she'll do that thing again with the little teeny pumpkins and jalapeño cheese? And the girls doing their Irish dancing?"

"Jesus, I hope not. Kevin said come any time after ten, so we can catch some of the parade. And we're supposed to bring cider."

"Cider?"

"Yeah –" Brendan pulled an ATM receipt from his pocket and squinted, trying to read something scrawled there. "Magyar Farms Organic Flash-Pasteurized Cider. Four gallons."

"Wow. Flash Pasteurized." Tony leaned back in his chair and grinned. "Thanksgiving. I can't hardly wait. Remember when we were kids, watching the parade and stuff? And that story your Uncle Tom always told, about the turkey who ate the Pepperidge Farm Man?"

Brendan laughed. "I forgot about that."

"And Chip Crockett ... Remember how Captain Kangaroo always used to have Thanksgiving dinner, like a real formal dinner – you know, Mister Green Jeans and Dancing Bear saying Grace with all the silverware and good china. And so Chip Crockett started doing that thing with Ooga Booga and Ogden Orff trying to stuff a kielbasa?"

Brendan speared a cherry tomato and shook his head. "Jeez, Tony. How the hell do you remember that stuff?"

"Chip Crockett Web page, man! It's like a memory enhancer. Or a time machine, or something." He hesitated, recalling that weird charged moment with Peter; thought of mentioning it to Brendan, but instead said, "Like when you smell something, or hear something – a song, or the way a balloon smells – and all of a sudden you flash back to when you were really, really little? Like Peter's age? But you can't remember exactly what it is that you're remembering, because you were so young then it was before you started remembering things. It's like that."

Brendan stared at him blankly. "Balloons?"

"Sure!" Tony leaned back a little too enthusiastically in his chair, nearly tipped before he came crashing back down. "Oops. Yeah, balloons."

"Tony? What the hell are you talking about?"

"I told you: Chip Crockett's Web page! It's all there. All that stuff you thought you forgot when you grew up –"

"Like where I put my Casey Stengel baseball cards?"

"Absolutely. And all those Bosco commercials? And Cocoa Marsh?" Tony pushed aside Brendan's salad and leaned across the table. "It's all in there. Bonomo Turkish Taffy. Enemee Electric Organs. Diver Dan and Baron Barracuda. 'They're Coming to Take Me Away, Ha Ha.' Ooga Booga. Ogden Orff. Everything."

"Right." Brendan closed his eyes, opened them, and slid his salad plate back where it belonged. "You know, Tony," he said between mouthfuls of mesclun and seared porcini mushrooms, "doesn't it ever strike you that some of this stuff is – well, sort of useless?"

Tony looked confused. "What do you mean?"

"All this baby boomer detritus. Beatlemania. Mickey Mouse Club hats.

Three Stooges T-shirts. It's all bullshit. They're just trying to sell you shit. It's all one big fucking infomercial."

"But that's not what I'm talking about." Tony shook his head, hair whipping round his face. "I'm talking about the stuff that was lost – all those people you never heard of again. Like Chip Crockett. All those puppets he made," he said plaintively. "And his characters. Ogden Orff. I mean, there's nothing left but these little tiny ten-second videoclips, but he's there, man! He's still alive!"

Brendan dropped his fork onto his plate and buried his face in his hands. "Tony." He cracked his fingers so that he could peer at his friend. In front of him, Tony's cheeseburger platter was almost untouched, the ghostly red outline of a heart just visible alongside the pickle. "Listen. I hate to be the one to give you the bad news about Santa Claus, but –"

"But this is real. Ogden Orff was real – or, well, Chip Crockett was. They were real," Tony repeated, pounding the table. "Real."

"Yeah, but Tony! They don't matter. They never mattered! I mean, it's cute and nice that you can find this stuff and look at the funny pictures and all, but Jesus Christ! You're forty-three years old! I got my access bill and you spent thirty-nine hours online in the last two weeks. That's a lot of Ogden fucking Orff, Tony. And to tell you the truth, I'm kind of –"

"I'll pay you back. I'll pay you right now, here –"

Brendan made a tired gesture as Tony fumbled in his pocket. Dollar bills fluttered around him, coins chinked across the table and onto the floor in a steady rain. "I don't want your money, Tony. I definitely don't want it in nickels and dimes – stop, for chrissake! Listen to me –

"I know you just started working again, but – well, you've got to, like, get a life, Tony. A real life. You can't spend all your time online, looking at pictures of Ogden Orff."

"Why not?" The look Tony gave Brendan was definitely hostile. "Why the fuck not? What do you think I should do? Huh? Mister Big-Time lawyer. What, are you pulling in thirty grand these days, after you make child support? Forty?"

"That has nothing to –"

"Yes it does! Or, well – no it doesn't, does it?" The hostility drained from Tony's face. Suddenly all he looked was tired, and sad, and every one of his forty-three years old. "Hey man. I'm sorry. I was out of line there, with that money stuff –"

"It's okay, Tony."

"Way out of line. 'Cause like, I know you could earn more if you wanted to. Right?" Tony raised his eyebrows, then looked away. "But, like, I understand that you don't want to. I identify with your integrity, man. I respect it. I really do."

"My what?" Without warning, Brendan began to laugh. "My integrity? My integrity? Oh Tony. You big dope!" Hard; harder than he'd laughed in a long time, maybe since before Peter was born. Maybe since before he was married, when slowly everything had stopped being funny – because what was funny about being married, especially when you didn't stay married? Or having a kid, even a perfectly normal boring healthy kid; or a job, a perfectly normal healthy job that you hated? There was nothing funny about any of that; there was nothing fun about it at all.

And there was Tony Maroni, with his soulful dopey eyes, his long greying hair and stretched Silly Putty face, his black leather jacket with its Jimmy Carter campaign button rusted to the lapel and the faxed copy of Chip Crockett's obituary still wadded in one pocket. Tony who remembered the words to every back-of-the-schoolbus song they'd sung thirty-five years ago; Tony who had dedicated a song to his childhood friends, and treasured Officer Joe Bolton's autograph as though it were the Pope's; Tony who'd nearly wept when PeeWee Herman got booted off the air; who did weep, as a kid, when he'd gotten the bad news about the North Pole.

Tony Maroni was fun. Tony Maroni was funny. Most of all, Tony Maroni had integrity. Sort of.

"What?" Tony tilted his head, puzzled. "What?"

"Nothing." Brendan shook his head, wiping his eyes. "Nothing – just, you know –" He flapped his hand and coughed, trying to calm down. "Me. You. All this stuff."

Now Tony sounded suspicious. "All what stuff?"

"Life. You thinking I have integrity, when –"

The laughter started up again: spurts of it, hot somehow and painful, like blood. Laughing blood, Brendan thought, but couldn't stop. " – when I'm just – a – a – terrible – lawyer!"

"Awwww." Tony rubbed his forehead and frowned. Then he started laughing, too. "'No, Ogden, no!'" he said, imitating Chip Crockett. "'Don't file that tort!'"

Brendan lifted his head. His pale blue eyes were brilliant, almost feverishly so; but there was a kind of calm in them, too. Like a beach that's been storm-scoured, all the sand castles and traces of an endless hot afternoon smoothed away, so that only a few still sky-reflecting pools remain.

Calm. That was how he felt. Their waiter passed and Brendan smiled at him, signaling for the check; then turned back to Tony. "Okay. So maybe you can show me that Web site."

Tony's face cracked into a grin like Humpty Dumpty's. "Sure, man! Absolutely!"

"And maybe you can write me a check – not now, jeez, Tony. When you get settled. More settled. Whenever."

The waiter brought the check. Brendan paid it. Tony left the tip, in little neatly-stacked piles of quarters and dimes and nickels. On the way out Tony held the door as Brendan shrugged into his heavy camel's hair coat, still smiling. As he stepped past him onto the sidewalk Brendan tripped, catching himself as he lurched between an immaculately dressed Capitol Hill couple who scowled as Brendan drew himself up, laughing, alongside his friend.

"That's my attorney," said Tony fondly. "Ogden Orff."

~ ~ ~

Thanksgiving Day dawned clear and warm, the air glittering with that magical blue-gold tinge Brendan recalled from his undergrad days – late-autumn light that seemed to seep into the pores of even the most disenchanted bureaucrats in their holiday-weekend drag of paint-spattered chinos and faded Springsteen T-shirts, rearranging leaves on vest-pocket lawns with their Smith & Hawken rakes. That was what Teri was doing when he went to pick up Peter at The House Formerly Known as Brendan's, way up Connecticut Avenue just past the Bethesda line.

"Hi, Teri," he said, stepping from the car and hopping over a brown heap at the edge of the driveway. "How you doing? Where's the boy?"

Teri paused, balancing the rake on her shoulder like a musket, and cocked a thumb at the house behind her. "Taking a nap. You can go wake him if you want."

Brendan nodded. His ex-wife as always looked harried, her short hair stuck with twigs and her dark eyes narrowed with a furious concentration that seemed expended needlessly upon innocent dead leaves. "Great," he said. "What're you doing today? Kevin said –"

"Leon's coming over. We're going out to Harper's Ferry."

Leon was Teri's paralegal, a wispy young man ten years her junior who'd been her companionate default since before the divorce was final. Brendan had never been able to figure out if Leon was sleeping with his ex-wife, if he were even heterosexual, or a careerist, or what? "That's nice," he said. "Well, Kevin and Eileen send their love."

"And Tony?" Eileen swung the rake down from her shoulder, plonked it in the ground in front of her and leaned on the handle. To Brendan it still looked like a musket.

"Tony?"

"Does Tony send his love? I understand he's living at your place these days."

"Tony! Oh, sure, Tony sends his love." Brendan kicked at the leaves, noticed Teri's wince of disapproval and quickly began nudging them back into place with his foot. "Loads of hugs and kisses from Tony Maroni."

"Hm." Teri eyed him measuringly. Then, "You should have told me."

"You know, Teri, I don't need to ask for —"

"I didn't say ask," she said calmly. "I said told. You should have told me, that's all. I don't care if Tony's living with you. I know it's — I'm sure it must make things easier for you. I just need to know, so I can arrange Peter's schedule accordingly."

Brendan frowned. "Accordingly to what?"

Behind Teri the front door of the little mock-Tudor house swung open. Peter stood there, yellow rubber duck in one hand. He smiled, staring at a point just above Brendan's head, then walked across the lawn towards him.

"We can talk about this later," said Teri. She wiped a smudge of dirt from her cheek and called to the boy. "Hi sweetie. Ready to go with Daddy?"

Brendan grinned as Peter came up alongside him. "Hey, Peter!" He caressed the top of his son's head, ever so gently, as though it were dandelion fluff he was afraid to disperse. "We're going to go see Kevin and the twins. Remember the twins? Give Mommy a kiss goodbye."

Peter remained beside his father. "I'll go get his stuff," Teri called as she started for the house.

"I'll bring him back Sunday afternoon. Is that still okay?"

Teri nodded. A few minutes later she returned with his knapsack and extra bag of clothes. "Okay. This should be everything. Here's the number where we'll be till Saturday."

She crouched in front of Peter and took his hands in hers. He writhed and tried to pull away, but Teri only stared at him, her eyes glazed with tears. "I'll miss you," she said. Her voice was loud and steady. "You have a great time with Daddy and Uncle Kevin and the twins, okay? I love you, Peter —"

Peter said nothing. When Teri kissed him and stood, he drew the rubber duck to his mouth, rubbing it against his cheek.

"All right then." Brendan started for the car, turning and beckoning for Peter to follow. "Wave goodbye, Peter."

The boy followed him. "Wave bye-bye," Brendan repeated, standing aside to let Peter climb into the back seat. Brendan strapped him in, then got in front. "Bye-bye," he said to Peter, the boy kicking at the seat in front of him. And, "Bye-bye," Brendan called to Teri, rolling down the window as he backed from the drive, "Bye-bye," as behind them she grew smaller and smaller, the rake just a rake again, his ex-wife just a mother, waving to her son as he disappeared down the street.

~ ~ ~

Kevin lived in an expensive contemporary house in Potomac, its cedar siding tinted a rich russet-brown and lushly overgrown with Virginia creeper and English ivy, its front yard a miniature forest of rhododendron and birch trees and azaleas. There were no stray leaves on the ground, save beneath a solitary Japanese maple whose bounty was scattered across the grass like crimson handprints.

"Uncle Brendan! Uncle Brendan's here!"

Two small girls, Cara and Caitlin, danced excitedly on the front porch. Twins, with long silken hair so deep a red it looked violet in certain lights, paper-white skin and green eyes. They were wearing smocked flowered dresses and their hair was ribboned with pink satin bows so immense it looked as though they were wearing throw pillows on their heads.

"Peter! Where's Peter! Hi Peter!"

The girls ran over to the car and began pounding on the window. Peter regarded them with the same reserved interest he'd shown the iguanas at the zoo, but when Cara yanked the door open and flung herself at him he kicked fiercely at the back of Brendan's seat.

"Cara! Hey, honey, come give Uncle Brendan a kiss — it's okay, Peter — come here, sweetie, remember he gets a little excited if —"

"Actually, you're our cousin." Caitlin stood watching him solemnly. "Not our uncle. Our first cousin once removed."

"Oh yeah? Well here, come give Uncle Cousin Brendan Once Removed a kiss –"

"Brendan!"

Another figure appeared on the porch, radiant in crimson velvet and ecru lace, her hair a gold corona framing a face even paler than the girls'.

"Eileen, hi – gee, you look great! Hi, Caitlin, Cara, hi hi hi hi –"

Brendan unfolded himself from the car and the twins' embrace, freed Peter from his carseat. Eileen clattered down to hug him, Peter sliding behind his father's legs as she did so; and Brendan felt that irresistible tug of lust and awe he always felt when he saw his cousin's wife.

"Wow!" He drew back to admire her dress, protected by a spattered apron with the legend *JESUS IS COMING: LOOK BUSY* . "You really dressed for dinner."

"Tell me about it." Eileen dabbed Brendan's chin with a finger, erasing a smudge of lipstick. "Girls, go get your father."

She swatted at the twins and sent them racing into the house. "And close the door! I've been doing this job out in Warrenton, redecorating Senator Weston's place," she continued, turning back to Brendan. "Almost broke my wrist on that goddamn chainsaw, the chain came off and –"

Brendan laughed. Eileen had been a lingerie model –"the Rosey Underwear girl," she called it – for the Rosellen's Boudoir Catalog, before quitting to have babies and then become an interior decorator for the horsy set out in Middleburg. Now she wielded a chainsaw and glue-gun like Martha Stewart on steroids.

" – oh, but you know what it's like," she ended.

"Breaking my wrist on a chainsaw in a senator's house? Actually, no."

"And how is Peter?" Eileen's tone softened as she took in Peter, sheltered behind his father and chewing his rubber duck. "Hi, darlin' – "

She glanced at Brendan. "Will he let me hug him?"

"No. But Peggy – his teacher at Birchwood – he'll let her hold him, now. Sometimes."

Eileen gazed down at Peter. "That's okay," she said softly. "That's just fine, okay Peter?" She turned back to his father, holding the front door open. "I'm glad he's doing so well, Brendan. Kevin told me, that new school is great and he's just making such great progress ..."

Brendan followed her inside, wondering what on earth Kevin could have said. The two cousins seldom confided anything more personal than Redskins scores. "Oh, and listen," Eileen went on, taking his arm. "Tony said not to worry, he got the cider."

"The cider!" Brendan slapped his forehead. "I totally forgot."

"That's what I'm telling you, Tony's bringing it."

"Tony? I thought he had to work."

"Change of plans. Here, Peter, you can put your things in here. Brendan, you too."

"Brendan! Peter! Glad you could make it −" Kevin loomed in the doorway, beaming.

"Yeah, great to be here, Kevin, thanks."

"Girls!" Kevin ordered. "You all go play nicely together, you and Peter." He turned and made his way down the hall.

"Sure Dad." Caitlin smiled respectfully at the younger boy. "Hi, Peter. Would you like to come watch TV with us? In the other room?"

"It's down here," said Cara, and started off. Peter shook his head, looking at the ceiling and patting his rubber duck against one cheek.

"You know what?" Brendan started to explain. "Sometimes he doesn't like to go off on his own. But maybe in a few minutes, if I go −"

Without a word Peter began walking. Still gazing at the ceiling, but following Cara into the cozy room where a TV was already turned to the Macy's Thanksgiving Day Parade.

"Hey, Brendan." Kevin stuck his head out from the kitchen. "What're you drinking?"

"Uh, club soda. Fizzy water, anything." Brendan's brow furrowed, and he crossed to where the children sat.

"He's watching with us," said Caitlin. On screen the camera panned a crowd of waving children, then swept up to take in a shapeless scarlet mass floating against a backdrop of skyscrapers and cobalt-blue sky. "Look Peter, it's Elmo!"

"Sesame Street. The universal language."

Brendan looked up to see Tony standing in the hall. He wore a black T-shirt, faded black jeans, and his leather jacket, augmented by four gallons of cider balanced very precariously in his arms.

"Tony. Hey, why didn't you tell me you were coming, I would've given you a lift." Brendan scooped up two of the gallons and took a step towards the kitchen. "I thought you had to work."

Tony shrugged. "Well, you know how it is." His gaze remained fixed on the television. "Gee, look at Elmo! He sure looks bigger in real life, huh? Hi goils," he called to the twins. "Look: it's Crazy Uncle Tony."

The girls glanced up, gave high-pitched squeals of glee, and raced over to hug him.

"Uncle Tony! Crazy Uncle Tony!"

"Hey," said Brendan. "How come he's Uncle Tony and I'm only Cousin Brendan?"

"Come on, guys," called Eileen from the kitchen. "Come hang out with the big kids. Girls, dinner'll be ready in an hour."

It was warm enough to sit outside on the deck, looking out onto a small stand of maples still clinging to their shaggy red leaves. Now and then one of the children would wander out, the girls looking for snacks (refused) or attention (given), Peter simply standing for a moment beside his father before turning and walking back inside.

"Tony said he's starting to read?" Eileen asked. She alone was drinking wine, a good Sémillon that gave off topaz sparks as sun struck her glass.

Brendan's mouth twitched in an automatic smile. "Actually, no, I don't think he's reading. Well, we're not sure he's reading. We have close-captioned TV, and he watches it, and Teri thinks maybe he makes out some of it. But I don't know," he ended, pressing his glass of club soda to his cheek. "I just don't know."

"Well, but everything has to be taken slowly, doesn't it?" Eileen leaned over and touched his knee. "Every little thing is sort of a major triumph with kids. Any kids."

"Sure." Brendan thought of Peter going in by himself to watch TV with the twins. "Every little bit counts."

"It's all important," agreed Eileen.

"Sure," said Kevin, standing. "But what's really important is football."

Tony looked stricken. "What about The March of the Wooden Soldiers?"

"Don't worry, Tony, we got it all set up." Kevin started for the kitchen. "And you know what else, Tony? This year you even get to sit at the grownups' table."

When dinner was ready they all moved into the formal dining room. At his father's side, Peter sat quietly as Brendan cut up turkey and green beans. For a little while the room was happily silent, except for grunts of "Great job, Eileen" and muffled requests for more stuffing. Seconds were dispersed, plates emptied, and soon everyone save Peter began talking at once – the twins eager to tell Brendan about some complicated arrangement they had for sharing hamsters, Kevin ribbing his cousin about the last football game, Eileen sharing her recipe for jalapeño-pumpkin dip with Tony.

And, gradually, despite Eileen's best efforts, the conversation began to turn to childhood. Brendan and Kevin and Tony's childhood, in particular; Chip Crockett, in even more particular.

"Kevin, man, you got to check out his Web site. I was gonna show it to Brendan the other night but it got too late. It'll blow your mind. Right, Brenda?"

Kevin sniffed. "Sounds more like something the girls'd go for, Tony. I personally don't watch a lot of Chip Crockett these days."

"Well, no one does," said Tony. He turned to Eileen. "You remember Chip Crockett. They had him over in New Jersey, right?"

"Oh sure. He was great – you girls would've loved him. I had a total crush on Chip Crockett," she added dreamily. "He was –"

"What was he like?" Cara broke in.

"He was just like your Uncle Tony," said Kevin. "Plus or minus a few brain cells."

"I was going to say," Eileen continued, "that he was like my father. Or what I wanted my father to be like. He was funny –"

"He was silly," said Kevin.

"He was wonderful. I still remember, after Kennedy was assassinated – that Monday morning Chip Crockett came back on the air and tried to explain it to us. He looked awful, but he was so gentle and sad – I never forgot that."

The twins looked bored. "Can we be excused? Please?"

Eileen nodded. "Yes. Of course, just clear your plates ..."

They were already out the door. A moment later Cara poked her head back in. "Peter? Wanna come? We have that movie –"

"The movie!" Tony shot to his feet. "Wait, girls –"

"Go ahead, Peter," said Brendan, smiling encouragingly. "Go with Tony." Peter slid from his chair and left.

"Tony! Clear your place!" Kevin shouted as Tony hurried down the hall. "God, he drives me nuts. Doesn't he drive you crazy, Brendan? Living with him?"

"Not really. Well, a little. He's very neat."

"Neat? Well, his life's a fucking mess. You know he got canned from Gigantor Music?"

Brendan blinked. "No."

"Yes. He showed up for work last night, they told him to go home."

"Kevin." Eileen's lacquered red nails poised menacingly above his wrist. "Shut up."

Brendan began to unwind a crescent roll. "What happened?"

"Who knows? Who cares? Look at him – forty-three years old, he's still wearing a leather jacket and hightop sneakers and waiting to collect his first royalty check. He's a fucking loser."

Eileen's eyes narrowed. "Yeah? Well, I've never seen anyone wearing a T-shirt with *your* face on it."

"He hasn't even played a pickup gig in three years." Kevin picked up his glass of non-alcoholic beer and stared at it. "He depresses me."

"He makes me laugh." In a swirl of red velvet and Chakra perfume, Eileen stood. "He's the only one who's still the way we were when we all met. I think he's a sweetheart."

"Oh yeah?" sputtered Kevin. "Well, then, why –"

"And you can do the dishes."

She stalked off, carrying the bottle of Sémillon. Kevin stared after her. "Christ. My wife's leaving me for Tony Maroni."

Brendan took a bite of his roll. "You know, it's a concept."

"What?"

"T-shirts with your picture on them. They could give 'em out at Green-peace rallies. You'd be bigger than Saddam Hussein."

Kevin gazed broodingly at the deconstructed turkey. After a minute, Brendan asked, "Why does he bother you so much?"

"Tony? Because he's superfluous. He has absolutely no place in the food chain."

"Then why do you stay in touch with him at all?"

Kevin sighed. "Because he's the only one of us who's still the same as when we met."

"Dad?" Caitlin stood in the doorway. "The tape's not working."

"I'll go." Brendan stood, put a hand on his cousin's shoulder. "You help Eileen with the dishes."

He followed the girl into the hall. "How's Peter doing, Caitlin?"

She shrugged. "Okay, I guess. He doesn't talk."

"That's right."

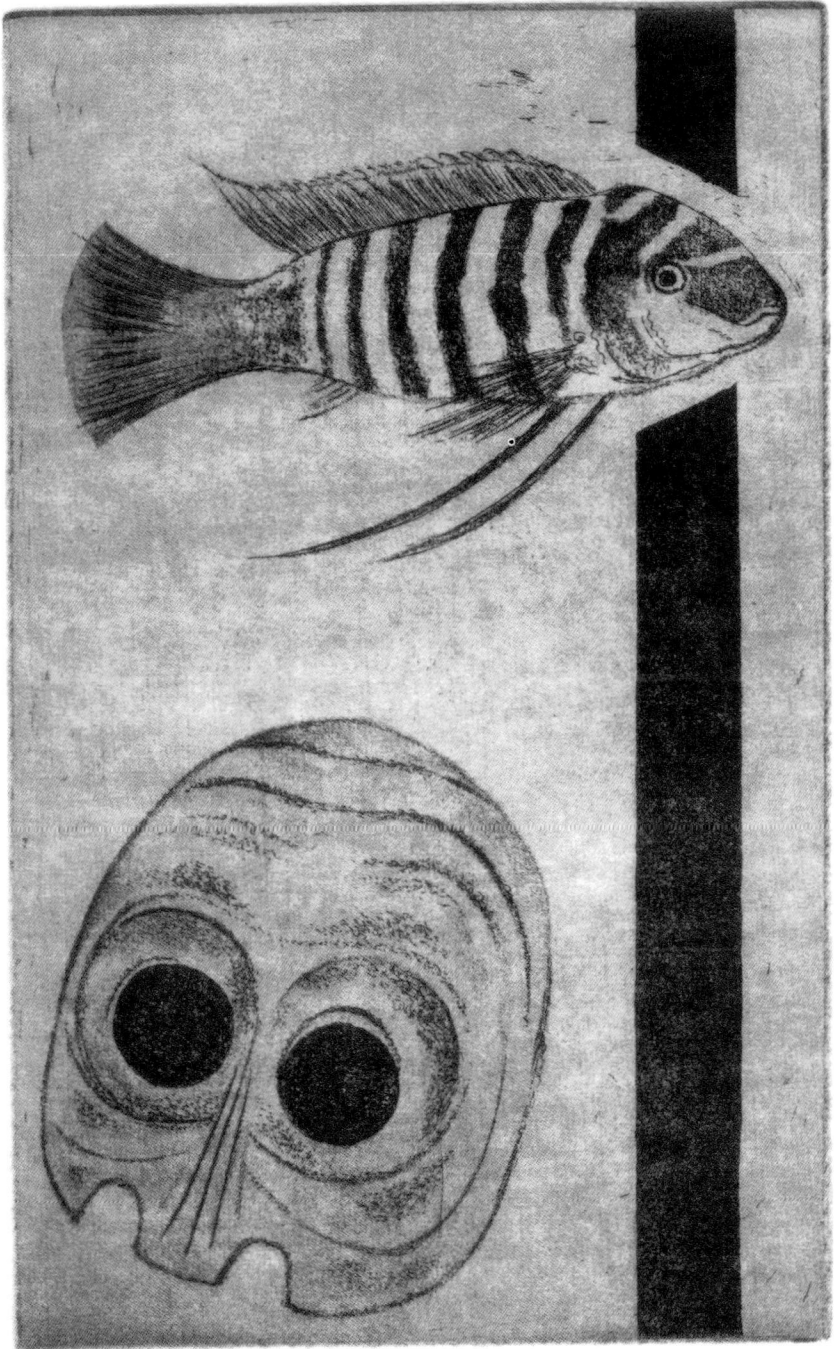

"Did he ever?"

"No, he didn't."

Caitlin stopped outside the door to the TV room. Peter and Cara were sitting on the floor with Tony sprawled between them, counting out Gummy Worms.

"Hey, guys," said Brendan. He stepped over them to the television and picked up the remote. "What's the problem?"

The screen blipped to blue, then black. In a flurry of electronic snow the tape started. Brendan sank onto the couch, balancing the remote on his knees. "There –"

Mother Goose appeared on the screen, warbling tremulously about Toyland. Heroes and villains were identified: Little Bo Peep, Tom Thumb ("That sap," said Tony), wicked Barnaby, and, last of all, Stan and Ollie lying side by side in bed sound asleep.

"Do they talk?" Cara frowned. "I don't like it when they don't talk."

"It's been colorized," said Brendan. "I hate that."

"I don't." Caitlin scrunched closer to the screen. "I hate black-and-white. No way ..."

"Way," said Tony. "Black-and-white is cool, man. You just have to get used to it. Here--"

He grabbed the remote from Brendan and started fiddling with it, pushing buttons and pointing it around the room. "Beam me up, Captain – oops, not that one ..." Caitlin and Cara giggled. Even Peter turned to watch. "Hmm. There's gotta be a way to do this ..."

Brendan shook his head. "It doesn't work like that, Tony. Older TVs, you can adjust the color to make it black-and-white again. But not anymore. Not with a remote, at least. Believe me, I've tried."

On screen, Stan Laurel froze, rose-pink mouth open in a wail.

"Uh-oh. Looks bad for Old Mother Hubbard." Kevin's massive frame filled the doorway. He looked down at the kids and smiled. "We used to watch this every year on Thanksgiving. But it wasn't in color then."

"Uncle Tony's fixing it."

Kevin glanced suspiciously at Tony. "Uncle Tony better not be breaking it."

" – see what this'll do –"

"Look!" Cara jumped up excitedly. "He did it! Uncle Tony did it!"

Stan's wail filled the room. He reached up to tousle his thatch of hair – black-and-white hair, black-and-white hand; black-and-white Ollie rolling black-and-white eyes in disgust.

"Now, Stannie, what'd you go and do that for?"

"That's impossible." Brendan shook his head. "You can't do that with a remote. I've tried. I've even called the video store –"

"You sure can't do it with that remote." Kevin strode over and snatched it from Tony's hand. "If you screwed this up –"

"Daddy, be quiet!"

"Shhh!" said Tony. "I like this part."

"Well, don't mess it up now, Kev, for Chrissakes." Brendan whacked at his cousin's knee. "At least wait'll it's over."

"Yeah, Daddy – come sit with us –"

Kevin sat. Tony flopped back, arms outspread and long hair tangled as he watched, a huge grin on his face. Brendan slid past him onto the floor and edged towards his son. Without taking his eyes from the screen, Peter moved away. Brendan stopped, feeling as though someone were squeezing his ribs. Then he turned back to the movie. After a few minutes, Eileen appeared and sat down next to Tony. She cupped her wineglass between her knees and put the half-empty bottle on the floor beside the couch.

"I love this movie," she murmured. "But I don't like the way they colorized – but hey! Who fixed it?"

"Tony!" everybody shouted.

Eileen raised her glass at him. "Way to go, Tony Maroni."

"Shhhh ...!"

Everybody shhhed. The story unfolded, like one of those card tricks you know in advance won't be much of a trick at all – Guess which one's the king, Daddy! – because they're all kings.

But no one cared. Cara and Caitlin and Peter watched, huge-eyed. Brendan sat as close to Peter as he could, feeling his heart constrict again when the boy winced at the Bogey Men.

"It's okay, Peter – they're just pretend. See – you can see the zipper on that one. Are you scared, honey? Do you want to sit with Daddy?"

Peter shook his head.

"This is the best part," whispered Tony. "Watch ..."

There was Santa's Workshop. There were Laurel and Hardy. There were one hundred wooden soldiers six feet high.

And there was the music. A solitary horn, high and sweet and strong, a sound Brendan still heard in dreams; an answering blare of trumpets and drums –

And the toy soldiers became real, black helmets lifting above impassive white faces, stiff black legs slicing the air as they began to march. As a child, this moment had always filled Brendan with such inexpressible joy that he had simply jumped to his feet and leapt up and down. Then Tony would do it, too, and Kevin, and all their brothers and sisters, until the rec room would be filled with giddy leaping children, and on the screen behind them rank upon rank of implacable, unstoppable soldiers making war upon the Bogey Men.

Now, for just an instant, he felt that way again: that tide of joy and longing, that same impulse to leap into the air, because he could not leap into the screen. Without thinking, he moved to put his arm around Peter. His son shrank away.

"Peter ..."

The name came out before Brendan could stop it, a sound nobody heard. The trumpets swelled, the soldiers broke ranks and began routing the Bogey Men. Brendan looked down and wiped his eyes. He glanced aside and saw Kevin doing the same, and Eileen, eyes fixed on the screen and their arms around their children.

"Mommy, will they win?"

"Of course, watch ..."

On the floor beside Brendan, Tony sat unnaturally still, his hands clasping his knees, his bare arms goosefleshed as the soldiers triumphed and the Bogey Men were driven back into the darkness and the lovers reunited before Old King Cole.

"That was a good movie," said Cara.

"Whaddya mean?" said Kevin. "That's the best movie –"

"I liked it when the soldiers saved everybody."

"I liked it when the soldier stepped on that guy's head."

"I liked it when the alligators ate Barnaby."

Brendan turned to his son. "What did you like, Peter?" he asked, struggling to keep his voice steady. "Did you like the soldiers? Were they cool?"

Kevin flashed the remote at the television. The tape began to rewind, soldiers marching backwards, crooked Barnaby wriggling back into his crooked house.

"Hey, look." Cara walked up to the screen. "It's in color again."

"Damn good thing, too," said Kevin. "This remote cost a hundred bucks."

"Come on, girls." Eileen yawned, looked dismayed into her empty wineglass. She set it in on the floor and stood. "Who wants dessert?"

A rush for the kitchen, the girls elbowing Tony as he pretended to hold them back. Kevin drooped an arm around Eileen and snuck in a kiss as the others raced down the hall, Peter trailing after them. Only Brendan remained sitting on the floor, staring at the empty TV screen. After a minute, he turned and reached for Eileen's empty wineglass; then angled around the couch until he found the half-empty bottle of Sémillon. He poured some into his glass and drank it, slowly but steadily. Then he refilled the glass and drank again, and then a third time, until the bottle was empty.

"Mmm."

For a minute he sat, feeling the muffled rush that came when he drank too quickly: like pressing a pillow over his face and jumping from the top bunk when he was a kid. Doing that always made his head ache, eventually, just like drinking did.

But not yet. Brendan got to his feet, feeling purposeful, perfectly focused, and walked down the hall. Away from the kitchen, to the huge back room where his cousin had set up a pool table and wide-screen TV, sofas and club chairs and the small liquor cabinet Eileen insisted on keeping for guests and clients.

Tony had wandered off as well, looking for the bathroom. He finally found it, a room bigger than any living room he'd ever had. More furniture, too, including a bookcase that contained reprints of vintage comic books. He got so caught up in Namor the Sub-Mariner that it wasn't until his Pokemon watch beeped six o'clock that he realized he'd been in there for half an hour.

"Damn."

He shoved the Sub-Mariner under his arm and hurried back to join the others in the kitchen.

The children had gone out onto the deck to eat. A floodlight cast a weird movie-set glow over them: the twins' hair pumpkin-orange, Peter's rubber duck a blob of yellow paint beside his elbow. Cara and Caitlin sat side by side at the picnic table, sharing a fluffy pink blanket against the November chill. Peter was on the other bench, alone, picking at apple pie and rocking slowly back and forth. Inside, Eileen had dimmed the kitchen lights and brought candles in from the dining room. It took a minute for Tony's eyes to adjust to the odd patchwork of light and shadow, the surreally bright window framing the children so that they looked like a film running behind their silent, candle-lit parents.

Only it wasn't really silent at all. As he entered the room, Eileen turned, her cheeks red and golden hair seemingly aflame.

"Here's Tony!" she said, too brightly. She lifted a bottle of mineral water and beckoned at a stool pulled up beside the counter. Kevin was leaning beside her, arms folded against his big chest, scowling with even more than his customary ferocity. "Here! I was just making some coffee to go with dessert!"

"Uh, thanks." Tony looked around uneasily. What the hell was going on? "Is there any more cider?"

"Cider? Sure, sure ..." Eileen hurried over to the fridge, and that was when Tony saw Brendan. He was sitting at the big round kitchen table, holding a wineglass and looking up at Tony and Eileen and Kevin with a dangerously fixed smile. Tony remembered that smile. He hadn't seen it in about ten years. The last time he had seen it, it had been followed by an empty bottle of Jameson's that nearly cracked Tony in the skull.

"Why, it's Tony Maroni," said Brendan. His eyes glittered, but his voice sounded as though he were talking through a cardboard tube. "Hey hey. Whoa whoa whoa."

This time the bottle wasn't Jameson's but white wine. It wasn't empty yet, either. The cork lay at Brendan's elbow beside Eileen's Williams-Sonoma corkscrew, and beside that was a steaming coffee mug, untouched.

"Hi, Brendan."

"Hi, Tony. Pleased to meet me?"

"Oh sure, sure." Tony nodded. Eileen walked over and handed him a glass of cider.

"There you go!" She turned to Brendan. "What about you, Brendan? Some cider?"

"Not on your fucking life."

Tony cleared his throat and lifted his glass. "Mmm." His mouth was so dry that when he took a sip, it tasted like raw sugar on his tongue. "Hey, great seeing that movie with the kids, huh?"

Eileen and Kevin both swiveled to stare at him. Tony flushed and looked over at Brendan. His friend's blue eyes had gone cold and distant: he looked like a distinctly less benign version of his son.

"Hey, no," said Brendan. "It actually really sucked. It actually made me feel really bad."

"Brendan." Eileen pressed a hand against her cheek. "I – maybe you could –"

"Never mind." Brendan took a drink of his wine. "It doesn't matter."

"I just thought, I can make some –"

"Why don't you put it down, Brendan."

Eileen sucked her breath in audibly as Kevin pushed past her. "Kevin, why don't you –"

"Why don't you let me handle this," he said harshly. "I told you, no wine –"

Eileen stood her ground. "You know what? I am not the one who –"

"Uh-oh." Brendan laughed. "The annual Thanksgiving dinner meltdown! Hey Tony, what would Chip Crockett say about that?"

"I know what Curly would say." Everyone turned, and Tony said, "Nyuk, nyuk, nyuk ..."

"Put it down, Brendan. You don't need that. Come on." Kevin looked down at his cousin. His arms were uncrossed now, half-raised before his chest. One hand was already unconsciously starting to curl into a fist. "You've got to drive."

"You can stay here," broke in Eileen. At Kevin's glare she said, "I just meant he wouldn't have to –"

"Give it to me." Kevin reached for the wineglass. Brendan continued to smile, continued to stare at some place in the air above a flickering candle. "You don't want it, Brendan."

"What do you know about what I want?" Brendan's smile grew broader, and he took another gulp of wine. "You have no fucking clue. You've never had a fucking clue. You –"

Kevin's hand clamped down on his shoulder. Brendan rocked back in the chair, teeth grinding as his smile became a terrible fixed grin. A drop of blood welled from his lower lip where he'd bitten it. In his hand the wineglass began to tremble, as Kevin's arm fell.

And froze in mid-air. Kevin turned, writhing, as Tony held him by the wrist.

"Leave him alone, Kevo," he said softly.

"The fuck you say! I'm not letting my goddam cousin kill himself and–"

"Leave him." Tony gazed calmly into Kevin's eyes, but under his black T-shirt his chest rose and fell, rose and fell, as though he'd been running. "Just leave him, Kev."

"You – !" Kevin tried to yank his hand free. But Tony moved with him, looking more like he was slamdancing than fighting one of his oldest friends. "Let go –"

With a muffled shout Kevin stumbled back against the table, sending it sliding across the floor. Brendan remained in his chair as the wine bottle toppled and then fell onto his cousin.

"Goddamit!" Kevin yelled, still struggling to pull himself from Tony. "You goddamn –"

"Oops," said Brendan, gazing at the spilled wine as Eileen darted over with a dish towel. Tony looked at Kevin, measuringly but without rancor, then let him go.

"I'll drive Brendan and Peter," said Tony. He turned to Brendan and nodded. "If that's okay? I'll drive you back. Just let me know when you're ready."

"I'm ready now."

Brendan sat in his chair. He stared at his cousin, his eyes cold; then turned and let his gaze flick from Tony to Eileen to the children, still oblivious on the porch. The acid light had poisoned everything, time had poisoned everything. He remembered that now, with the taste of wine souring on his tongue and the return of the dreadful drunken clarity that had fed him for so many years. Why had he ever forsaken it? For an instant he felt like Superman, his eyes burning into those of his family, scorching right through Kevin, leaving Eileen a little charred around the edges, skipping the children completely: they were all doomed anyway. He grinned, his lips pulled tight across his teeth, and got to his feet. "Sure, Tony. I'm ready."

The room seemed watery and amber-tinged, though maybe that was his eyes? He blinked, and suddenly everything came back into focus. Or rather, it lost the bright malign shimmer the alcohol had given it. The wine had burned right off; someone had snuck Kryptonite into the kitchen. He blinked again, this time because he could feel tears starting, and took an unsteady step towards the door. He reached blindly for the back of his chair, fumbling so that he knocked it over. Tony caught it, stepping forward to put a hand on his friend's shoulder.

"It's okay, man. You're just a little tired. I'll drive. Maybe you could get Peter and I'll, like, meet you by the car."

"That's a great idea, Tony." Eileen paused on her way out to the deck. "It's time for the girls to get ready for bed, too."

They prepared to leave. Peter began to scream when Brendan tried to put his coat on, and the twins watched with great interest until Kevin shouted at them to go upstairs. Brendan finally gave up with the boy's coat and simply picked him up and carried him, shrieking, to the car. The effort exhausted him. He flung the back door open and strapped Peter in, then staggered out again and threw himself into the front passenger seat, his head throbbing. He was dimly aware of Eileen and Tony hugging farewell on the front steps, Kevin's brooding figure looming behind them. The wind rose, cold and smelling of wood smoke, and sent leaves whirling up into the darkness. Then Tony was beside him, adjusting the seat for his longer legs and playing with the radio.

"Check it out." Tony beamed as the Volvo filled with the strains of "Mister Grinch." "Christmas music!"

Brendan closed his eyes. "Are you going to drive?" he asked after a minute had passed.

"Not until you give me the keys."

"Oh. Right. Here."

Tony drove. Brendan sat beside him with his eyes shut; but after a moment he rubbed them, blinking, and turned to stare at his friend.

How had the car radio been on, if Brendan hadn't given Tony the keys? Was that possible, even in a late-model Volvo? Brendan shook his head, framing the question; then thought better of it. He was the drunk, after all. He sank back down in the seat, gazing numbly out the window as they made their way back through the silent suburbs, trees dark and bare as lampposts, lampposts already woven with sparkling Christmas lights and plastic greenery. Houses prim as Peter's Lego towers, butter-yellow windows and an occasional flash of the grand meal in progress, heads thrown back in laughter, dishes being passed, televisions blinking in the background. Brendan shut his eyes again, praying that he might fall asleep.

He did not. Tony kept fiddling with the radio, scanning between oldies stations and the left of the dial, finally settling on a station whose playlist seemed to consist almost entirely of guitar feedback. Brendan winced and sighed loudly; shifted, trying to shut out the sound. At last he gave up, sliding down in the seat and shielding his eyes with one hand, wondering if there was a single human being playing on this song, or even working at the radio station.

"Doesn't it ever bother you?"

Beside him, Tony nodded in time to a beat Brendan couldn't hear; but after a moment he glanced aside. "What?"

"You know. This —" Brendan gestured feebly at the radio. "I mean, you were in *Newsweek* and *Rolling Stone*, and that movie. Everything just seemed like it was going to be so great. Doesn't it ever bum you out?"

Tony stared straight ahead. His long hair had slipped from its ponytail, catching inside the collar of his battered leather jacket. He turned the car onto Connecticut Avenue, drove for several minutes in silence. Finally he said, "Well, sure. Especially after Dickie went, you know? I kept thinking, fuck, what'm I waiting for? Put a bullet in my fucking head."

Brendan turned to lean against the door and stared, surprised, at his friend. "No shit?"

"Well, yeah. What'd you think?"

Brendan shrugged, embarrassed. "I don't know. I guess – I don't know."

Tony smiled but said nothing. They slid in and out of traffic, until finally Brendan asked, "Why didn't you?"

"What? Kill myself?" Tony shook his head. He poked at the radio, blips of noise, chatter, static, treacly ballads, relentless country twang, guitar. He stopped, finger poised above the scanner. A twelve-string jangled, and he hit the volume.

"Like that," he said, and grinned that loopy Tony Maroni grin. "Now and then, you hear something. You know? And then you think, well, what the hell."

Brendan shook his head bitterly. "Yeah, but it only lasts for three minutes."

Tony rolled his eyes. "Well, sure! What do you expect?"

Brendan stared at him, and suddenly they both started to laugh. The song played on, Tony sang along until it ended. In the backseat, Peter grunted and kicked, but when his father looked back at him the boy was yawning, staring out at the streetlights. Brendan turned back, rubbing his forehead and smiling ruefully. "What did I expect," he said, and they drove on home.

~ ~ ~

Tony slept on the couch that night, as he always did when Peter was there. He didn't even bother pulling it out; just lay facedown, still in his leather jacket, and pulled a blanket over his head. Within minutes he was asleep.

He woke, so suddenly that for a moment he wondered if he'd even been asleep at all. He lifted his head, hair falling in his eyes, then gingerly raised the edge of the blanket to peer out. Beyond the edge of the couch wan grey light was filtering through the rice-paper shades. The street was unusually quiet: no rush-hour traffic or trash pickup on the day after Thanksgiving. No street people, either; they'd all still be down by the Fourteenth Street shelter, finishing off their turkey leftovers and getting in line for breakfast.

Then what had awakened him? With a frown Tony sat up, the blanket sliding to the floor. It was so still he could hear the faint tick- of his wristwatch on the VCR, and the rustling of leaves along the sidewalk; nothing more.

Still, he'd heard something, or dreamed it – a bird, or maybe a cat. Though whatever it was, it was gone now. He stood, stretching, then padded down the hall to the bathroom.

And stopped. The sound came again, a pinched high-pitched cry, like a trapped animal struggling to breathe.

But Tony knew it wasn't an animal. He turned, and saw the open door of Peter's room.

"Peter?" He walked over hesitantly, squinting. "Hey, man, you having a bad dream?"

Peter's bed was pushed against the wall. A white Ikea bed with high rails, it gleamed in the soft glow of a night-light shaped like the moon. On the floor beside it, a large pillow had fallen. At first Tony thought it was Peter, but it was too big. And now he could see Peter, lying on his side with one hand cupped against his cheek. He looked tiny, dark hair and eyes smudged against pale skin, his rubber duck clutched to his chest. And he was having a nightmare – the noise was louder here, a harsh wheezing that stuttered and then started up again. Tony shook his head, stood on tiptoe and took a step inside.

"It's okay," he whispered. "Don't be scared ..."

On the floor beside the bed, the pillow moved. Tony froze. A pale rope looped up from the shapeless heap that was not a pillow, wobbled in the air above the boy's head, and finally materialized into an arm grabbing at the bedrail. There was a gasp, a terrible sound that made Tony dart back into the doorway again. The rest of the heap fragmented into blots of shadow: a thatch of unruly hair, a maroon t-shirt, another arm: a man, his shoulders heaved forward and shaking.

"Brendan?"

Tony wasn't even sure if he'd said the name aloud. It didn't matter. His friend clasped both hands around the bedrails, so tightly that the entire bed shook.

"Peter ..."

Tony flinched, turning his head so he wouldn't have to see Brendan there in his sweatpants and Redskins T-shirt, rocking back and forth until the bed began to racket against the wall. But he could do nothing to shut out the sound, Brendan crying out wordlessly, unrelentingly, his fingers weaving through the rails and tugging helplessly at the blankets.

" ... come back – please come back –"

Tony turned and stumbled down the hall. His own breath came in such short sharp bursts that when he reached the kitchen he slid to the floor and sat there, heart pounding, waiting for Brendan to suddenly burst in and turn that awful spotlit glare of grief upon him.

But Brendan did not come. Tony waited for a long time, watching the dawn brighten from grey to pearl to white. Gradually the echo of his friend's weeping died away, into the faint rattle of the first buses on Maryland Avenue. And with that small reassuring sound, Tony felt better. He got to his feet, a little unsteadily, opened the fridge and grabbed a carton of orange juice. He downed it, shoved the empty carton into the trash and then stuck his head back out into the hall, listening.

Silence. He waited, then very softly crept back down to Peter's room.

On the floor beside the bed sprawled Brendan, seemingly fast asleep, one hand against his cheek. Above him, Peter's body was curled into the same posture. The rubber duck had fallen from his grasp, and his hand had escaped between two of the rails to rest upon his father's shoulder. For a minute Tony stood and watched them. Then he turned away.

He went back to the living room and did a peremptory check of the television, half-hoping to find some remnant of Thanksgiving Past buried in the strata of infomercials and commercial sludge he sifted through. Except for the fade-out of *It's a Wonderful Life*, there was nothing. He clicked it off, singing "Auld Lang Syne" under his breath as he wandered down the hall. By the time he'd settled in before Brendan's computer, he was humming "Rudolph" and beating time with a pair of unsharpened pencils.

He checked his e-mail, the usual notes from friends and several of the effusive, occasionally lunatic, letters from Maroni fans that made up the bulk of his correspondence. There was also a brief message from Marty Berenstein, a.k.a. Mony Maroni.

Dear Tony,

Just wanted to let you know that our latest effort to extricate the catalog from EMI went down in flames, again. Sorry.

Otherwise things here are fine. Jocelyn's doing her junior year abroad in Madrid, so Helen and I are having a second honeymoon, of sorts. Actually, make that a first honeymoon. All the best to you and yours for the holiday season –

Marty

"Ho ho ho," said Tony. "Another day, another lawsuit. Now –"

He started clicking around, looking at the *New York Times* headlines, checking Amazon for the standing of the first three Maronis albums. Even twenty-odd years later, these sold well enough to generate modest but reliable royalties – if, of course, any of the surviving band members could have collected them. He was just starting to compare the sales figures for various musical rivals, when a shadow drifted across the keyboard.

"You know, I always figured there'd be a Tony Maroni Web page."

Tony looked up to see Brendan, holding a glass of water. He still wore his sweatpants and rumpled T-shirt, his face stubbled and eyes bleary as though he'd been on a three-day toot, rather than the losing end of a minor skirmish with three quarters of a bottle of expensive Sémillon. "You guys were so big in Japan," Brendan went on, pulling up a chair. "I would've thought you'd at least have a Web site."

"Well, yeah, sure. I mean, actually, there's a lot of them. A lot for me, I mean. I don't know about the others."

Brendan raised an eyebrow. "What do you mean, a lot? Like how many?"

Tony bounced out of the Amazon page, nibbling thoughtfully at a long strand of hair. "I dunno. Like fifty, maybe? I forget."

"Fifty? Fifty Tony Maroni Web pages?"

Tony looked embarrassed. "Well, yeah. But, I mean, none of 'em's authorized."

Brendan laughed. "How come none of 'em's ever helped you get the rights back to your stuff?"

"I dunno. Sometimes they offer to, you know? Like some big LA lawyer writes me about it. But – I guess I just don't care so much anymore, with all the other guys being gone." Tony sighed. "We wrote all that stuff together. It just wouldn't feel right."

Brendan nodded. "Yeah. Well, I guess I can see that."

He leaned forward, and Tony caught the faint reek of wine and sweat and unwashed clothes, that sad tired smell he associated with church meeting rooms and the long tearful exegeses of weekend binges – conventions where sales reps got locked out of their hotel room after closing time, college students missing the crucial exam after a beer bash, mothers forgetting to feed their kids. Brendan sipped his water and Tony waited, hoping there wasn't going to be an apology.

There wasn't. Instead, Brendan ran a finger across the computer screen, raising a little trail of electrified dust. "Okay." He cocked his finger at Tony and smiled. "So, like, where's Chip Crockett's Web page?"

Tony's head bobbed up and down. "Aw right," he said, relieved. "Check this out, man, you're gonna love this –"

Tony hunched over the keyboard, fingers tapping eagerly. Brendan sank back into his chair and watched him. He rubbed his forehead, hoping he looked better than he felt – although what he felt wasn't even hung-over so much as some pure distillation of humiliation, depression, and exhaustion, with a healthy dollop of anxiety about just how Teri was going to react when she heard about him falling off the wagon. It hadn't happened once in the years since he'd joined AA, and somehow he suspected it wouldn't happen again. Brendan didn't drink because he was depressed, or lonely, or even just out of habit. He used to drink when he was happy, in that long joyous sunny rush of years between high school and the failure of his marriage. Back then he'd drink with his friends, in bars and at the beach, at ballgames and concerts. He drank because he liked it, and everyone else he knew liked it. He drank because it was fun.

Even now Brendan wasn't sure what had gone wrong. He suspected there was some sort of malign convergence between his body chemistry and the way the world had suddenly changed, round about the time he saw Lou Reed shilling for Honda motorbikes. After that, when he drank he saw the world differently. It was as though all his worst fears were confirmed, and after a while, he was drinking just so they would be confirmed. Marriages were doomed. Mothers drowned their children. Your father developed Alzheimer's disease and died without remembering your name. That guy you used to play softball with wasted away with AIDS, and you never even knew. Your favorite TV show was canceled, your dog had to be put to sleep. The music you loved seeped away from the radio, and all of a sudden when you walked down a street where you'd lived for twenty years, there were strangers everywhere. One day you had a toddler who'd always been a little colicky, but who smiled when he saw you and crawled into your lap at night. The next day you had a changeling, a child carved of wood who screamed if you touched him and whose eyes were always fixed on some bright horizon his parents could never see. The terrible secret Brendan kept was that he hadn't quit drinking to save his marriage, or himself, or even his child. He'd quit because he now knew, irrefutably, that the world had become the wasteland. And he no longer needed any confirmation of that.

"Okay, Brenda Starr." Tony pecked at one last key, grinning. "Technical difficulties, please stand by. I control the horizontal, I control the vertigo ..."

"Vertical," said Brendan.

"Whatever. I control it." With a flourish Tony straightened. "Do not adjust your screen! We have liftoff!"

Brendan blinked. On the monitor in front of him, that morning's *New York Times* headlines glowed, flickered and disappeared. For an instant the screen was black. Then, very slowly, a scrim of sky blue and white scrolled down. The white became clouds, the sky shimmered and melted like summer afternoon. In the center of the screen a small rectangle appeared, holding the black-and-white image of a man leaning on a stage-set Dutch door. He had neatly combed blonde hair, side-parted, and a boyish, smiling face. He wore the kind of suit Brendan associated with the second Beatles album, a light-colored Glen plaid, and beneath that a white shirt and skinny dark tie. Above his head, small letters floated in a streaming red banner:

WELCOME TO CHIP CROCKETT'S WEBPAGE!

"Well," said Tony. He sucked at his lower lip and looked sideways at Brendan. "There he is."

Brendan didn't say anything. He stared at the screen, then reached out and traced the outline of Chip Crockett's picture. The monitor crackled a little at his touch, and he shook his head, still silent.

Because there he was. He hadn't seen him for – what? thirty years, at least – but now it was like looking at a picture of his father when he was young. The same haircut; the same skinny tie. The same magically complicit smile, which he'd only seen on his father at the Fourth of July or Thanksgiving or Christmas, but which Brendan had seen twice a day, every day, on *The Chip Crockett Show*.

"Wow," whispered Brendan. "Chip Crockett."

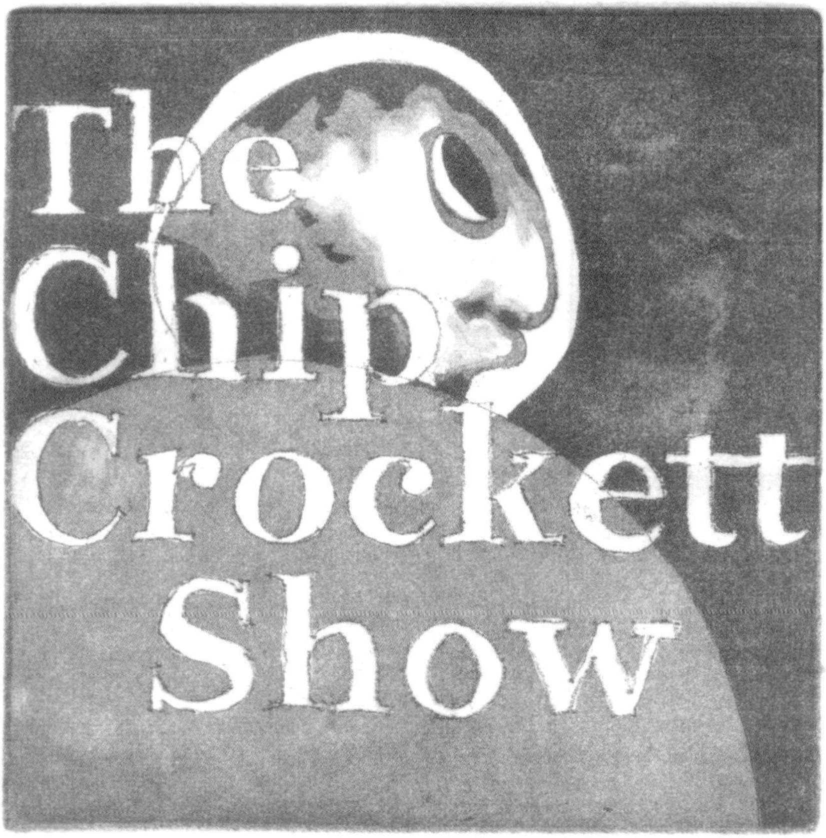
The
Chip
Crockett
Show

It was like dreams he had, that his dog was alive again. He pulled his chair up closer, inadvertently nudging Tony aside. "Sorry – but hey, this is great." His voice was husky; he coughed, took another swig of water and cleared his throat. "This is really, really great."

Tony laughed. "That's just a picture. Actually, it's the same picture from the obituary in the News. But here –"

He moved the mouse, and more phantom letters filled the screen. Brendan recognized the printout Tony had brought to the Childe Roland a few weeks ago.

- *BROADCAST HISTORY*
- *ARTICLES & OBITUARIES (NEW)*
- *THEME SONG*
- *THE GREAT FIRE OF 1966*
- *CHIP CROCKETT'S CHRISTMAS SPECIAL*

Without thinking, he reached over and took the mouse from Tony's grasp. "Oops – sorry – but you, would you mind if I –"

Tony smiled. "Go for it."

Brendan clicked on *THEME SONG*. The screen shifted, blue sky fading to a grainy black-and-white backdrop, much enlarged, showing a cheap soundstage. Long white drapes covered the back wall. There was a painted plywood table, and strewn on top of it were a number of puppets. By today's standards, they were slightly intimidating, more crackbrained Punch and Judy than benign Muppet. One looked like a pirate, with a patch on his eye and a gold hoop earring and a cigarette; another was a little guy with white fuzzy hair and a scholar's mortar. There were more – a spaceman, a beatnik, a dog – but the only puppet that was upright was a figure with small beady eyes and an enormous nose, his mouth cracked in a huge, slightly demonic grin, his tiny cloth hands clapped together as though he were about to witness – or perform – something wonderful.

"Ooga Booga," whispered Brendan. "Holy cow. I totally forgot what he looked like – I'd even forgotten his name, till you showed me that obituary."

He drew a long breath and leaned forward, clicked on an icon. A moment when all was still. Then the song began: a jouncy chorus of horns and strings, those unshakably chipper background voices you heard on records in the early '6os. Elevator music, but this was an elevator that only went up.

"Bum bum bum bum," sang Tony happily. "Bum bum bum bum!"

Brendan started to cry. Knowing it was stupid, knowing it was the sort of thing you did on a jag, when you'd lost it completely, when you were so far gone you'd sit around all day long surfing the Net for the names of girls you'd had a crush on in the second grade, or listening to Muzak and commercial jingles.

Didn't matter, didn't matter, didn't matter. He squeezed his eyes shut, eyelids burning as he willed himself to stop: another Irish Catholic trick that Teri hated. Back when they'd first started trying to understand what was wrong with Peter, back when they barely even knew there was something wrong – back then, it was one of the first things Teri had accused him of –

"This fucking Irish Catholic thing, you guys can never cry, you can never show anything, any emotion at all – and now, now – look at him –"

Pointing at the silent toddler crawling across the floor, but crawling in that awful horror-show way he had, dragging himself on his elbows and knees, head canted sideways so he could stare at the ceiling but not at what was in front of him; and never, ever, at his parents.

"– look at him, *look at him* –"

Her voice rising to a shriek, her fists pounding against her thighs as she stood there screaming. And Peter never looked, never even noticed at all, and Brendan –

Brendan walked away. Only into the next room, saying nothing, feeling rage and grief and sorrow swelling in his head until he thought blood would seep from his eyes; blood, maybe, but never tears. His entire body shook, but he wouldn't cry; just stood there like a human Roman candle waiting to ignite; waiting for the house to grow silent once more.

"Wanna hear something else?"

Brendan blinked. The theme song was over. Before he could say anything, Tony clicked on another icon, and the faint oozy strains of Chip Crockett's closing theme began to play.

"... *danke schoen* ..."

"Jeez ..." Brendan shuddered. "I forgot about that."

"Yeah. Maybe we better not. Here, listen to this one."

Tony clicked on OGDEN ORFF. A faint voice echoed from the speaker, declaiming proudly.

"That's my boy – Ogden Orff!"

"Let me!" Brendan poked Tony's arm. "C'mon, c'mon, c'mon, To-neee –"

Tony laughed. "Be my guest."

Brendan looked at the pictures, black-and-white publicity stills of Chip Crockett as his most notorious character: the weirdly Edwardian Ogden Orff, a man dressed as a boy in black jacket and trousers, with a long floppy tie and his hair slicked down. Ogden never spoke; only listened as Chip Crockett's sonorous off-screen voice offered him advice and the inevitable admonition –

"No, Ogden, noooo!"

– but always ending with the same triumphant announcement –

"That's my boy – Ogden Orff!"

There were other characters, too. Ratnik, the beady-eyed beatnik puppet who carried around a copy of *No Exit* and ended each of his scenes by failing to find his way off the set. There was Captain Dingbat, navigating the Sloop *John B* through New York Harbor and calling the Statue of Liberty a Hotsy-Totsy. There was the Old Professor, quoting Groucho Marx instead of Karl; and Mister Knickerbocker lip-synching "Mr. Bassman." And last of all there was Chip Crockett himself again, sitting with a copy of *Millions of Cats* on his knees and reading to a studio audience of a dozen entranced children.

Only of course these were only pictures. No voiceovers, no soundtrack, no living color, except in Brendan's head. Just pictures. And there were only nine of them.

"That's it?" Brendan tried to keep his voice from breaking. "What about, you said something about some video clips?"

"Yeah. Well, sort of. There's nothing from the actual show, just a couple of outtakes. But they're not very long. Everything was lost." Tony sighed. "Just – lost. I mean, can you believe it? They just taped over all of it. That's like taping over the moon landing, or Nixon's resignation or something."

"Not really," said Brendan, and he grabbed back the mouse.

The videoclips were about the size of Brendan's thumbprint, framed within a little grey TV screen.

COCOA MARSH COMMERCIAL

FUNORAMA BLOOPER

CHIP'S THEME

"Wow," said Brendan. A timer underneath the little screen indicated how long each clip was. Sixteen seconds. Twenty-seven seconds. Thirty-two seconds. "There's not a lot of him left, is there?"

"Nope. But you know, I was thinking – like, maybe there could be like a hologram or something, you know? Like cloning someone. You have a tiny piece of their DNA and you can make a whole person. So, like, you'd only need a tiny piece of Chip Crockett, and you could bring back a whole episode."

"Tony." Brendan stopped himself before giving his automatic answer of thirty-odd years: Tony, you're an idiot. "Tony, you're the Steve Wozniak of Massachusetts Avenue. Do I just click on this?"

Tony nodded. Brendan clicked. A swirl of black-and-white-and-grey dots filled the tiny screen, danced around jerkily while a hollow voice intoned something Brendan could barely understand, though the words "Cocoa Marsh" seemed prominent. It took nearly sixteen seconds for Brendan's eyes to force the pixels into an image that resembled a man's face and a puppet. By then the clip was over.

"That's it?"

"That's it."

Brendan played it again. This time he could make out the image more easily, a closeup of Chip Crockett and Ooga Booga, the puppet holding a glass and trying to drink from it while Chip encouraged him.

"That's right, Ooga Booga! Drink your Cocoa Marsh –"

Bam: the image froze, the screen went blank. Brendan ran it six more times, trying to fix it in his mind's eye, see if it stirred any memory at all of the original commercial. It didn't; but just that tiny clip was enough to bring rushing back the wonderful sound of Chip's voice, the deep and deeply humorous tones that were the echo of some great benign Everydad. You could imagine him telling knock-knock jokes over the barbecue grill of your dreams, holding Ooga Booga as he tucked you into bed at night, taking sips from a can of Rheingold between verses of "They're Coming to Take Me Away, Ha Ha!" You could imagine all of this, you could live all of this, and sometimes it seemed that you had.

"Check these out, man!"

He started, as Tony ran the other clips. They resembled the first: fuzzy black-and-white pointillist figures, tinny voices beamed from a million light years away; cheap sets. The last few notes of Chip's theme song faded and the screen cut to Ooga Booga nestled against Chip's face, his little hands clapping spasmodically and Chip's lips moving, seemingly by remote control.

"... now Ooga Booga, tell all the boys and girls what you just told me –"

The image froze. It was over. No matter how many times you played it back, you'd never hear Ooga Booga's secret.

"Man, this really bites," said Brendan. He replayed the blooper clip, Chip bumping into a boom mike and pretending to wrestle it. "There's really nothing else?"

"Nope." Tony pulled his hair back, making a ponytail with his fingers. "But if you read through all the letters people have sent, there's, like, all these rumors of other stuff. Like a couple of people say they've heard about some bootleg tapes that were shown on Italian TV in the '70s, tapes of actual shows that somehow got shipped over there or something. So there's this entire Chip Crockett Mafia trying to track them down, a bunch of fans and this retired video cameraman from New York. If they find them, they can broadcast them over the Net. They could probably broadcast them on TV, one of those stations that plays old stuff all the time."

"I doubt they could do that, Tony. Even if they found the tapes. Which they won't."

Tony swept the curtain of hair from his face and gave Brendan a hurt look. "Hey, don't believe me. Here, look —"

Another click, and there were the e-mails from devoted fans: kids grown to doctors, lawyers, teachers, garbage men, rock stars, TV weathermen, editors.

I'm 45 years old and boy, was I amazed to find an entire Web site devoted to Chip Crockett ...

They were all pretty much like that, though surprisingly well-written and grammatically correct for e-mail. Brendan imagined an entire invisible electronic universe seething with this obsessive stuff, billions of people crowding the ether with their own variations on Chip Crockett – obscure baseball players, writers, musicians, cars, books, dogs. He scanned the Chip Crockett messages, all variations on the themes of Boy, was I amazed and Gee, I remember when and Oh if only, a long lamentation for videos perdus.

If only they'd saved them!

If only WNEW knew what they were losing when they erased those tapes!

If only the technicians had done something!

If only I'd been there!

Brendan sighed and ran a hand across his face. "You know, this stuff is sort of depressing me. I think I'm gonna get the coffee going."

Tony nodded without looking away from the screen. Reflexively, Brendan glanced back, saw a brief message that seemed to be the very last one.

Happy T'giving, everyone! Has anyone else heard about a bootleg of 'Chip Crockett's Christmas Carol' that's supposed to air on Christmas Eve? I'd like time/station info so I can tape it.

"You know about that, Tony?"

"Uh-uh." Tony frowned, leaning forward until his nose almost touched the screen. "That's kind of weird. Where would you hear about something like that? I mean, apart from this site?"

"Probably there's a thousand other sites like this. You know, weird TV, collectors' stuff. Christ, Tony, move back, you're gonna go blind."

He put his hands on Tony's shoulders and gently pulled him away from the screen. "Come on. Time for breakfast. Time for Cocoa Marsh."

"Yeah. Yeah, I'm coming." Tony stood, reluctantly, and yawned. "Christmas. Wow. How could I forget it was Christmas?"

"It's not Christmas. It's the day after Thanksgiving," said Brendan, seeing the first faint flickers of that other movie starting to burn around the edges of his head. Very deliberately he blinked, snowflakes melting into slush, a forest of evergreens flaming into ash and smoke, a black boot disappearing up a chimney that crumbled into rubble. "You have a whole month to remember Christmas." But Christmas was what Brendan was already trying to forget.

~ ~ ~

The truth was, over the last few years Brendan had become an expert at forgetting about Christmas. A few days after the start of the Official Holiday Shopping Season, the ubiquitous background soundtrack of "Silver Bells" and "Silent Night" and "Christmas at K-Mart" had diminished to nothing more than a very faint whining echo in his ears, choir boys and rampaging reindeer and Bing Crosby relegated to that same mental dungeon where he banned homeless people on the Metro, magazine ads for starving children, stray cats, and junkies nodding out at Dupont Circle. It didn't snow, so a whole gauntlet of joyfully shrieking kids on sleds or snowboards or big pieces of cardboard could be avoided. But it was cold, that frigid dank D.C.

cold that seeped into your pores and filled the newcasts with reports of homeless people freezing in alleys and cars stalling on the Beltway on their daily exodus to the sprawl.

It sure didn't feel like Christmas to Brendan Keegan. But then, he'd been successfully inoculated against the holiday two years ago, right about the time they'd been busy playing that popular parlor game, What's Wrong With Our Baby? Peter had been a toddler that December, and it was Christmas that had finally triggered Brendan's realization that something was wrong.

"Hey, what do you think of this tree, huh, Peter? What do you think, is this the greatest tree ever or what?"

It was a beautiful tree, a blue spruce that had set Brendan back almost a hundred bucks; but hey, what was Christmas for? There were presents hidden away that he'd bought back when Teri first told him she was pregnant, a baseball mitt and football helmet, plush Redskins mascot and oversized jersey, copies of *Winnie-the-Pooh* and *The Hobbit* and a videotape of *The March of the Wooden Soldiers* that his cousin Kevin had given him. Most of the presents were still too old for Peter, he knew that; but he also knew that this was the age when kids started getting into tearing off the wrapping paper and gazing at Christmas ornaments and stuff like that. A sort of synaesthetic experience of Christmas; and Brendan wanted to be right there, video cam in hand, when Peter got his first look at a real Christmas tree, his very own real Christmas tree.

Well, Brendan was there, all right, and he got it all down on tape. A few months later, playing it back for doctors and psychiatrists and a few close family members, it amazed Brendan that he hadn't grabbed Peter and driven directly to GW Hospital.

Because what the tape showed was a fantastically decorated tree, branches drooping beneath the weight of popcorn strings and cranberry strands, Shiny Brite balls salvaged from Brendan's own childhood, hand-carved wooden Santas from a shop in Georgetown, and, most wonderful of all, an entire North Pole's worth of fabulous glass ornaments from Poland – clowns and dragons, cathedrals and polar bears, banana-nosed Punchinellos and one vaguely ominous St. Nick. Eileen and Teri had spent hours hanging baubles and carefully hiding each tiny bulb so only its glow was seen, magically, from within the secret forest of dusky blue-green needles.

"Close your eyes!" Teri had cried, covering his face with her hand as she led him into the room. "Now –"

When Brendan saw the tree, he got gooseflesh: that atavistic sense of looking down some endless tunnel, past the window displays at Mazza Gallerie, past the Cratchit children exclaiming over the plum pudding, past the manger and the Romans and the circled stones: all the way back to a forest clearing and falling snow, cold flung against his limbs and the unspeakable wonder of flames leaping beneath an evergreen. He blinked back tears, touched Eileen and Teri each on the arm and mumbled something about incredible, amazing, beautiful; and bent to scoop up his son.

"Look, Peter, look –"

But Peter wouldn't look. His gaze shifted, then his head, and finally his whole body, so that no matter how Brendan turned and twisted, trying to hold Peter so he could have the perfect view of the perfect tree – no matter what he did, his son would not look. It was as though the tree did not exist. Indeed, the more Brendan tried to direct his gaze, the more his son struggled, until he was thrashing in his father's arms, making those soft nnnhh nnnhh sounds that, so far, were his only efforts at speech.

"Look, honey, see where Daddy is? Look! Look at the pretty Christmas tree! See where Aunt Eileen is pointing – look at the bird! You like birds – look, look!"

Look. They had played the tape for Dr. Larriday, after she observed Peter in her office. Waiting for her comments, Brendan and Teri held hands so tightly that Brendan's knuckles ached for two days. For hours they perched at the edge of the precipice, the doctor's diagnostic terms whizzing past them like stones –

LACK OF AFFECT ...

LITTLE RECEPTIVE LANGUAGE ...

LITTLE OR NO EYE CONTACT ...

IMPAIRED MOTOR SKILLS ...

RITUAL BEHAVIOR ...

FAILURE TO SPEAK ...

MORBID FEAR OF CHANGE IN ROUTINE ...

Peter had struggled and screamed in his father's arms while Dr. Larriday went down her list. Finally he had fallen asleep. They had brought an evaluation from their family physician, along with seven hours of videotaped footage of Peter – Peter crying, Peter sleeping, Peter crawling on his knuckles and toes, Peter obsessively pulling himself up and down, up and down, on the edge of his crib. Peter stacking one block on top of a second – clumsily, the wooden pieces flying from his unwieldy grip between pinkie and thumb. Peter sitting in front of the glass door, moving his head back and forth, back and forth, watching the flicker of movement from the corner of his eye. Hours and hours of tape; but Dr. Larriday was most interested in the earliest one, the Christmas tape.

"Let's see what we have –"

And there it was, glistening branches blocked by Brendan's struggling figure as he crossed and recrossed the living room, towheaded child screaming in his arms. Even now, almost three years later, Brendan couldn't bear to think of that tree; any Christmas tree. Because watching the tape again in Dr. Larriday's office that July afternoon, it was apparent that Peter had not been ignoring the tree.

He was avoiding it. He was terrified of it.

MORBID FEAR OF CHANGE IN ROUTINE ...

Teri had wept, sobbing until the words were lost. "Oh, Christ, how could we – I mean, look at him, it looks like he's being tortured ..."

Dr. Larriday looked, and took notes. Brendan stared straight ahead, his sleeping child in his lap, Peter's damp face pressed against his arm and his own tears falling, unheeded, onto his son's cheek.

That was the end of Christmas for Brendan. The end of everything, really – his marriage, his dream of himself as a father, his dream of a child. Oh, he still did everything he was supposed to, buying presents for Peter, encouraging him to open them under the small artificial tree at Teri's house, its sparse aluminum branches threaded with a few red plastic balls. Opening the presents for Peter, when he showed no interest in them himself; following the behavioral therapists' directives as to modeling play behavior with the new blocks and games and trucks.

But Christmas? Christmas was gone. Brendan didn't even hate it, because how could you hate something that was dead? Instead he focused on his work, and tried his best to ignore whatever demands the season put upon his senses, if not his time.

"Mr. Keegan?" His secretary's voice came through the intercom. "It's Toys for Tots again."

"Thanks." He put the phone on monitor, his gaze still fixed on the computer screen, a half dozen heavily scrawled-upon yellow legal pads scattered on the desk before him.

"Mr. Flaherty?" A cheerful voice boomed from the speaker. Brendan winced, reaching to turn the volume down. "This is Don Huchison from the Capitol City Chapter of Toys for Tots. As I'm sure you know, we –"

"This is Mr. Keegan, not Mr. Flaherty. And I don't take solicitation calls at the office –"

"Well, Mr. Keegan, I'll be happy to note that and request that someone call you at home, at your convenience and when you have time. When might that be?"

"Never."

Don Huchison laughed, a sympathetic, Ain't that the truth! chuckle. "I hear you! This time of year, there's never enough time to –"

"I mean, never call me. Again. Anywhere." Brendan flipped through a legal pad with one hand, with the other reached to turn off the monitor.

"Mr. Keegan, I'm sure you're aware of the difficulties many families have at this time of year, meeting their children's expectations for a happy –"

"I don't give a shit about anyone's expectations. Remove me permanently from your list, and please don't call here again."

Click.

That evening he walked home. The cold spell remained unbroken. Pockets of slush filled potholes and broken edges of sidewalk. The eastern sky had a blackened cast to it, like a scorched pan; behind him, the last glowering trails of sunset streaked the horizon blood-red, so that the walls of the Library of Congress seemed to burn as night fell. Clouds of vapor surrounded the crowds hurrying home from work, giving everyone a ghostly familiar. But they were cheerful ghosts haunting cheerful people: even the rat-tailed mongrel who kept Dave the Grave company on his bench in Stanton Square Park raced excitedly back and forth, rising on its hind legs and walking backwards when smiling passersby tossed coins into Dave's battered Starbucks coffee mug.

"God bless ya, god bless ya –"

Brendan gritted his teeth, staring stonily at a down-clad woman who stooped to put a five-dollar bill into Dave's hand. "You're wasting your money," he said loudly. The woman looked up, startled; Dave swayed back and forth on his bench, his litany uninterrupted. He still wore Tony's coat – Brendan's coat – though it was black now with grime, the sleeves and collar disintegrating. "He's a wino. You're just feeding his addiction."

The woman stared at Brendan coolly. "It's Christmas. And it's none of your damn business what I do with my money."

"Ha ha!" Dave laughed; the dog did a back flip, to applause from several of Dave's cronies drinking malt liquor on the brittle grass. "God bless you, darlin', that's right ..."

Brendan started to yell after the woman's retreating back, but then he noticed that people were stopping to stare at him. Instead he glared contemptuously at Dave, spun on his heel and stalked home.

"Merry Chrissmas!" Dave called after him, and the other homeless men raised their voices raucously. "Merr' Chrissmass!"

He had left work earlier than was his habit. Since his divorce, he'd adjusted his schedule so that he seldom left the office till after dark; an exception had always been those days when he had Peter. No word of his Thanksgiving fall from grace had reached Teri – Brendan silently blessed Kevin and Eileen. But since then, his visits with his son had been cut back, at Brendan's own suggestion, to every other week. Just until the new year, he assured Teri, pleading pressure from work, a case long pending that now looked as though it would be settled out of court but there was still paperwork, and client interviews, and of course it was the holidays –

And of course that was it, exactly. Teri had seen it in her ex-husband's face when they had last met a week earlier, staring out at her from the front of the Volvo.

"Don't you want to come in for a minute? It's so cold."

Brendan shook his head. "I'm not cold," he said, his voice tight. He continued to stare resolutely at the steering column. "Is he ready? I have to get going."

"He's ready." Teri looked at the house, where Peter stood impassively on the steps, then turned back to the car. "Will Tony be there?"

"You got a problem with Tony, take it up with your lawyer." Brendan's knuckles whitened as he clasped the wheel. "I don't give a –"

"I am not being hostile." Teri's voice shook. "I'm glad Tony's there. At least Tony is capable of something resembling an emotion. At least Tony remembers what time of year it is. You know why you don't feel the cold, Brendan? Do you know why?"

Brendan turned the key in the ignition. "Get him in the car. I'm leaving."

"Because –"

He tapped the accelerator. The engine roared. On the porch Peter began to cry. Without a word Teri walked back to the house and got her son.

"You have a good time, sweetheart," she murmured as she buckled him into his car seat. He had stopped crying almost immediately, and she tucked a scarf around his shoulders. "You have a good time with your Daddy ..."

She drew away from the car and stared at Brendan in the front seat. In the back Peter pushed off the scarf, letting it drop to the floor. "You could do something with him, you know." Her voice was perfectly calm now. "He's doing so well at school these days. You could take him to see the White House tree, or Santa out at White Flint. Peggy said that might be a good idea. She said –"

Fuck what she said, thought Brendan. He glanced back to make sure Peter was buckled, then rolled up the window. He had already started to pull away when Teri ran up beside him and pounded at the glass.

"What?" He stopped and rolled the window down a crack. "Now what?"

"I wanted to make sure you hadn't forgotten and made other plans for next week."

"What's next week?"

"Christmas." Teri's smiled tightened. "You said you wanted to have him Christmas Eve – last summer, remember? When we –"

"I remember."

"I thought – I hoped that we could all be together. To give some, some continuity. For Peter. I asked Kevin and Eileen –"

"Oh, Christ –"

"And I wanted you to ask Tony for me. If you don't mind." Teri's voice had taken on the same brisk oldest-daughter tone she used with her elderly clients. "If you don't want to stay you don't have to. They're going to come after church, mid-morning. You can just drop him off if you want. Or you're welcome to stay."

"We'll see. I'll let Tony know."

But tonight, walking up the sidewalk towards his apartment, he remembered that he never had let Tony know. Not that he suspected him of having any big plans for the holiday. Occasionally Brendan could hear music from behind the closed door of his room, Tony playing guitar and singing softly to himself; but that seemed to have stopped with the onset of the holiday season. Unemployment didn't just suit Tony better than any job he'd had since fronting the Maronis. It was as though he had actually found another job, one that involved getting up each morning promptly at six AM, showering, shaving, dressing in black jeans and T-shirt and leather jacket, then eating a modest bowl of Grape-Nuts before getting down to work.

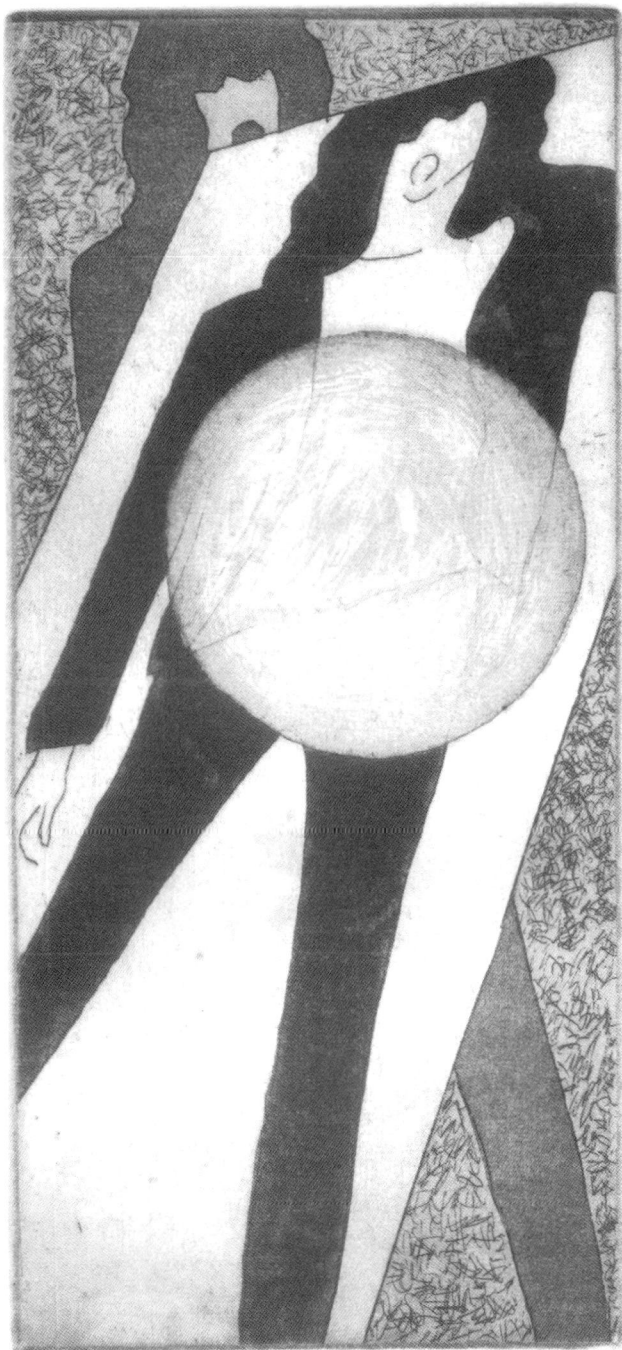

Which, in Tony's case, seemed to consist of watching every single Christmas special that every single television station on Earth chose to air between the first and twenty-fifth of December. No program was too obscure or too terrible for Tony's viewing pleasure – not *The House Without a Christmas Tree* or *The Bishop's Wife*; not Andy Williams's Christmas Special, or Elvis's, the King Family's, and Barbara Mandrell's; not *A Very Brady Christmas!* or *Mickey's Extra Special Christmas Eve* or *The Little Drummer Boy Returns*.

And certainly not Rudolph, the Grinch, Charlie Brown, Frosty the Snowman or Mr. Magoo. Tony had *It's a Wonderful Life* committed to memory; what was harder to take was that Tony knew every word of *Santa Claus Versus the Martians*, as well as *The Christmas That Almost Wasn't* and *Fuzzy the Christmas Donkey*.

"That one ought to be called *The Christmas Jackass*," Brendan had snapped one morning when he woke to find Tony already sitting transfixed on the living room couch, steaming coffee mug beside him.

"You should check this out." Tony shot a quick grin at Brendan, then hunched closer to the edge of the sofa. "Shh, this is the sad part –"

Now, as he hurried up the steps, Brendan saw the familiar blue-grey wash of light through his apartment window, the telltale flicker of shadow on the wall behind the sofa where he knew he would find Tony in the exact same place he had left him that morning.

Only this time when Brendan walked inside it was different. On the floor, staring at the television with the same rapt expression, was Peter.

"Peter." Brendan shut the door and dropped his briefcase. "Tony? What's going on?"

Tony looked up and smiled. "Oh, hey, man! You're home early. That's good, I'm glad –"

"What's he doing here? What happened?" Brendan quickly stepped over a small mountain of Peter's things, knapsack and overnight bags, his pillow, his lunchbox, his duck. "What –"

"There was a problem ..."

"Problem?" He knelt beside his son, fighting the need to hold him, to shout at Tony gazing at them calmly from the couch. Peter edged away, making a small humming sound, his gaze fixed on the TV. "What problem? What happened? Is he –"

"No, no – Teri had the problem. She tried calling you but she couldn't get through –"

Brendan sighed with relief, then nodded. "Right – Ashley left this afternoon, she'll be gone till next week. But –"

"I dunno, some client thing? Teri said she'd call from the airport –"

Right on cue the phone rang. Brendan grabbed it.

"Brendan." Brendan could hear her swallow, fighting tears. "Jesus, Brendan. I called and called –"

"I know. What happened?"

"Oh, Christ, some stupid thing. Well, not really – old Mr. Wright died, everyone was expecting it but not right before Christmas, I mean he was ninety-three. But I have to go out there to deal with his wife and ex-wife and his sister and his kids. I'm at Dulles now, this case is a mess, you remember me telling you –"

"But Peter's okay?"

"Peter's fine. He really likes Tony, doesn't he?"

"Yeah, yeah, sure. So what's the deal here?"

Silence. He heard airport noises in the background, the squawk and boom of flight announcements. "The deal is, Brendan, that I have to be out of town on business right now. And –"

"How long?"

"Just till tomorrow. It was impossible to get a flight, they're completely booked, but –"

"And Peter's schedule? All this talk you had about how fucking important it is for everything to be –"

"Look, Brendan, stuff happens. You can't control everything. Or maybe you can, but I can't. Peter is with me every hour, every day, every week –"

"Except when he's with me –"

"– you have no idea how exhausting it is, being with him all the time. It's killing me, Brendan, it's –"

Her voice broke, drowned in a spurt of static as another flight announcement thundered somewhere behind her. " – I can't, Brendan, not anymore, he's –"

Brendan shut his eyes and took a long breath. "Teri? Teri?" He turned so that Tony and Peter wouldn't see him. "Can you hear me? Listen, I'm sorry, really. Don't cry. We'll be fine. I know you're with him all the time, I know how hard it is. He'll be fine –"

"Shit. That's my flight. I'm sorry, Brendan, this is so crazy. But I really did try to call. He's got school, I gave Tony the schedule. Except for Christmas Eve, but you knew that. His medicine's in the blue bag with the dinosaurs. Okay, shit, I have to run – kiss him for me, I'll call you, bye –"

So.

"So." Brendan put down the phone, turned. In the living room, Peter sprawled on the floor, fingers pulling at a thread in the carpet. On the couch behind him sat Tony, pointing excitedly at the screen.

" – see, remember? Those are the real Three Kings, and that guy there, he's one of the real shepherds. But that other guy with the black beard who's sneaking up on the little donkey, he's a Sears shepherd –"

"Tony. You were here when Teri dropped him off?"

Tony looked over at Brendan, surprised. "Oh. Hey, I forgot you were home. Yeah, sure I was. I was right here, Peter and I settled down to some serious holiday cheer. Right, Petie?"

Peter continued to make the same soft nasal humming sound he always did. His eyes were still glued to the screen: when the bad shepherd grabbed the little Puppetoon donkey and stuffed him in a sack, Peter flinched. His father didn't notice; he was already going through Peter's bags, looking for the pages of instructions he knew would be there.

"Well, thanks. What the hell was she going to do if you weren't here? Why didn't she go by my office?"

"She did. She couldn't even get in the building."

Brendan grimaced. "Damn, that's right. Christmas party next door, they all went down to the Hawk & Dove. And I wasn't picking up the phone."

"You didn't go to the Christmas party?"

"No, Tony, I didn't go to the Christmas party. I mean, what's the point? They don't give you a present."

Tony looked shocked. "They don't give you a present?"

"No, you bonehead." Brendan bopped him on the shoulder with Teri's instructions. "Of course they don't give you a present. That was a joke. But I really am glad you were here when she came. C'mere, Peter –"

He reached for his son, steeling himself for the boy to turn away or, worse, fail to acknowledge him at all. Instead Peter remained where he was, watching TV. When Brendan touched his arm, he could feel the ripple of muscle beneath his son's bare skin. Or maybe it wasn't muscle at all; maybe it was nerve, maybe that was how exposed it all was to Peter, bound sheaves of neurons and ganglions and dendrites, veiled with nothing more than that soft white tissue of baby skin, the tiny hairs like a dusting of snow, the sweet powdery smell of him. For an instant he was close enough to smell him, so close it made him dizzy, made him forget for a moment where or when it was – like when Teri was still breastfeeding and they would lie in bed together and he could smell all of them at once, his own sweat, and Teri's, and Peter's scent, a scent he had always thought came from baby powder – strange and warm, like honeysuckle, or bread – but which he knew now came from babies.

"Peter," he whispered.

For a split second, Peter did not move away. Brendan held his breath until it hurt, until he could feel his own nerves shimmering alongside his son's, the two tines of a broken tuning fork suddenly and miraculously vibrating together. Peter's skin was warm, warmer than Brendan's own; there was a sticky spot within the crook of his elbow, jelly or paste or generic childhood crud. He was close enough to see the small red crescent just below his hairline, where another child had accidentally struck him with a block. Still holding his breath, Brendan let his fingers move ever so slightly down his son's arm, towards his hand –

– but it was too much. The nasal humming became a grunt, of annoyance or fear or pain; and the boy shrugged him off.

"Peter." Brendan spoke his name, louder this time. Peter nodded – a half-nod, really, jerking his chin downward a fraction of an inch – and scooched closer to the television. Brendan watched him, biting his lip; then turned to Tony. "Well. One big happy family. I guess I'll make dinner."

He waited for Tony's usual offer to help, or clean up, or bring out the trash. But Tony only sprawled on the couch and stared at the television, lips moving as he recited along with King Melchior.

"... *greatest gifts are always those that cannot be bought with gold or silver ...*"

"Ugh." Brendan rolled his eyes. "I'm outta here."

He made dinner, pasta with butter sauce for Peter, with pesto for himself and Tony. While it was cooking he rummaged around for that morning's Post. It was gone. When he looked outside the back door, the entire stack of papers waiting to be recycled was gone, too.

"Tony? You do something with today's paper?"

"Um, well, yeah. I did." His expression was distinctly furtive.

"Um, well, yeah. Could you tell me where it is?"

Tony shifted uncomfortably, knocking a pillow onto the floor. "Uh. Actually, no. I mean, it's gone."

Brendan frowned. "But the pickup isn't till tomorrow." Although, now that he thought about it, he hadn't seen any newspapers out there all last week, either.

"I know. I just needed them for something."

"What?"

"Just something. A surprise."

"A surprise. Right." Brendan sighed. "Well, tomorrow leave the damn paper for me to read, okay? I don't need any more surprises."

Peter went to bed with surprisingly little trouble that night. Usually any change in his routine was enough to send him into a fit of heart-splintering screams, but except for the usual tantrum over brushing his teeth, the evening was calm. Brendan read to him in bed, *Goodnight, Moon* and "The Owl and the Pussycat"; and before he was finished his son was asleep, hand knuckled up against one cheek, the much-gnawed rubber duck nestled against his breast.

"Don't you read him Christmas stories?"

Brendan gently tugged the blanket up around Peter's shoulders, motioning Tony to be quiet. "No," he whispered, and joined him in the hall. "I don't have any here."

"Teri packed some. I saw them. *The Grinch, The Night Before Christmas* –"

"Tony." Brendan poked his friend in the stomach. "You know what? I'm going to tell you a secret. Christmas depresses me. It makes me sad. It totally bums me out."

"But why?"

He sucked his breath in angrily; but when he looked into Tony's eyes he saw only genuine puzzlement. Brendan sighed, drew his hand back and ran it through his thinning hair.

"It just does," he said. "Okay? I just don't get in much of a Christmas spirit anymore."

"You're not kidding," said Tony.

Still, after he'd finished cleaning up and going through his email and sorting out Peter's clothes for the next day, Brendan found himself in the living room again, sprawled beside Tony on the couch. Outside, icy rain spattered against the windows and tossed red and green confetti onto the ground beneath the traffic light. On the TV screen, snow whipped around a man with shoulders hunched against the cold as he hurried down a narrow lane, rosy-cheeked urchins singing merrily in his wake.

Brendan nudged Tony with his foot. "Who's this one?"

"George C. Scott. The Reagan-era Scrooge. See? His clothes are expensive – nice cut, nice fabric? He just can't be bothered helping anyone else. Classic Republican Scrooge. As opposed to Alistair Sim, the classic Dickensian Scrooge, who was a genuine miser." Tony wiggled his fingers. "Holes in his gloves, stuff like that. Then there's Mr. Magoo, the great Broadway Musical Scrooge."

Brendan laughed. "What, are you a Scrooge scientist?"

"Sure, man. Lionel Barrymore, Reginald Owen – vintage Hollywood. And Scrooge McDuck – what can I say? Quite simply one of the greats."

"Yeah? What about me?"

"You?" Tony scrutinized his friend, rubbing his chin. "You're the classic post-po-mo Scrooge. Involved with the text, yet denying your own place within it. Definitely post-post-modern."

Brendan snorted. "Right." He leaned forward, picked up the *TV Guide* from the floor and began flipping through it. "Where do you find all this stuff? I mean, half of it isn't even listed in here."

"I dunno. But I can always find it. Sometimes it takes a while, but …" Tony shrugged. "It's there."

"What about that Chip Crockett Christmas thing? Ever hear any more about that?"

"No." Tony looked sad. "I keep checking, but nobody seems to know anything except these sort of vague rumors. I figure I'll just, like, stay up all night Christmas Eve and see what happens."

"Great idea, Tony." Brendan took a deep breath. "But you know what? I've kind of had enough of Uncle Ebenezer. I'm going to bed."

Tony nodded absently, engrossed once more in the movie. "Sure. 'Night, Brenda."

It was a scramble to get Peter ready for school the next morning. He refused to eat anything, screaming and throwing first a bagel, then Cheerios, toast, English muffin, cantaloupe, and instant oatmeal on the floor, before his increasingly desperate father gave up and began the struggle to get him dressed. When Peter stayed on the weekend, Brendan always let him wear his pajamas until lunchtime. Now it took both Brendan and Tony a full fifteen minutes to get the boy into his clothes, and even then Peter ended up wearing the same T-shirt he'd gone to sleep in the night before.

"Hey, Pete, man, calm down," said Tony when the ordeal was finally over. "It's only clothes."

Brendan shook his head, red-faced and panting, and started shoving plastic containers and juice boxes into Peter's knapsack. "That's just it. It's not just clothes. It's everything – everything is a battle." He found himself blinking back tears, and turned to the kitchen counter, waiting until he could speak without his voice breaking. "I swear to God, I don't know how Teri does it."

"No lie." Tony sighed and began to scoop congealed oatmeal from the floor. In the living room Peter sat rigidly on the couch, watching Cookie Monster eat an aluminum plate. "Does she have to drive him in every day?"

"Yeah. And she – shit." Brendan straightened, smacking himself in the forehead with his palm. "How'm I going to do this?"

"Do what?"

"Well, I can't take him on the Metro in rush hour. And it'll be so late, I'll never find a parking spot by the office after I drive him in. Let me think, let me think –

"I know." Brendan snapped his fingers, pointed at Tony. "You're not doing anything, right? You mind coming with me? Then you can drop me off at the office and drive back here, and I don't have to worry about parking."

Tony frowned, glancing at the television. "Yeah, I guess. Do I have time to –"

"No. If the Grinch is on you can damn well tape him. Let's go – come on, Peter, sweetie, time for school. ..."

Out on Maryland Avenue, the city's ineffectual road crews were doing their usual job of making the morning commute even worse. The night's sleet had been reduced to a pureé of salted slush and dead leaves clogging the roadside, and numerous tow trucks were still doing a brisk business on the narrow side streets.

Yet despite the mess, the commuters crowding the sidewalks were cheerful, men and women in trenchcoats and lightweight parkas waving to each other as they hurried towards Union Station and the Capitol grounds. Strands of white lights spun through trees and hedges and outlined the fronts of brick rowhouses and storefronts. In Stanton Square Park, an evergreen glittered green and blue and red where some street people had strung together empty beer cans and bottles with strapping tape and bits of aluminum foil.

"Hey, check it out!" said Tony as the Volvo crawled past. "That looks nice, doesn't it?"

Brendan grunted. On a bench by the sidewalk, Dave the Grave and his dog were already settled with a paper bag between them. Dave's battered tweed jacket had been augmented by a long red muffler and some tinsel; his dog lolled beside him, the ends of the comforter tucked between his paws. At sight of Brendan's car, Dave lifted his bottle and shouted a greeting.

" 'Aaay, whoa whoa! M'ry 'issmiss!"

Tony rolled down his window and leaned out. "Merry Christmas, Dave!"

"Shut up, Tony." Brendan pressed a button and sent Tony's window sliding back up. "He's a goddamn bum."

"Aw, give him a break, man! It's Christmas."

"Yeah, well, he can go to the shelter with everyone else, then. Or freeze on a grate."

"Jeez, Brendan!" Tony shook his head in dismay. "What about all those poor people in the missions we used to collect for at Sacred Heart? You never wanted them to freeze on a grate."

"If they'd been outside my house, I'd have wanted them to freeze. And their little dogs, too."

"Boy, what a grouch. Hey, Peter, you ever know your old man was such a grouch?" Peter said nothing; only chewed thoughtfully on his yellow duck and stared out at the bottle-decked tree behind Dave the Grave.

Brendan continued to be a grouch the whole way to the Birchwood School, immune to Tony's admiration for the White House Christmas tree, the decorations in the windows of the restaurants at Dupont Circle, the group of kids from Gonzaga High School singing by a subway entrance. In the front seat Tony rocked and sang, too, turning to pick up Peter's duck when it fell and yelling encouragement at some boys trying to slide down a driveway on a cafeteria tray.

"Keep your weight in the front – the front –"

"They're going to kill themselves," Brendan said, turning up the side road leading to the school. "And then their parents will hire me to sue the company that makes those trays."

"Don't you remember doing that? Only we had those flying saucers?"

"Yeah. And we had snow. All right, here we are. Let's make this snappy, I have a client coming in at ten."

Tony slid from the front seat and began gathering Peter's things. "How come you're so busy right before Christmas?"

"Because I want to be," Brendan said tersely. "Okay, Petie, here we are at school."

Inside, everything looked pretty much as it always did. There were green-and-red cutouts on the wall, a few reindeer and trees, some yellow cardboard stars and blue Menorahs; but no Christmas tree, no lights, no scary Santas. There were fewer kids than usual, too, and half as many teachers.

"Peter! Hi!" Peter looked up, a faint smile on his face as Peggy knelt before him. "I missed you when your Mom picked you up early yesterday – hi!"

She reached forward and gave him a hug, holding him very tightly for just a moment and then withdrawing. She stood, brushing the hair from her eyes, and smiled. She was wearing a long green sweater with stars on it, and a small red-and-green-striped wool cap. "Brendan! I haven't seen you for a while –"

"I know, my schedule changed, I –" Brendan was still staring at his son. "He let you hug him?"

"Yeah, that's a new thing, just this week. But we've been working up to it for a while. He's really doing great, you know, he's been making some incredible progress just these last few weeks. Do you have a minute? 'Cause I can –"

She looked over and for the first time saw Tony. "Oh! Hi, I'm sorry, I work with Peter here, Peggy Storrs."

She stuck out her hand. For a moment Tony just stared at her, with an expression Brendan had last seen when he'd received the new Advent Moth promo. Then,

"Very pleased to meet you," he said, grabbing her hand and pumping it. "Anthony Kemper. I'm an old friend of Brendan's. We went to high school together. In Yonkers. Actually, we're living together now, if you ever –"

"That is very temporary." Brendan glared at him, then turned back to Peggy. "Actually, Peggy, I'm kind of in a rush this morning, but –"

But Peggy was still looking at Tony, her brow furrowed. "You know, you look very familiar. I mean, really familiar. Have you, like, been in here before? Although I don't remember –"

Brendan sighed. "Peggy, meet Tony Maroni."

"Tony – Maroni?" Her blue eyes got huge. "You're like, the real Tony Maroni? Oh my god. You are. I don't believe it! God, I saw you guys when

I was in high school! In Seattle, I guess it was – jeez, it must be fifteen years ago! God, you guys were great, that was like the greatest show I have ever seen in my life!"

Tony smiled dreamily. "Yeah, yeah … I remember that. The Limehouse. That was right before we went to Japan. That was, like, the last time we really played together," he added wistfully. "I mean, all of us, in the States."

"You left after that …" Peggy ran a hand over her cap. "God, I was so bummed out. I was only fifteen, and that was it, I felt like I'd missed everything. Tony Maroni." She shook her head. "This is so amazing. I guess I'd heard once that you lived here in D.C., but –"

Brendan cleared his throat. "You know, I hate to break up the Rock Trivia Show, but I have a client coming in half an hour and I need Mr. Maroni here to drive me back to my office."

"Oh sure, sure." Peggy glanced down at Peter, then up at Brendan again. She was actually blushing. "But I just can't believe that –"

"Oh, please, believe," said Brendan. He wondered what Peggy would think if she knew that Tony considered *This Is Spinal Tap* a model for behavioral therapy. "Look, I'm in a real hurry today, that's all. Maybe tomorrow when I drop him off, we could go over some of this great stuff you're talking about."

"Oh, but there's no school tomorrow. Christmas Eve. So many kids and teachers are going away or have family stuff, Deirdre decided that we'd just close until the 28th. We have early release today, at noon. It was in the newsletter …"

Brendan swore under his breath. Peggy hunched her shoulders. "I'm really sorry – you didn't know? That was why Teri was so freaked out about having to go away …"

"Right, right. It's okay, not a problem …" Brendan turned and stooped beside his son. "Peter, Peter, Peter. What am I going to do about you?" he murmured.

"I'll be there." Tony's voice was so loud that several of the other teachers turned. "I mean, hey, what else do I have going on? It'll be great, we'll do Christmas stuff."

"Christmas can be a little intimidating for some of these kids." Peggy smiled. "But you probably know that already if you're hanging out with this little guy here at home. I still can't believe you and Brendan went to high school together."

Brendan stared at the floor and shook his head despairingly. Tony nodded, bopping back and forth on his heels.

"You know what?" he said. "I can come pick him up at noon, and you can tell me what I need to know about being with him. I mean, whatever I don't know already."

"Which would fill an encyclopedia," Brendan muttered darkly. "Listen, Elvis, I really do have to get back to the office. Peggy, Peter will be fine with Tony, you just tell him anything you think he needs to know, okay?"

Peggy nodded. "I don't think you're on the sheet as an authorized pickup, are you, Tony? So maybe you could just come to the office and fill out a form, and Brendan can sign it, and we'll be all set," she said, and started for the office.

"Sure, sure!" Tony loped after her.

"Do you believe this, Peter?" Brendan shook his head. "I graduated fourth in my class at Georgetown. Plus, I thought she was gay."

Peter said nothing. Though if his father had turned his head, he might have seen something like reflected light shining in his son's eyes, as Peter gazed sideways at Tony jouncing up and down outside the office.

"Listen, sweetie. Daddy has to go to work now. Uncle Tony's going to pick you up at lunchtime. Can you remember that? It won't be me and it won't be Mommy –"

"Okay. I'm signed on, Captain Kirk," Tony announced, sweeping up behind Brendan. "You ready? Want me to drive?"

"No, I'll drive." Brendan sighed. "Yeah, I guess I'm ready. Remember, Peter." He stood, pointed at Tony. "Uncle Tony here will pick you up."

Tony nodded. "Noon, right?"

"Actually, if you can come a little earlier, it'll make it easier in case he's having a rough day." Peggy smiled. "Or if I am."

Brendan groaned. "Let's go –"

"Bye, then – see you around noon. Hooray hello, Tony!"

"Whoa whoa whoa!" Tony called. "Ouch! Jeez, I'm coming, Brenda, for chrissakes –"

Brendan drove back to Capitol Hill. Tony bopped and drummed on the dash-board and sang "Christmas (Baby Please Come Home)" until Brendan threatened to throw him out and make him walk from Foggy Bottom.

"Okay, okay, I've stopped, see? Man, I just can't believe that girl Peggy, huh? She's great, she's like so great ..."

But Brendan was brooding over how Peggy had been able to hug his son. Automatically he glanced into the rearview mirror, looking for Peter in his car seat. For a split second he had a flash of panic, seeing it was empty –

But of course Peter wasn't there. Peter was at school, bonding with strangers. Panic subsided into a wash of despair, and Brendan gripped the wheel until his hands hurt.

"How come you never told me about her?"

Brendan swallowed, let his breath out. "You never asked."

"I can't believe she saw us at the Limehouse. That was probably the best show we ever did, you know that? I can't believe she saw it."

"At least she's old enough to vote." Brendan pulled over near his office. For a moment he just sat there, waiting to see if the despair would fade. It did not. A young woman pushing a stroller around puddles on the sidewalk stopped, pointing at the window of the Trover Shop. Swags of fresh holly hung there, their berries so deep and glistening a red they looked like drops of blood. Brendan shut his eyes, then turned and reached into the backseat for his briefcase.

"Listen, Tony. Get there early like Peggy said, okay? But don't forget Peter. Make sure he eats something when he gets home – actually, bring something in the car, there's some juice boxes and peanut butter crackers in the kitchen. Ask Peggy to check if he needs any medicine before you leave, okay? I'll try to get out early but probably I won't be back till five or so."

"Sure man, sure, no prob." Tony clambered into the driver's seat as Brendan climbed out. "Don't worry, we'll be great, it'll be fun."

"Make sure he's in his car seat!" Brendan shouted as Tony pulled away, an arc of slush rising behind him. "Get there early. And be careful – !"

Tony was careful, and he got there early. In fact, he got there about an hour after leaving Brendan on Pennsylvania Avenue. It would have been even sooner, but he stopped at the flower vendor's at Eastern Market and bought a small crimson poinsettia in a green plastic pot shaped like a Christmas tree.

"Hi," he said breathlessly when he arrived back at the Birchwood School. A half dozen children were settled at separate tables around the room, each with a grownup and a cookie and a little paper cup full of juice. Peggy looked up from where she sat across from Peter, holding the cookie for him.

"Tony! You are early."

"Here. This is for you. Merry Christmas." Tony plonked himself on the floor beside Peggy and handed her the poinsettia. "Unless you're not allowed to accept gifts."

"Oh no, gifts are highly encouraged. Look, Peter! See? This is a poinsettia. A flower – this is a flower –"

"So. Any instructions?" Tony turned and smiled at Peter, stretched his hand out to within a few inches of his face and waved gently. "Hey, Petie. You ready to come home with me? Watch Mister Magoo?"

Peter moved his head so that he faced away from Tony; but his gaze edged sideways, watching.

"Mister Magoo!" exclaimed Peggy. "God, I loved that – it used to be my favorite Christmas show. But they never run it anymore. Did you rent it?"

"Uh-uh." Tony wiggled his fingers at Peter.

"Is it on Nickelodeon or something?"

"No. I mean, I don't know. I guess."

"Huh. Well, I'll check it out when I get home, maybe I can catch the end."

"Wanna come over with me and Pete here? Cause then you could watch it with –"

Peggy shook her head. "I wish I could. But I have to write up all the weekly reports and stuff like that. Maybe another time." She smiled across the table at Peter. "So, Peter, are you ready? Tony here's going to drive you home today. Then your Daddy will be back later. Okay? Let's finish our snack and get everything ready to go ..."

Tony went with her to gather Peter's things. "So. Is he, like, really doing better? I haven't seen so much of him the last two weeks, 'cause he's been with Teri."

Peggy nodded. She turned from the wall of brightly-painted cubbies and leaned against it, cradling Peter's jacket to her chest. "You know, he really is. We work so intensely with the kids here, and it can take years, but sometimes all of a sudden you just have a breakthrough. And I really think that could happen with Peter. Although," she added, lowering her voice, "probably I shouldn't say that. People get very, very sensitive about the issue of 'curing' autism."

Tony stared at Peter, standing off by himself and staring at a knothole in the wall. "Right," Tony said softly. "Well, I know his Mom and Dad love him no matter what."

Peggy bit her lip, then nodded. "Oh, sure," she said. "Though I think Brendan has some unresolved issues. He seems a little – distracted lately.

Not as focused. But like I said, I shouldn't be saying this ..."

"It's okay. I'm, like, family," said Tony. "And let me tell you, Brendan really loves that."

He laughed and bent to pick up Peter's knapsack. "Okay, Petie. Let's go watch Mister Magoo's Christmas Carol. One of the very best –"

Peggy walked them to the front door. A few other parents were waiting by the office now with wrapped packages, greeting teachers and waving at their children.

"Yvonne! I'll be right with you –" Peggy touched the shoulder of a woman in a faux-mink coat, then turned back to Tony. "That's the mother of my other student. I should go. But thanks so much for coming by, Tony."

"So, are you, like, around? After the holidays maybe?"

Peggy straightened her little wool cap and smiled. "Maybe. Thanks for the poinsettia. Tell Mister Magoo I said hi. And Peter –"

She stooped and gave him another quick strong hug. "You have a wonderful Christmas, Peter. I'll see you very soon. Very, very soon..."

They walked outside, Peter stopping once to stare ruminatively at a spiral of oil sending spectral currents across a puddle. Tony waited with him. "Hey, pretty cool, huh?" he said, and continued to the car. "You know, you're a lucky guy, Pete."

Tony held open the Volvo's back door and watched as Peter slowly climbed in. "Having a babe like that for a teacher. Man oh man."

They returned to Brendan's apartment. The sky was inked with clouds like slate-colored smoke, the air had that metallic bite that precedes snow. Peter was careful not to look into Tony's eyes when he glanced back at him. He seemed not to hear Tony when he asked a question or pointed out something – Christmas lights, sidewalk Santa – and after they parked the boy walked in front of him, dragging his backpack and making rhythmic huff-huff noises.

"Okay. Lunchtime," announced Tony when they got inside. He cut up an apple and smeared the slices with peanut butter. Peter refused to sit, so Tony fed him standing. Tony ended up eating most of it, but he did manage to get Peter to drink some milk, only half of which ended up on the floor.

"All right. Now Uncle Tony has to check his email. Come on –"

Peter ignored him. He walked into the living room and sat on the floor and began pulling at a thread in the carpet. Tony frowned, then turned and walked down the hall.

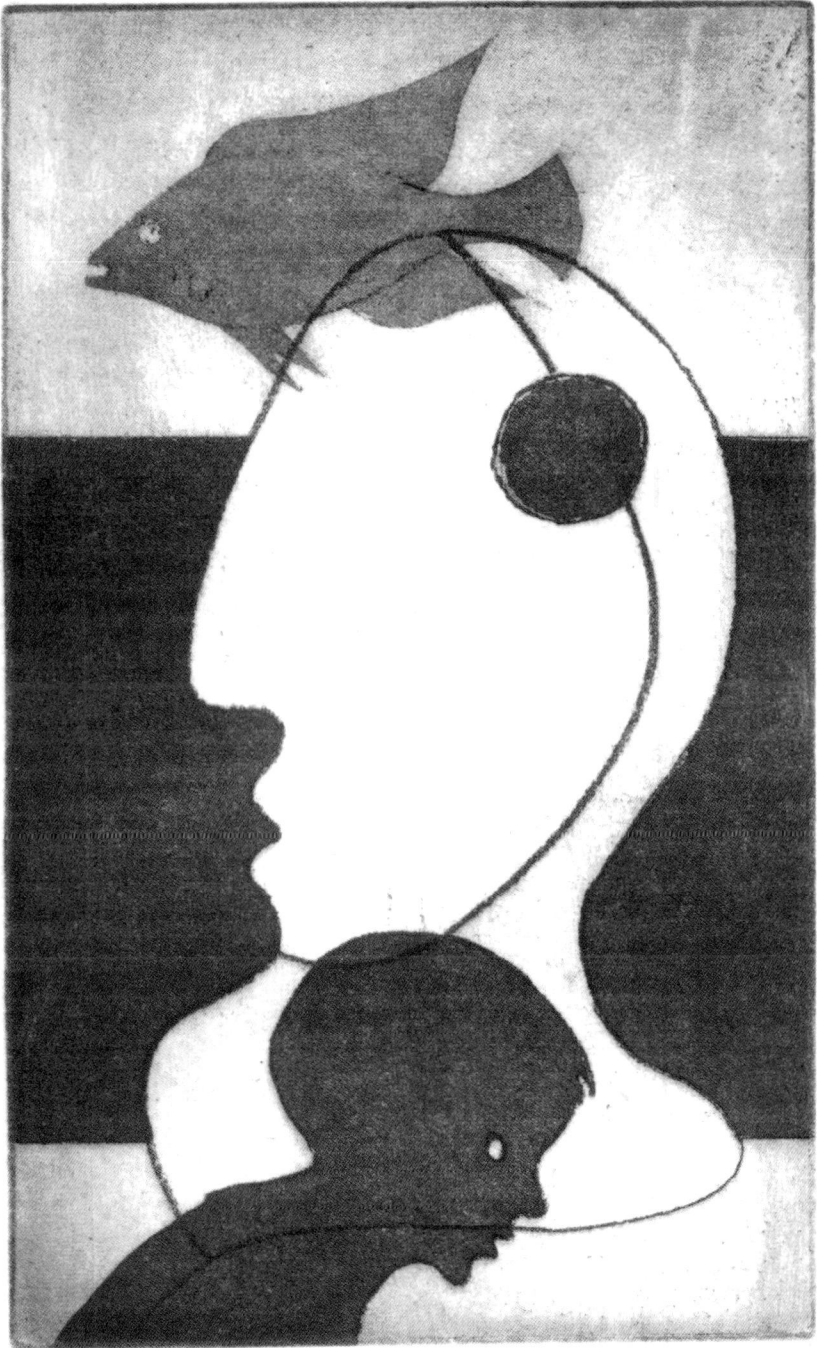

"I'll be right back. You come on down here if you want, okay?"

He checked his mail and spent a few minutes reading the headlines, then went to Chip Crockett's Web site. Nothing new there. A few messages from a week ago, Tony's own unanswered request for information about Chip's Christmas special. He was just going to log off when he heard a soft huff-huff behind him.

"Hey, Peter. C'mere, want to check this out?"

Peter stepped forward, keeping a good distance from where Tony sat. There was still peanut butter on his face, and a clump in his hair where he'd twiddled it into a knot.

"Look," said Tony. "See? That's Chip Crockett. Your Daddy and I liked him when we were little. Like you like Cookie Monster."

Peter avoided his eyes, but when Tony turned back to the computer the boy stepped forward, staring at the monitor. "And that's Ogden Orff. Listen –"

Tony punched a key. Static; then, *That's my boy – Ogden Orff!*"

Peter moved closer.

"Wanna hear it again?"

Tony played the sound bite again; then drew up the black-and-white image of Chip Crockett dressed as Ogden Orff. "See? That's him? Ogden Orff. And look – here's Captain Dingbat. And this one, this is my favorite. Ooga Booga. Isn't he great? Check out that schnozz, man – ever see a nose like that? Hey, you're blocking me!"

Peter stepped in front of him, his face scant inches from where the black-and-white image of a puppet with bulbous nose and tiny hands filled the screen.

"Pretty cool, huh?" asked Tony. Peter shook his head and continued to stare. "Ooga Booga. Good ol' Ooga Booga."

Tony sighed, swiping the hair from his eyes. "But you know, we oughta go check out Mister Magoo. Come on, let me turn it off now."

He started to move the mouse, but as the screen changed Peter shook his head again, and when the screen went blank he made a sharp angry sound.

"Hey man, I know; but I promise, we can come back later. Let's go watch TV now. Come on, it's Mister Magoo – you'll like him, he's like Ooga Booga only he moves."

Tony started for the living room. Peter remained where he was, gazing at the empty monitor.

"Come on, Petie," Tony urged. "Let's go ..."

At last Peter followed him. Tony put the television on and slumped onto the couch, remote in hand. Peter sat on the floor. Tony began flipping through the stations until he found what he was looking for.

"Hey, great, it's just starting! Watch, Petie, you're gonna love this show–"

That was how Brendan found them when he got home hours later. They were onto the Grinch by then, the floor around them scattered with popcorn and broken crackers.

"Tony. Peter." Brendan shut the door, shaking moisture from his overcoat. "Man, it's getting cold out. Hi, guys."

"Hey, Brenda Starr! You're just in time. Look, he's stealing the Christmas tree!"

"Yeah, great." Brendan rolled his eyes. He looked back down at the handful of letters he'd just picked up from the floor beneath the mail slot. "Here, you got something."

He handed Tony a letter and set his own mail on the kitchen counter. Tony glanced at the envelope, then shoved it into a pocket.

"Did he have anything to eat?" asked Brendan. He ran a finger along the counter top, frowning: someone had spilled something there, flour it looked like, or maybe salt. "Beside what's on the floor?"

"Some peanut butter and apple and some milk. And a lot of popcorn."

"All the major food groups. Well, we've got frozen pizza for dinner." Brendan stepped back into the living room and stood behind his son. "What do you think, Peter? You like this Grinch guy?"

Peter shook his head slightly. On screen the Grinch covered his ears against the sound of villagers caroling. Brendan crouched down to pick up bits of popcorn.

"I do," he said. "I can really relate to him. You know why? Because there is too much noise. Turn it down, Tony."

Still, after Peter was in bed the rest of the evening was quiet – too quiet for Tony, who wanted to watch David Bowie and Bing Crosby singing "The Little Drummer Boy" but was forbidden to by Brendan.

"For the next forty-eight hours, this is a Christmas-free zone," he announced, shooing Tony from the couch and changing the channel to CNN.

"Forty-eight hours? Jesus, Christmas'll be over by then!"

"You got it." Brendan stretched out on the couch and yawned, then wrinkled his nose. "What's that smell? Paint?"

Tony shrugged. "Mmmm, yeah." He stood in the hall, looking lost and disconsolate. His T-shirt was spattered with white powder, his hair pulled back in a sloppy ponytail. "I told you, I'm working on something. I just wanted to take a break and hear –"

"Forget it, Tony."

"But –"

"Good night, Tony."

That night his father came to him. At first Brendan thought it was Peter, but as the sound of footsteps grew clearer he recognized it unmistakably as his father's tread, that familiar pause as he went into the bathroom and after a minute or two returned to the hall, heading down towards Brendan's room. Brendan was lying in bed, staring at the ceiling where the soft mingled lights from the tree fluttered like blue and green and red moths. He couldn't wait, how could anyone wait? Surely it was morning now ...?

And yes, of course it was, because his father's shadow filled the doorway, just as it always had. Brendan started, then with a cry sat up. Joy scalded him, and amazement: because there he was, wearing the red L.L. Bean nightshirt he'd gotten for Christmas one year, its sleeves worn and hem frayed, his bare legs still muscular though the hair on them was grey now. His face, however, was young, the way it looked in old family pictures, the way it looked in Brendan's mind – and that was the other amazing thing, not just that his father should be here, alive, but that he was young. Brendan gasped with delight, realizing anew what he had forgotten since the last time this had happened: that people didn't really die, or even if they did, you could still be with them again, it didn't matter that they were dead after all! Relief poured over him like water and he shook himself, feeling the sheets sliding from his arms as he tried to get to his feet, to cross the room and hug him. Because his father saw him, too, it wasn't like it had been those last two years in the nursing home, he saw Brendan and recognized him and he was smiling, one hand half-raised in the familiar greeting that mimed tossing a baseball, the other stretched out to his son.

"Dad! Dad –"

But the words didn't come out. All the air had been sucked from him, and all the light too – the room was black again, or no, his eyes were closed, he could still see those phantom lights pulsing behind his eyelids and somewhere behind them his father stood, waiting, and all he had to do was open his eyes and he could see him, he could leap from the bed and in two steps he would be there, he would see him again –

But his eyes would not open. When he tried to cry out his throat closed and he could only grunt, horribly, thrashing at the bed and struggling to rise while his hands sank down and the darkness pressed upon his face like a door falling on him. He screamed then, and as the sound echoed around him he opened his eyes and found himself sitting up in bed. A narrow slab of light fell into the room where the door was cracked, then disappeared as it was flung open.

"Brendan?" Tony stood there in his boxer shorts, hair a wild nimbus around his face. "You okay?"

Brendan shook his head, then nodded. When he opened his mouth air rushed in to fill his throat, and he gasped.

"Jesus ... I had a nightmare. Or – no –"

He ran his hands across his face, feeling how cold his skin was, and moist. "– just a – this dream. But I'm fine. Go – go back to bed. I'm sorry I woke you."

"I wasn't asleep." Tony remained in the doorway, his face creased with worry. "You sure you're okay? I thought someone was, like, breaking in or something."

"No, really, it was just a dream. I – I'll just check Peter. Go on –"

He stood shakily, the sheets falling to the floor around him. Tony moved to let him get by, and as he passed him Brendan paused, then put a hand on his shoulder. "Hey. Tony. Sorry I woke you."

"No prob, man." Tony smiled. In the half-light leaking from the bathroom his raggedy features looked gaunt, his hair more silver than grey; and for the first time Brendan thought, he's old. The notion shook him almost as much as the dream had. He stood there for a moment, gazing at his oldest friend as though trying to recall his name; and finally smiled back.

"Yeah. Well, 'scuse me –"

"Hey, you know what today is?" Tony called after him softly. "Christmas Eve!"

Brendan took a deep breath. "Yeah," he said, pausing to lean against the bathroom door. For an instant spectral lights flickered around the perimeter of his vision, red and green and blue, the shadow of a tree. He drew a hand across his face and winced. "Thanks. I – I remembered."

~ ~ ~

The morning was cold and heavy with moisture, the sky leaden and a few fine flakes already biting Brendan's cheeks as he hurried to work, his fingers numb where they curled around the handle of his briefcase. He'd forgotten to wear gloves – refused to, actually, indulging in some absurd belief that if he didn't dress as though it were winter, it wouldn't be.

But the day promised more miserable weather, more sleet and freezing rain, maybe even snow. Dave the Grave and his cronies had gotten an early start on the holiday, gathering on a corner opposite the Library of Congress and bopping up and down against the cold. Dave's wiry dog nosed at a pile of refuse spilling from a trash can, and Dave himself looked pale and rheumy-eyed, the filthy tweed jacket hanging loosely from his stooped shoulders. One of his friends held him up as he waved at passersby. Brendan saw him and started across the street, Dave's cracked voice trailing forlornly after him.

"Where's Whoa Whoa? Whoa ... c'mere, goddamit ..."

"Shut up, goddamit." Brendan hopped onto the curb, glanced up and saw a well-dressed man passing him with a suspicious look: he must have spoken aloud. He glared back and the man hurried on.

There was no one in his office when he arrived. He let himself in, trying to summon up some sense of well-being at having the place to himself. But everything looked desolate and abandoned, the computer monitors staring blankly from his partners' desks, Ashley's tiny Norfolk pine dropping yellowing needles onto the floor, its branches drooping beneath the weight of three miniature glass balls. Brendan spent a good minute staring at it glumly, before picking the tree up and depositing it in the wastebasket. Then he set to work.

He'd made a point of scheduling back-to-back client appointments all morning, starting at nine. At just past eight-thirty the phone began to ring with the first of the day's cancellations.

"Brendan Keegan."

"Yes – hi, Mr. Keegan, this is Paulette Yates? I was supposed to see you this morning? About a personal injury suit?"

"Yes, Miss Yates." Brendan swiveled so that he could gaze out the window, took in the Capitol's scaffolding glazed black with snow and ice, and immediately swiveled back to glance at his appointment book. "Let's see – yes, that's at nine."

"Well, you see, I – I have to cancel? I forgot it was Christmas Eve, and I have to get the train to see my parents, and –"

"You're canceling the appointment."

Nervous silence. Then, "Yes. I'm really sorry, I just –"

"Would you like to reschedule now? Or, no, it'd be better if you called next week, my secretary's out."

Her voice brightened with relief. "Oh! Sure, sure –"

"Fine. And, um, Miss Yates: you know I have to charge you for the missed appointment."

Another silence. "You do? Even though I called?"

"Well, you called at twenty-five to nine. I can't put someone else in that slot now."

"But – how much?"

"The hourly rate, one twenty-five."

"One hundred –" He heard a brisk intake of breath, and then a softer, muffled sound. "Oh, jesus. That's, like – can't you –"

"I'm afraid I can't. Now, we can reschedule after –"

Click.

He read the morning *Post*, rescued before Tony could find it and spirit it away for whatever knucklehead purpose he had. He made phone calls, setting up meetings and hearings for after the holiday, responding politely to the *Greetings of the Season* and *Best Wishes For*, all carefully worded these days and especially in this place, make sure no one feels excluded: Merry Christmas, Chanukah, Kwaanza, Solstice. In the background, laughter and music, recordings announcing *We Will Be Closed Until*; receptionists answering phones with breathless voices, already anticipating the afternoon's office party, early release, Midnight Mass.

And alone of everyone he spoke to, Brendan felt grounded, sober, adult; already looking to next year, a new year. Like someone on a long international flight, everyone around him fidgeting restlessly while he slept, his watch already set ahead seven hours, his mind at peace, untrammeled by excitement, and cold to the allure of gratis wine, chocolates, movies, smiling fellow passengers.

Three of his other appointments canceled as well; two, actually, with the other a no-show. Brendan carefully noted all this in his book, copying the information out for Ashley for billing purposes. He researched a case that would be going to trial in February – the thought comforted him, February a nice no-nonsense month, nothing there to worry about except for Valentine's Day, and God knows that had never been much of a threat.

At lunchtime he ventured out for a sandwich. Big wet flakes were falling now, whitening black overcoats and Timberland parkas but turning to slush as soon as the flakes made contact with the pavement. The takeout shop was crowded; everyplace was crowded, nothing, seemingly, being out of the running for consideration as a last-minute Christmas gift. Brendan waited impatiently while the man behind the counter prepared cold-cut platters and wrapped a roast beef sandwich in green butcher paper with a gold bow.

"I'll have one of those." Brendan pointed at the sandwich. "Only without the wrapping paper."

"That'll be about five minutes – I've got to get this party platter over to Senator Easton's office –"

"Forget it." Brendan jabbed his finger at the glass front of the counter. "Just give me a Kaiser roll."

The roll was tasteless. He ate it on his way back to the office, dodging Senate staffers rushing for cabs and giddy interns hugging each other goodbye on their way to the airport. When he got back inside, there was a message on the machine from Teri, giving him her flight arrival time and reminding him to come by with Peter the next morning at ten o'clock for Christmas cheer.

"Cheer," Brendan repeated, erasing the message. "Cheer cheer cheer."

The phone rang. He answered it, still shrugging out of his wet overcoat and shaking crumbs onto the floor alongside dead Norfolk pine needles. "Brendan Keegan."

"Brendan. Kevin."

"Kevin." Brendan hung up his coat, slid into his chair. "How are you."

"Well, I'm good. Been thinking about you. See the game the other night?"

"Wasn't that something," Brendan said, his voice sounding like a hollow echo of his cousin's bluff tone. He hadn't spoken to Kevin since Thanksgiving. "What's up?"

"Well, Eileen and I wanted to invite you and Peter over this evening. If you're not doing anything. The girls would love to see you. You could even stay over if you want. We're going to Teri's tomorrow and we could all go together, if you feel like it."

"Well, thank you." Brendan cleared his throat: why did he and Kevin always sound as though they were trying to arrange a subpoena? "I mean, that would be nice, except that I don't know when you last talked to Teri –

she had to go out of town, and so Peter's with me until tomorrow morning, and I think probably we'll just stick to our original plans."

"Peter's there with you right now?"

"No, no – he's at home, with Tony." Brendan cleared his throat again and adjusted the contrast on his monitor. "As a matter of fact, I better get going – I should get back early, make sure everything's okay."

"Oh." Kevin's voice rose slightly. He paused, then added, "Well, you know, Tony would be very welcome, too. Eileen's got a ton of food, there's plenty of room –"

"Thanks, Kevin. But, you know, I have a client waiting. We'll just see you tomorrow, okay?"

He waited a long moment until Kevin finally replied. "Sure. Sure, Brendan. Give Peter a hug, okay? We'll see you tomorrow. Merry Christmas –"

"Right. Thanks, Kevin –"

He hung up. Around him the room was dim, the windows ash-colored: he'd forgotten to turn the lights back on. He didn't do so now; just hunched closer to the computer screen, scrolling down a list of dates and names as he punched his home number into the telephone. Tony answered just as the answering machine kicked in, sounding out of breath.

"Tony? It's me, Brendan. Everything okay?"

"Oh, hey, hi. Yeah, it's okay, I guess. I don't know what it is – yesterday he was great, but today he doesn't want to eat at all. He doesn't want to do anything. I finally just parked him in front of the TV, he seems to be all right there."

Brendan felt conflicting emotions, a bitterly gleeful *I told you so!* and anxiety for his son. "Well, he can be a handful. Are you sure you're all right?"

"No kidding he's a handful. But I think we're okay ..."

There was no concomitant bitterness in Tony's voice; only exhaustion. And suddenly Brendan wondered what, exactly, he was doing here in his office; what had he been thinking, leaving his child at home alone with a stranger? What the hell was wrong with Teri, taking off like that at the last minute, not even talking to him first? His concern spiked to rage, thinking of Peter hungry, Peter suffering, Peter –

"Brendan? I gotta go check on him – I'll see you later, okay – ?"

And Tony was gone. Brendan started to call back, to demand to know what was happening; but as quickly as it had come his anger disappeared.

He drew a long shuddering breath, replaced the phone in its cradle. He should have stayed home today; he should be there now. Even thinking of Teri and trying to transfer this granite load of guilt to her didn't make Brendan feel any better.

"Ah, shit."

He switched his computer off, and for several minutes sat alone in the dark. Snow and freezing rain hissed against the window; now and then he could feel the walls shake as wind buffeted the building. He had to go home, he should never have left this morning, how could he even have dreamed of doing so?

But the thought of returning there, of facing the hours of tedium and cleaning up and fruitless insistent arguing with a child who never spoke – his child, his son, a boy who would scream if Brendan tried to look him in the eye, a boy who would only bear his father's touch when he was asleep – the thought of being with Peter in that desolate apartment on Christmas Eve filled him with such despair that he moaned aloud.

And, at last, stood and dressed to go home. What else could he do? He could no more blame Peter for his own grief than he could blame Teri. And of course Peter did recognize him, he wept sometimes when Brendan dropped him off at school, and when he left the room after tucking him into bed at night; he woke up some nights whimpering, and would only go back to sleep after Brendan spoke to him, murmuring nonsense, snatches of half-remembered nursery rhymes, the words to "Meet the Mets." And of course Peter loved him, there was no doubt about it, he was his father. Brendan tried not to hear Teri saying that, or the therapist they'd seen; tried to hear the words in his own voice inside his head; tried to imagine them coming from his son ….

But at that his imagination balked; the thought of Peter speaking made his father feel sick and dizzy with hopelessness. It was too much like his dream; too much like giving in for a few moments, even in sleep, to love and belief and hope. You could not steel yourself against disappointment and loss and grief in this life, if nothing else Brendan knew that; but you could arm yourself against the rest of it. You could arm yourself against desire and hope, you could be a fucking fortress and never fall, never let a single arrow through. And so as the sleet gave way to snow and every radio in the city began to sound, gently or noisily, its welcome to the imminent feast, Brendan Keegan picked up his briefcase, locked the door to his office, and began to trudge home.

It was a miserable walk. Just as Brendan had spent the last few years trying to ignore the sigils of the season, so he had attempted to ignore its weather, refusing to invest in anything more winter-worthy than his Brooks Brothers overcoat. No down parkas, no Thinsulate-lined gloves, no sturdy L.L. Bean boots with leather uppers to shield his expensive wool trousers from the surging tide of slush and curbstone filth that inevitably caught up with him. In this he was not alone: much of the city's workforce, save those hardy Congressional underlings from places like Maine or Minnesota, continued to indulge the hopeful but ultimately unsupportable notion that they lived in a Southern city, with weather befitting retirement communities along the Gulf Coast. In reality D.C.'s weather could be as extreme as it was unpredictable, a fact now underscored for Brendan by the sight of two laughing, red-cheeked young women in Park Police mufti, making their way past Eastern Market on cross-country skis. He shuddered and tugged his collar up around his neck, averting his eyes. It was harder to avoid the row of cut evergreens leaning against the brick facade of the Market itself, or the plastic buckets full of fresh-cut holly and box, the ropes of princess pine and balsam and the ghostly clouds of mistletoe dangling from oak branches sawn from trees along Skyline Drive. He skirted the line of greenery, stepping off the curb into the street; but the fragrance of balsam and boxtree dogged him, along with the sound of pleading children, the faint thrum of a church organ and an unsteady soprano struggling with "O Holy Night."

"God damn it," whispered Brendan through chattering teeth. He spoke aloud, as much to drown the music of the world in his ears as to protest the cold. But it was so cold, and the expectant world was so tightly wrapped around him, that he kept it up the whole way home, the mean rigorous chant rising and falling as he scurried across streets and past driveways packed with cars, kicking at mysterious boxes that had already disgorged their secrets to garages and attics, jostling passers-by who unwisely wished him Merry or Happy, his head down and eyes fixed on nothing but the grey ice-scummed sidewalk before him. "God damn, god damn ..."

Finally he reached the corner of Seventh and Maryland. For a long moment he stood there, heedless of his neighbors hurrying past, and stared at the defiantly barren windows of his rowhouse apartment. There were no lights there; no spangled promise of a tree within; no fake plastic candles; no Menorahs or Kwaanza candles. No wreath on the door; just a red paper flyer from the Capitol Hill Food bank –

*SORRY WE MISSED YOU! WE ARE STILL ACCEPTING
DONATIONS OF CANNED GOODS FOR OUR HOLIDAY HUNGER
DRIVE, PLEASE DROP OFF AT –*

He tore it down, crumpled it and tossed it onto the steps behind him; then went inside.

The apartment was silent. All was calm, all was bright. Actually, all was an incredible mess.

"What the – ?"

Brendan frowned, putting down his briefcase and surveying the living room. The TV was on: scampering reindeer, an elf. He switched it off, turned to survey the galaxy of spilled popcorn sweeping from wall to wall, mingled with cracker crumbs and an apple core, an empty juice box, videotapes. There were shreds of newsprint everywhere, a trail of apple juice leading to the kitchen, and smudges of white powder on the carpet.

And where the fuck was Tony? Brendan could feel the rage knotted inside him starting to uncoil, a slow serpent suddenly awakened. "Peter?" he called. "Tony?"

"In here, dude – we're in the bathroom –"

Brendan shook his head, then lowered himself into a crouch. He dabbed a finger in the white stuff on the floor, brought it to his mouth and hesitantly touched it to his lips.

"Blech." He grimaced, standing. Well, at least it wasn't cocaine. Or heroin. "Tony – ?"

He found him in the bathroom leaning against the tub in a white-streaked RAW POWER T-shirt. Peter sat on the toilet, pants around his ankles, nuzzling his rubber duck and humming to himself.

"Hey, Brenda." Tony lifted his head and smiled weakly. For an instant Brendan thought he'd apologize for the mess, but no, he was just tired. "Jeez Louise, I'm glad to see you. We –"

"What the fuck is going on?" Brendan stared at him, his eyes too bright, his hands white and raw from the sleet outside.

"Huh?"

"'Huh' nothing. What's this mess? The whole place is a goddamn mess–" He moved his hand, too quickly, to point to the living room, and bashed it into the door. "Ow – god damn it –"

"Hey, man –" Tony glanced uneasily at Peter, then at Brendan. "Take it easy, he's had kind of a rough day, like –"

"Oh yeah? Well, I've had kind of a rough week. I've had kind of a rough fucking life –"

"Hey, whoa! C'mon, man, you're too loud, you'll scare him, Peggy said–"

"The fuck what Peggy says. What is this goddamn mess?"

He stepped forward and grabbed the shower rod. His entire body shook. In his hand the plastic rod bent, then snapped, and the curtain flopped down around Tony's head.

"Whoa, man, who's making the mess now? Jeez, Brendan! I was just –"

He smashed the curtain aside, grabbed for Tony's shoulder; but before he could touch it Tony's hand curled around his.

"Brendan," said Tony, softly but urgently. Tony's grip was tight, his hand bigger than Brendan's and his grasp, Brendan realized with a small shock, far stronger than his own. "Calm down, man, I'll clean it up! But he wouldn't eat anything, I tried all day until finally he, like, ate a whole gallon of popcorn and I think he got a stomach ache. That's what we're dealing with now."

Behind him, Brendan could hear a low *nhhhh nhhhh nhhhhh*. Tony nodded, tipping his head toward Peter; then gazed back at Brendan. His brown eyes were not puzzled so much as they were utterly without comprehension. He stared down at Brendan's hand, gripped in his own like some remnant of a life-size toy, and abruptly let it fall. He shook his head. "Hey, man – it's Christmas."

Brendan stared back at him; past him, at his own shadow on the shiny white tiles of the shower stall. By some trick of the overhead light Tony's shadow dwarfed his, but when Tony turned away Brendan's shadow sprang back up, filling the empty space and the corners of the ceiling. He swallowed, the inside of his mouth tasting sour and chalky, his lips aching and chapped from the cold. "Get out," he said. It hurt to talk, it hurt to say that but he turned, bending to put his hand gently on Peter's shoulder where he sat. "Get out."

"But." Tony watched as his friend gazed down at his son. Without looking at his father, the boy twisted, trying to slip from Brendan's touch. After a moment Brendan let go of him, and Peter began to cry. Tony bit his lip, then turned away.

"Okay," he said quietly.

"Thank you." Brendan remained standing above the child. Like Tony's shadow moments before, his son seemed to shrink. Brendan shivered, a wave of dizziness flooding him; then steadied himself by grabbing the back of the toilet. The dizziness passed; his anger hardened, grew small and cold and compact, a stone he swallowed, just one of thousands. He blinked, feeling granite in his chest, a deadening behind his eyes. His child was crying, and he reached for him automatically but knowing he would not give him comfort, could not, not ever. Tony was gone, there was the sound of a door closing and once more Brendan was helping Peter, cleaning him and dressing him and waiting for the boy to follow him from the bathroom back into the kitchen. It was a night like any other, cold, dark, sleet slashing the windows and the curtains drawn against what was outside, the apartment silent, the sounds of song and voices muffled by the steady dull pounding of his heart. He cleaned the living room; Peter stood and watched him from the sides of his eyes but his father did not see him, did not seem to know he was there. When he was finished he dumped the dustpan full of grit and flour and popcorn into the trash, then started on the kitchen, wiping up spilled juice and more kernels and fishing an uneaten apple from beneath the table. He straightened, his hair still damp and unkempt from the walk home, and gazed across the room at the child leaning against the wall: his fist curled against his cheek, the yellow rubber duck with its gnawed head resting against his chin.

"Peter," he said. A moment; the boy shook his head, once, his gaze oblique, fixed on a tendril of dust hanging from the side of the refrigerator. "Peter. I'm sorry. I'm sorry, Peter. ..."

No reply.

He put him to bed. There was no fight over changing his clothes, because Brendan didn't change them; just slid the purple socks from his son's feet and pulled the blankets over him. Peter kicked them off. Brendan pulled them up again, but when the boy began to thrash he moved aside, letting the blankets fall to the floor.

"You'll be cold," he said. His eyes stung. He reached and turned off the small bedside lamp, Hickory Dickory Dock, and closed his eyes, waiting for the tears to pass. When he opened them he saw the small rigid figure of his son, lying on his back with his head slightly turned away. He was staring at the ceiling, moving the rubber duck back and forth across his lips. "Goodnight, Peter," Brendan whispered. He leaned down and kissed his son's forehead, let his hand light upon the child's cheek, cool and smooth as a pillowcase. "Goodnight."

He started for bed, but in the hallway he paused, listening. He could hear a faint ringing music, and at first thought a radio had been left on somewhere. Then he noticed the thread of light beneath Tony's closed door. He had not left, after all. Brendan took the few steps towards the door, stopped. The music continued, still faint but loud enough that he could make out the chiming chords, sweet and familiar as church bells, and the low, almost whispered sound of Tony singing, his nasal voice hoarser now but still that voice you would never mistake for any another, still that song –

> *I know that you remember*
> *How we made our mark*
> *Oh we had a great time*
> *Down at Tibbets Park ...*

Brendan blinked. He remembered the first time he'd heard it, not at the Maronis' legendary first show at the Coventry in Queens but years earlier when they were all still kids, him and Tony and Kevin, practicing in Brendan's basement. He'd had a little snare drum set, bright red with that weird metallic finish, and Kevin had some cheap Sears guitar. Only Tony had a real instrument, a Mosrite that he could barely hold, let alone play. The guitar was a going-away present from his older cousin; the going-away part had been to Viet Nam, and the cousin had not come back. Tony had saved up and bought a small amp, and he'd stuck knitting needles into the front of it, so that it would sound like a fuzztone. He'd made up the song one winter afternoon when they'd all been sitting around watching *The Three Stooges* and "Officer Joe" Bolton, trying to learn the chords to "Pleasant Valley Sunday" during the commercials. Finally Tony leaned over and kicked at the little Kenmore Lift'N'Play Record Player, sending the Monkees 45 flying, and started to sing.

> *Hey hey, whoa whoa whoa*
> *Gonna tell you now*
> *Where I wanna go*
>
> *Running with my friends*
> *Playing in the dark*
> *Gonna have a good time*
> *Down in Tibbets Park!*

"That's retarded," Kevin shouted over the din of Tony's Mosrite. "That's the stupidest song I ever –"

It had ended in a scuffle, as usual, Brendan breaking things up even though he secretly agreed with Kevin. But now ...

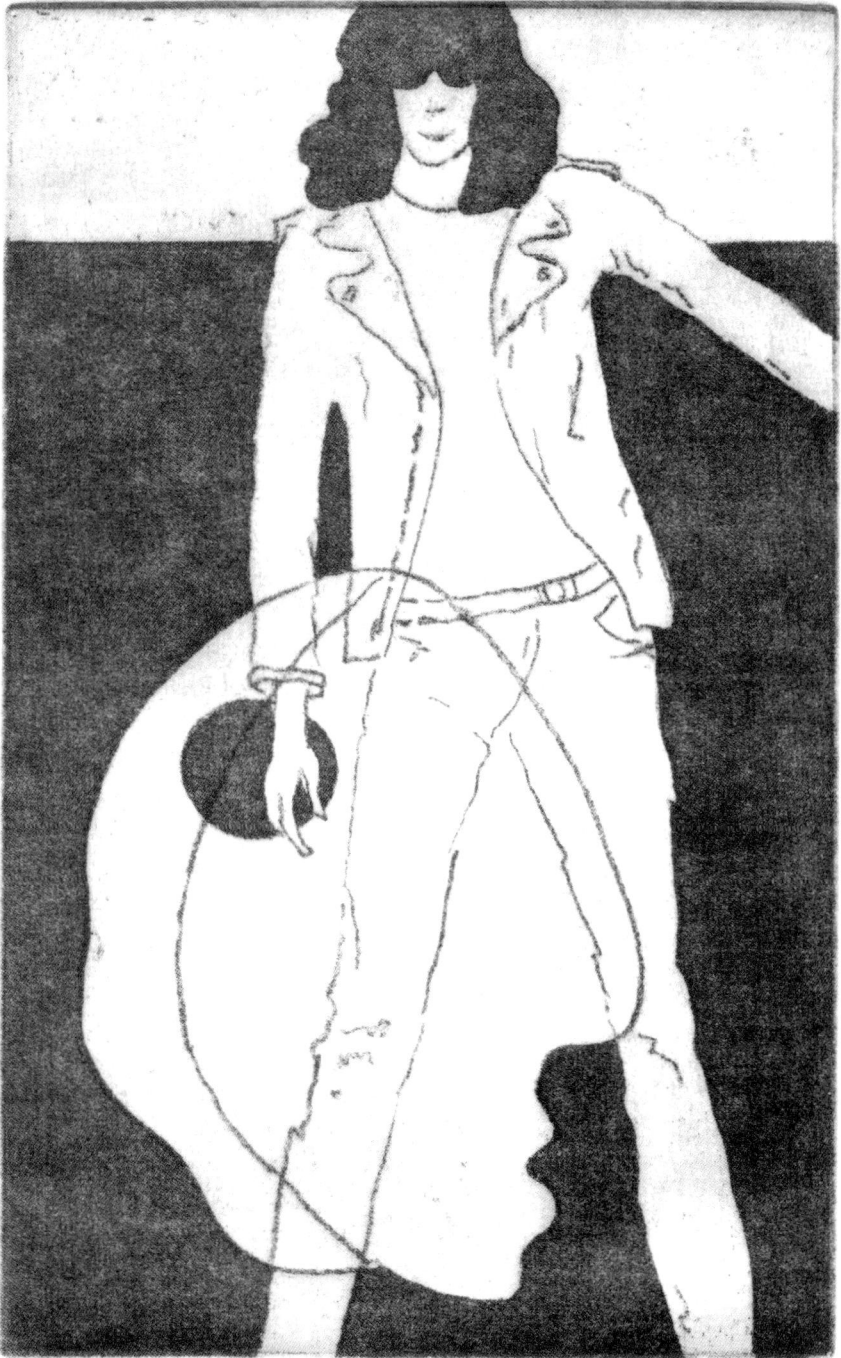

Now it made him cry. Without a sound, one hand pressed against the wall with such force that his wrist grew numb but he just stood there, listening. The song ran on and the darkness grew complete, he could see nothing before him but a blurred tunnel and, very far away, a gauzy gleam of red and green. The joke had always been that Tony knew only three chords but he had them down straight; yet now when he finished the one song he began another. Strumming the slow somber chords, his voice cracking as he stumbled over the words even as Brendan struggled to recall the song's name ...

> Lully, lulla, thou little tiny child,
> By by, lully lullay.
> How may we do
> For to preserve this day
> This poor youngling
> For whom we do sing,
> By by, lully lullay?

"Ah, shit," Brendan whispered. The "Coventry Carol" ...

He drew his hands to his face. They had learned it in third grade, for Midnight Mass at Sacred Heart. Now Tony was still trying to sing the boy soprano's part, his falsetto breaking into a wan croak at the chorus.

> Herod the king,
> In his raging
> Charged he hath this day
> His men of might
> In his own sight
> All young children to slay.

> That woe is me,
> Poor child for thee
> And ever mourn and may
> For thy parting
> Neither say nor sing
> By by, lully lullay ...

He could not bear it. He fled down the hall, knocking over a side table and stumbling into his bedroom. The door slammed shut behind him. The lights were already off. He yanked down the shades, shoving them against the window so that no light would get in and then turning to fling himself onto his bed. He groaned, kicking his shoes off and throwing his suit jacket onto the floor, burrowed under the covers and pressed his hands against his ears the way he did during airplane takeoff, trying to drown out the roar of engines, the implicit threat in any flight. Still the phantom lights pulsed behind his eyelids. A child's hand moved monotonously back and forth, back and forth, tracing the pattern of a solitary dance upon his lips. And a boy's high clear voice lifted, impossibly sweet and far away, welcoming the first arrivals to Midnight Mass.

He woke, hours later it seemed. It was a minute before he remembered where he was – the shock of being in his own bed with his clothes on but sober, no remnant of a hangover. It was dark; he recalled that it was Christmas Eve. With a subdued sort of dread he realized that it might even be Christmas Day. For some minutes he lay there, gazing blankly at the ceiling. Now and then he wondered if he actually was staring at the ceiling – it was so dark, the room devoid of anything that might delineate between the abyss behind his eyes and that which awaited him when he rose.

Which, at last, he did. His limbs felt heavy; his arms, when he sat up and rested them at the edge of the mattress, seemed swollen and cold to the point of numbness. But he had to get up: the thought of lying in bed suddenly filled him with an unease that was close to horror. Because if he was at last able to feel nothing, even on this night – especially on this night – he might as well be dead, he knew that. He might indeed be dead, and unaware. It was this awful thought, unbidden by the customary sirens of alcohol and rage, that spurred him to his feet, and out into the hall.

Immediately he felt better. The apartment was empty and mundane as ever: no leaking ceiling, no damp footprints on the bare wood floor, no disorder in the few photographs of himself and Peter and Teri in happier days hanging on the wall. He walked slowly, with each step feeling himself grow stronger and more fully awake. He must have had a nightmare, though he could not remember it, and very purposefully he made no effort to. He stopped and peeked into Peter's room. His son was on his side, sound asleep, his mouth parted and hand cupped before his face. His hand was empty. The beloved yellow duck lay on the floor beneath. Brendan walked in silently and picked it up, placed it gently back into the child's grasp. Peter's fingers curled around it and he sighed, deeply; then breathed as before. Brendan stiffened, feeling stones shift within his chest: he had bought no presents for his son this year, not one. Cruel reassurance sprang up immediately – Peter would not notice, he never had – and before grief or sadness could claw at him Brendan hurried back into the hall, closing the door behind him.

The door to Tony's room was shut, too. There was no light showing beneath it, and for a moment Brendan thought of looking inside, to check on his friend. Then he thought of what he might see. What if Tony actually did sleep in his leather jacket? Or worse, in a Maronis T-shirt?

Instead he felt his way through the dim hall to the kitchen. He was fumbling for the light switch when he noticed the blinking light on the answering machine. He touched it and played back a single message, from Teri. She had arrived safely though her flight was four hours late, she was completely exhausted, she was going right to bed, she'd see them in the morning. I love you Peter. Merry Christmas.

"I forgot to tell you, she called."

Brendan started, cracking his head on a cabinet. "Ouch! Jesus Christ, you scared me!" He rubbed his head, wincing. "Tony? Where the hell are you?"

"Sorry, man. Actually, you were here when she called, but I guess you were asleep, or something ..."

Tony's voice trailed off awkwardly. Blinking, Brendan made his way warily through the kitchen, until he could just make out Tony's lanky form on the edge of the couch. The glowing numerals on the kitchen clock showed 12:17. In the darkened living room the TV was on, its screen empty of anything but hissing grey static. Tony had his hands on his knees, angular shoulders hunched as he gazed at the television. He didn't look up when Brendan came in to stand next to him.

"Tony? What are you doing?"

Tony continued to stare at the screen. Finally: "Just checking to see what's on," he said.

Brendan glanced from the TV to his friend, wondering if this were a joke. Tony's expression was intent, almost fierce: apparently not. "Tony. You know what? It doesn't look like anything is on."

Tony nodded. He turned to gaze up at Brendan. "I know." He smiled sadly, then slid over on the couch, patting the cushion beside him. "C'mon in and set a spell, pardner."

Brendan did. There were bits of popcorn on the sofa; he brushed them aside, leaning back and sighing. Tony continued to stare at the screen. After a moment he reached over, absently picked up a handful of the popcorn and ate it. "What time is it?"

"Midnight. A little past."

"Huh." Tony sat quietly for a while longer. Finally, "Well, Merry

Christmas," he said.

Brendan hesitated. Then, "Merry Christmas, Tony."

Tony nodded but said nothing. Brendan squinted, staring at the television and trying to determine if he was missing something. "Do you want me to, like, change the channel?"

"No. Well, not yet."

Brendan waited. He thought of calling Teri, weighing up the peril of waking her against the notion of his sincerely apologizing for – well, everything. I'm sorry I'm such an asshole, sorry I was such a bad husband, lousy father, shitty lawyer, mean middle-aged baby boom critter who sneers at street people and doesn't recycle. I'm not making any promises. I'm just sorry. That's all.

"Tony?"

"Mmm?"

"I'm sorry."

"Huh?" Tony turned, startled. "What?"

"For being such an asshole. I'm sorry. For everything."

"Well, jeez. It's okay." Tony shrugged. "Hey, you weren't such an asshole. I mean, not always, at least."

Brendan looked at him hopefully. "What do you mean, not always?"

"Well, like, not for the entire last twenty years." Tony turned away again, brow furrowed as he stared at the hissing set. Suddenly he relaxed, all the lines of his face smoothing as he let his breath out.

"There," he said softly. "Look."

Brendan looked. On the television there was a test pattern, something he hadn't seen for twenty years, at least. Black-and-white and grey, the familiar bull's-eye pattern with large black numerals counting down in the middle.

-10-

"Hey," he said, pointing.

-9-

-8-

"that's really weird, it's a test"

-3-

-2-

-1-

The screen cleared. Instead of the ancient Atomic Era Mondrian of numbers and circles, there was now a fireplace. A big fireplace, black-and-white and filled with black-and-white flames, holding a heap of crackling black-and-white logs with white glowing embers beneath. Superimposed on it was a circle with the letters WPIX-NYC written inside.

"Whoa," whispered Brendan in awe. "It's the Yule Log."

Tony could only nod. His eyes were huge and round, his open mouth another cartoon O. The crackling of the logs faded in and out of the crackling of the TV. Brendan's mouth hung open, too, but before he could say anything a man's voice echoed from the screen.

"Broadcasting from Gracie Mansion, home of the Mayor of New York City, where we are bringing you our viewers the Christmas Yule Log."

An instant of silence. Then music swelled to fill the room. The 1,001 Strings, "The First Noel." Tony and Brendan turned to each other, gaping; and began to laugh.

"It is the Yule Log!" Tony's hair whirled around his face as he bounced up and down on the couch. "And listen!"

"The First Noel" segued into "Jingle Bell Rock." The fire crackled, the music swelled; a section of the yule log broke and fell onto the hearth. The screen went slightly jerky, and there was the same log – but unbroken now, the tape loop had begun again – still burning merrily in black-and-white.

" – that's the Jackie Gleason Orchestra!"

They listened, to the Carol of the Bells and the Vienna Choir Boys, the Hollywood Strings and Guy Lombardo. All that soupy stuff you never heard anymore, except as a joke, maybe, or archived on some ToonTown Web site. The tape loop of the yule log played and replayed, interrupted now and then by the same ponderous announcement.

"From Gracie Mansion ..."

Brendan felt as though he were dreaming; knew at least once that he was dreaming, because he woke, not with a start but with eyes opening slowly, sleepily, to monochrome flames and the back of Tony's leather jacket, Tony's hair the same silver-grey as the screen, his cracked marionette's face silhouetted against the little bright rectangle in the front of the room.

Then, abruptly, there was silence. The television went black, scribbled with a few white lines. Brendan sat up and frowned. "What's the matter? It's over?"

"Shhh," hissed Tony. A moment when they were both balanced at the edge of the sofa, staring intently at an empty screen.

And suddenly it went white; then grey; then white again. The grainy photographed image of a man's face appeared, his eyes wide and surprised, his mouth a perfect circle. A Santa Claus hat was superimposed on his head. As Brendan stared, black letters danced across the screen and the first bars of peppy music sounded.

CHIP CROCKETT'S

CHRISTMAS CAROL!

"Holy shit," whispered Brendan. He didn't even feel Tony's hand clutching at his. "It's *on*."

The words faded. The screen showed a small black-and-white stage, made up to look like a bedroom. A potato-nosed puppet in a long white nightshirt and nightcap stood in front of an open cardboard window, papier-mâché hands clasping a rock.

"Merry Christmas, Merry Christmas, ha ha ha!" the puppet shouted, and flung the rock out. Silence; then the crash of broken glass and a scream. *"Humbug!"* shouted the puppet gleefully. It bopped across the stage, picking up more rocks and throwing them.

"It's Ooga Booga!" cried Brendan.

"Scrooga Booga," said Tony. "Shhh ..."

Brendan started to shhh him back, but a sound distracted him. He turned and saw Peter standing in the doorway, staring at the TV.

"Oh, jeez – poor Peter. We woke you –" Brendan stood, without thinking swept over and scooped up the boy. "Shoot, I'm sorry. But it's okay, honey, come on, come in and watch with us ..."

For once Peter didn't fight; only gazed at the screen. When his father sat back down on the couch the boy slid from his grasp to the floor, scooching a few inches away and then sitting bolt upright, watching.

"See?" exclaimed Brendan as the puppet tossed a final rock onto an unseen passer-by. "See? There's Ooga Booga, see? Ooga Booga. He's a real grouch. Just like your dad." He glanced over at Tony. "Fuckin' A," he said, and laughed.

"Shhh!" said Tony. "Watch."

They watched, Tony and Brendan leaning so far over it was a wonder they didn't plummet, face-first, like one of the puppets onto the floor. Peter sat at their feet, silent, now and then shaking his head and looking sideways, the yellow rubber duck pressed against his chin. Onscreen the old old story played out with a few additions – Ratnik in the role of Christmas Past, and of course, Chip himself doing Ogden Orff as Bob Crockett. Brendan whooped, grabbing Tony's knee and punching his shoulder, laughing so hard his eyes burned and his throat hurt. Ogden Orff decorated a tree with cake frosting. Officer Joe Bolton made a surprise cameo appearance as Jacob Marley and Scrooga Booga hit him in the head with a flashlight. There were commercials for Bosco and Hostess Cream-Filled Cupcakes. Captain Dingbat appeared as the Ghost of Christmas Yet to Come, accompanied by a chorus of dancing, chanting finger-puppets.

Don't be a meanie,
Show us your bikini!

And at the end, all of them were onstage together, miraculously – Ratnik and Ooga Booga and the other puppets, Ogden Orff breaking character to become Chip Crockett laughing over some invisible technician's backstage antics, a boom mike hovering over Chip's head and fake snow falling, first in tiny flakes, then in handfuls and finally in huge clumps, until the entire soundstage was adrift with it.

"Merry Christmas!" shouted Chip Crockett, as the closing music began to play. *"Merry Christmas, and God help us, everyone!"*

Brendan and Tony roared. Peter bounced up and down. When the screen went black he began to cry.

"Oh honey, don't cry, don't cry – it's okay, Peter, look, there's the Yule Log –"

Brendan pointed, bending down to take Peter's shoulders and gently pulling him round to see. "It's okay. It's – it will be on again," he said, then swallowed. He looked over at Tony, who was watching him. Tony shrugged, gazed down at the floor and then at the TV.

"Yeah. Well, maybe," he said. For a moment he looked immeasurably sad. Then he hunched his shoulders, his leather jacket slipping forward a little, and smiled. "But hey. We got to see it. Right? I mean, it was on."

Brendan nodded. "It was on," he said. He smiled, bent forward until his face was inches above his son's head. He shut his eyes, moved his mouth in a silent kiss and felt the brush of Peter's hair against his lips. "It was great."

"And it even lasted more than three minutes!" said Tony.

Brendan felt his heart lurch. He shut his eyes, feeling the fire burning there, black-and-white; opened them and saw the room again, his son's yellow duck, the soft auburn cloud of his curls, Tony's grey hair and the ragged black cuff of his jacket. Onscreen a yule log crackled. "That's right," he whispered hoarsely, and reached to touch his friend's hand. "It even lasted more than three minutes."

~ ~ ~

He had no idea when he fell asleep. When they all fell asleep, Brendan and Tony on the couch, Peter curled on the floor at his father's feet. But when he finally woke the sun was shining, the windows slick and brilliant with frost flowers and ice, the floor speckled with bits of popcorn he'd missed the night before. He moved slowly, groaning. Beside him Tony lay slumped and snoring softly, his mouth ajar and a strand of hair caught on his lower lip. In front of them the TV was on, Regis and Kathie Lee wearing red hats and laughing. Brendan reached over and switched it off. On the floor Peter stirred, sat up and looked around, surprised; then began to whine wordlessly.

"All right, hang on a minute. What time is it? Oh, jeez –"

Brendan turned and shook Tony. "Tony, hey Tony – we got to get up. If you want to go to Teri's with us, we have to go, it's past nine."

"Go?" Tony blinked and sat up, stretched, moaning. "Aw, man, it's so early."

"Well, it's Christmas. And it's nine-fifteen, so it's late. Teri's going to kill me, come on come on come on ..."

He unearthed Peter's knapsack, tore through it until he found a red-and-green sweater and bright red corduroy pants. Peter's whining turned to shrieks when his father started dressing him, but Brendan only shook his head and pulled off the boy's T-shirt and pants, pulled on the clean clothes and then started on the socks and shoes. Tony stumbled past, rubbing his eyes, and disappeared into his room. A few minutes later he reappeared, hair disheveled and a bulky plastic bag tucked under one arm.

"Aren't you going to change?" asked Brendan, yanking on one of Peter's sneakers.

Tony frowned. "I did change." He pulled open the front of his leather jacket to display a black t-shirt and faded black jeans. "See?"

"Right. Well, do me a favor, sit with him for a minute so I can get changed."

"Sure, man. C'mere, Petie. Did you like watching Chip Crockett? Yeah, he was pretty good, huh! Did you see Ooga Booga? Huh? Good ol' Ooga Booga..."

Brendan dressed quickly. He shaved, forgoing a shower, then raced back into the kitchen. For a moment he stood gazing longingly at the coffee machine, but finally turned, gathered up his keys and overcoat, and headed for the door.

"Grab his coat, will you, Tony? You don't need to put it on him, just bring it, and his knapsack and that other stuff –"

Tony got Peter's things, and Brendan got Peter. "Merry Christmas, Merry Christmas," Brendan said, hurrying outside and holding the door for Tony. "C'mon, put a spin on it, Tony!"

"Consider it spun, man," Tony yelled. He jumped down the steps to the sidewalk. "Ooof ..."

They headed for the car, Peter digging his heels into the sidewalk and starting to cry, Brendan pulling him after him. "We're going to see Mommy," he said desperately, as a family in their Yuletide best hurried past him, on the way to church. "Come on, Peter, we'll be late –"

At last they were all in the car. Peter was strapped safely in his carseat, Tony was hanging out his open window, waving.

"Merry Christmas!" he called as another family walked past. The parents smiled and waved back, the children shouted Merry Christmas. "That's a beautiful coat, ma'am, Santa bring you that?"

The woman laughed and did a little pirouette on the sidewalk, showing off a bright red duster. "You bet!" she cried.

"Get your arm in, Tony, before it gets cut off," yelled Brendan as the engine roared. He backed up and did an illegal U-turn, and started for Teri's house.

"Hey, look at Dave the Grave!" Tony waved furiously. "Dave, my man! Nice lid!"

On his park bench, Dave the Grave sat with a bottle in his lap. As they drove by he doffed a green-and-red-checked fedora. "Whoa Whoa!" he cried. His dog yelped and jumped onto his lap, and Dave pushed him down again. "Murr' Curssmuss, mrr' crussmuss – !"

Brendan smiled in spite of himself. The sun was so bright his eyes hurt, and he drove a little too fast, running a red light. He no longer felt like apologizing to Teri – that would just scare her, probably – but he felt quiet, almost peaceful. Well, not peaceful, really, but resigned, and somehow satisfied. It wouldn't last, he knew that. Terrible things would happen and just plain bad ones, and most of all the relentless downward toboggan run of his own life as a just-good-enough father and barely tolerable ex-husband. But for now at least the sun was shining and the road crews had somehow managed not to totally screw up holiday traffic. His developmentally challenged child was in the backseat, chewing on a yellow rubber duck, and his oldest friend, the village idiot, was leaning out the window and startling churchgoers as they passed the National Cathedral.

And, somehow, this was all okay. Somehow it was all good, or at least good enough. Later he knew it would be different; but for now it was enough.

They arrived at Teri's house a little after ten. Kevin and Eileen's red Range Rover was parked in the driveway, and a car Kevin didn't recognize, an ancient Volvo sedan with a rusting undercarriage held together by virtue of about thirty-five different liberal Wiccan feminist No Nukes bumper stickers.

"Whose car is that?" asked Tony.

"I have no idea." Brendan pulled in behind it, crossly, because now the end of his car was sticking out into the cul-de-sac. "But maybe as a Christmas present you can teach them how to park."

He got out, and there on the doorstep was Teri, pale, her eyes shadowed, but smiling in a short black dress with the crimson cloisonné necklace he'd given her their first Christmas together.

"Peter!" she cried, and ran to greet them. "Brendan, hi, hi, Tony. Merry Christmas!"

Brendan hugged her stiffly, drew back and smiled. "Merry Christmas, Teri." He turned and helped her open the back door of the car. "Here's your present –"

He reached in for Peter. Teri waited until Brendan set the boy on the driveway, then stooped to hug him. "Peter! I missed you!" She looked up at Brendan and smiled again. "It's just what I wanted."

Peter slipped from her grasp and ran up the drive to the house. Brendan looked after him and saw Kevin and Eileen in the doorway, beside the twins in their Diane Arbus Christmas dresses. "Hi," he said, and waved.

"Merry Christmas!" shouted Tony. He reached back in the car for his plastic bag. "Hiya, goils!"

On the steps, the twins separated to let Peter pass. Another face appeared above theirs, masses of chestnut hair spilling from beneath a long green ski hat. "Hi, guys!"

"Peggy?" Tony gaped, then whirled towards Teri.

"I called Peggy to check on things after you picked Peter up Tuesday," she explained, smiling. "And she said she wasn't doing anything. So I got all the Christmas orphans." She glanced at Brendan. "That okay with you?"

Brendan shrugged. "Sure. Well, it'll be a very Maroni Christmas, I guess, huh Tony?"

But Tony was already loping towards the house.

"Brendan. Come on in," said Teri. She stared at the snow-glazed lawn, then looked up at him. "Thanks for dropping him off."

"Oh. Well, I thought I'd stay," Brendan said awkwardly. "Just for a little while. If you don't mind."

Teri continued to stare at the grass, finally nodded. "Sure. Sure, of course." She smiled. "That would be really good for Peter. For everyone, I think."

They walked inside. Eileen greeted Brendan at the door, enveloping him in yards of velvet and lace and perfume and hugging him as though it were her house. "Brendan! And you brought Tony!"

"Oh well, you know. Wouldn't be Christmas without Tony Maroni."

He smiled; his face was starting to hurt from smiling. Beside Eileen, Kevin stood in a tweed suit and tie with a blinking Rudolph on it. He was clapping Tony on the back.

"Get a damn tie, Tony, don't you own a tie?" he bellowed, then flopped his own tie in Brendan's face. "Merry Christmas, cuz! Check out the eggnog –"

"Eggbeaters," said Eileen, nodding. "Totally fat-tree and no cholesterol, Eggbeaters, Olestra, sugar substitute –"

Kevin made a retching sound. Brendan laughed. He stepped into the room, shading his eyes as he looked for Peter. He sighted him off by himself near the TV. It was on but the sound had been turned off. Peter stared at it, puzzled, then slapped the screen gently with his palm.

"The place looks nice, Teri," Brendan said as Teri passed him, heading for their son.

"Thanks." She stopped and pointed to the small artificial tree by a window. Dark green, its branches slightly furred to resemble, very fleetingly, real evergreens. A handful of green plastic Christmas balls hung from its branches, and there was an enormous pile of presents beneath. "Peggy said maybe we might try a tree again. A little one. And of course I got him too much stuff."

She sighed, then bit her lip, watching Peter as he once again pressed his hand against the mute TV screen. "Do you think he'll be okay with it?"

"He doesn't seem to have noticed."

"So maybe that's good?"

"Maybe."

They joined the others in the living room. The twins darted between grownups, sharing details of presents already received and glancing around hopefully for new ones. Brendan sampled Eileen's ersatz eggnog.

"Is that good?" asked Peggy. She was wearing a long shapeless wool dress, wooden clogs and a very large button that was rusting around the edges. The button had an old black-and-white picture of Tony's face on it, and the words HOORAY HELLO WHOA WHOA WHOA!

"No," said Brendan. He discreetly put his cup on a table and turned back to her. "Wow. A real Tony Maroni button," he said, tracing its edges with a finger. "That's, like, a genuine antique."

Behind her Tony appeared, still holding his plastic bag and balancing two crystal cups brimming with eggnog.

"Here, try this, it's great," he said, handing one to Peggy. "I don't know how Eileen does it."

"Jet fuel," whispered Kevin as he passed them on the way to the kitchen.

"Well, Peggy." Brendan cleared his throat and looked at Tony. He had an arm draped around Peggy's shoulder, and his long grey hair was wisping into her face. "I guess we'll have to have you over soon. So you can check out Tony's pad."

Tony shook his head. "Hey, no." He smiled at Peggy, then looked apologetically at Brendan. "I, like, totally forgot to tell you –"

He shifted, careful to keep his arm around Peggy, careful not to lose the plastic bag still in his hand; and in a complicated maneuver dug into his back pocket. "I got this. That letter you gave me the other day?"

He held a crumpled envelope up for Brendan and Peggy to see. The return address was from a law firm in Century City. "From, like, this attorney. A guy Marty hired?" Tony paused, breathing slightly fast, then went on. "They settled. We settled. Out of court."

Brendan looked at him blankly. "You what?"

"The lawsuit. Our catalog, all those royalties. We're getting a settlement."

"You're kidding!" Peggy turned to stare up at him. "You −"

"Yeah, really." Tony looked at Brendan and shrugged, then grinned. "Amazing, huh?"

Brendan just stared at him. Finally he said, "That's incredible. I mean, that's fantastic. Tony!"

He grabbed him by the front of his leather jacket and pulled him forward, until their heads cracked together. "Ow!" yelped Tony.

"How much, what'd they give you − ?"

"A ton. I mean, there's Dickie's ex, she's got his kids, and the other guys who're left, but −"

Tony looked down at Peggy. "I can definitely get my own place." He started to laugh. "I can get thirteen places −"

"Tony! Omigod, that's incredible, that's just so incredible −"

Peggy hugged him, and Brendan turned away. In the kitchen, Eileen was helping Teri get things out of the refrigerator. Kevin and the twins were lugging shopping bags full of presents from the foyer into the living room. Peter was still standing by the silent television, frowning, his hands at his sides.

"Peter?"

Brendan started towards him, then thought better of it. Peter was being quiet. This was Teri's house. Instead, Brendan turned and walked slowly over to the artificial Christmas tree. It smelled strongly of pine car deodorizer. He reached out to touch one of the plastic ornaments; then craned his neck and squinted, peering into the heart of the tree. There was no magic there, no hand-carved Santas or meticulously hidden lights; only neat rows of microfiber branches like dark-green spokes, rising to a point.

"Some tree," he murmured. Suddenly he felt exhausted. His head ached; he thought of everything that had happened last night, and how he hadn't gotten much sleep. No matter how you factored it all in, he was tired.

And sad. Behind him he could hear the twins giggling, the crumple of paper and Kevin scolding one of them.

"Not yet! And anyhow, those aren't for you, those are for Peter −"

"Peter!" Tony's voice cut through the chatter; as from a great distance Brendan could hear him stomping across the room. "Peter, I almost forgot, I brought you something. Look, Uncle Tony brought you a present …"

Brendan sighed and drew a hand over his eyes. There was a rustling, the girls' voices squealing; then sudden quiet.

"What is it?" said Cara.

Brendan took the end of one of the tree's branches and pinched it. The whole thing started to pitch towards him and he let go, so that it settled softly back in place. He was dimly aware that the room behind him was still silent. Then:

"Tony." Eileen's voice cracked. "What – where'd you get it?"

"I made it."

"You made it?"

"Sure. I mean, yeah …"

At Brendan's feet something crunched. He looked down and saw the corner of a present that he'd stepped on. He closed his eyes, his throat tight. He hadn't gotten Peter anything, anything at all …

"Deh."

One of the girls touched his elbow. He flinched, took a deep breath and tried to compose himself. "Yeah," he whispered hoarsely. "Yes, I'll be right there –"

"Deh …" The touch came again, insistently. "Deh. Sss."

Brendan looked down. A bulbous-faced puppet stared back up at him, black button eyes and enormous nose, little cloth arms capped by hands like crudely sewn mittens. Its face was uneven, bumps and ridges where the papier-mâché had refused to smooth out, spots where the paint had globbed together and dried unevenly.

"Deh," the voice came again. A low voice, hoarse, as the puppet nudged his chest. "Deh –"

It was Peter.

"Deh," he said.

Brendan stared at him, the boy's pale blue eyes gazing at his father from behind the puppet's head, for just a fraction of a second. Then Peter looked away again, back at the puppet in his hand.

"Ssss? Oog buh." The puppet thrust upward into Brendan's face, so close that he could smell it, flour and newsprint, tempera paint. "Deh," the boy said, impatiently. "Oog buh!"

"Peter?" Brendan dropped to his knees, his hands shaking, his head; all of him. He stared past the puppet at the boy who held it. "Peter?"

In the room behind him Eileen gasped. The twins squealed, Kevin made a low sound.

"Peter?" cried Teri. "Did he – ?"

"Peter," said Brendan. "Oh, Peter."

The boy glanced away, smiling faintly, and bopped him with the puppet.

"Oog buh," he said again. "Sss, Deh? Sss?"

"Yes," said Brendan. "Oh yes."

He smiled. Through his tears he saw them all above him, framed by bits of plastic greenery and the flickering outline of the TV screen, Teri and Kevin and Eileen and the twins in their halos of lace, Peggy with her hands pressed against her head and beside her Tony, grinning and nodding, the plastic bag and torn wrapping paper dangling from his fist; and last of all his son, still thrusting the puppet at him and chattering, the sounds so thick they were scarcely words at all but Brendan knew, he could understand, suddenly he could see –

"Sss, Deh? Sss?"

"Oh yes, Peter, that's my boy, oh Peter," Brendan gasped, hugging him and laughing even as he wept and turned to the rest of his family. "I do see it. I see you now. I can – I can see it all."

~ ~ ~ ~ ~ ~

Chip Crockett's Christmas Carol
Author's Afterword

Three ghosts haunt this story. The first, of course, is that of Charles Dickens, whose *A CHRISTMAS CAROL* is one of the ur-texts of my life, both personally and as a writer. Just like Brendan and Tony, I grew up in Yonkers, New York, which during my childhood in the late 1950 and early 1960s seemed a kind of children's paradise: always Christmas and never winter, to paraphrase C.S. Lewis. My father loved (still loves) Alastair Sim's great version of *A CHRISTMAS CAROL:* the movie, screened every year on one of the local TV stations, and later Dickens' book, became part of my literary DNA.

Those same TV stations – WNEW, WPIX – formed their own Edenic suburbs with their afternoon children's hosts. Officer Joe Bolton and the Three Stooges, Captain Jack McCarthy and Popeye, the guy who introduced Diver Dan, Sonny Fox and Wonderama.

And best of all, Sandy Becker. Sandy's kiddie show was on twice daily, morning and afternoon, the missing link between the classic age of screwball comedy and the brave new world that was just coming into its own with *MAD Magazine* and the films of people like Richard Lester and Blake Edwards. Sandy Becker was brilliant and anarchic, sometimes alarming, a child's version of Ernie Kovacs or Sid Caesar; handsome, charming, and intensely human, as when he spoke to millions of children on live TV after President Kennedy's assassination. My brothers and I (my sisters were too young) watched his show religiously every day, and for years I was haunted by the memory of Sandy's version of *A CHRISTMAS CAROL,* with his beautiful, slightly scary handmade puppets filling in for Scrooge and Bob Cratchit and the Ghosts of Christmas Past, Present, and Yet To Come.

When my parents phoned me in 1997 to tell me of Sandy's death, I was so saddened. Shortly afterward, I dreamed of Sandy, a dream I could never recall clearly — but I woke up laughing. and almost immediately sat down and began work on what became *CHIP CROCKETT"S CHRISTMAS CAROL.*

Which brings me to the third ghost, that of Joey Ramone. Joey was still alive when I wrote *CHIP CROCKETT* And while I'll never be sure, I suspect that he and Johnny and DeeDee, growing up in the same NYC nexus as I did, must have watched Sandy Becker. They certainly were part of the Uncle Floyd family – Uncle Floyd was an ironic Newark TV host much influenced by Sandy, and the Ramones performed on his program several times over the years.

I was and am a fairly unrecontructed punk from the old school. The first time I heard the Ramones, I fell on the floor laughing. Here was what I'd been waiting for my whole life, the missing link between three-chord rock and The Three Stooges! I played their first album so loudly in my college dorm room that other students called the police and threw rocks at me.

Those were the days.

I only saw the Ramones perform once, in October 1976, at their first Washington D.C. gig. There was a tiny audience, and what must have been one of the very first mosh pits. One of my friends got the Ramones to sign a napkin for me – I was too shy to approach them, although I certainly could have. A few years ago I finally got the napkin framed. They played for twenty minutes that night, and my ears buzzed for a week afterward. It was an experience so perfect and pure that I never felt the slightest desire to repeat it.

That was when I first started making jokes about the Maronis and Tony Maroni, a sort of cut-rate Joey Ramone. When *CHIP CROCKETT'S CHRISTMAS CAROL* sprang full-blown from my dreaming mind, Tony occupied it front and center. I wrote the story at white heat, putting aside whatever I was supposed to have been writing (the very early stages of *MORTAL LOVE,* probably) until the story was done.

At which point it broke my heart. I loved it, my agent loved it; more than anything, I wanted to see it published as a Christmas book. I'd always wanted to write a Christmas book, an homage to Dickens; and here it was. But publishers passed on it – I'm still not sure why – and it was too long for conventional publication in a magazine. Finally Ellen Datlow ran it as a serial at *SciFiction* in December of 2000. Ellen had also grown up in Yonkers (so did Avram Davidson), and she remembered Sandy Becker with as much love as I did. God bless her, everyone! The story was subsequently published as part of my collection *BIBLIOMANCY,* but I still longed to see it as a stand-alone volume.

Which brings me to the book you're holding now, with Judith Clute's exquisite etchings and Roger Robinson's elegant design. Without their support and encouragement, as well as that of my partner, John Clute, this book wouldn't exist, and – if this doesn't sound too hokey – one of my dreams wouldn't have come true. My gratitude is boundless.

Joey Ramone died in 2001. I cried when I learned of his death. I never knew him, of course, but he seemed to radiate the kind of innate goodness and good will that makes for secular saints, whether they are fictional, like Ebeneezer Scrooge, or real, like Joey Ramone. I think this is why kids love the Ramones – I know mine do – and it's certainly one reason why I do.

As a postscript to all this – after *CHIP CROCKETT'S CHRISTMAS CAROL* was publshed online, I discovered Christopher Gross's great internet homage to Sandy, *www.christophergross.com/becker/becker.html* Through the site, I was able for the first time in over forty years to see images of what had been a treasured childhood memory. I was also able to contact Cherie Becker, Sandy's widow, and had a warm correspondence with her. When *BIBLIOMANCY* came out, I sent her a copy. And a year or two ago she wrote me one winter night to say she had taken the book down from the shelf and reread *CHIP CROCKETT'S CHRISTMAS CAROL*.

This is really a treasure, she said; Sandy would have loved it.

That was one of the best Christmases presents I could ever have received.

Sandy Becker's Christmas Carol aired on Saturday, December 23, 1961, which means that the publication of this book brings full circle something begun when I was four years old. For everyone who made that possible, including the guiding spirits of Charles Dickens and Sandy Becker and Joey Ramone, all my love and thanks.

God help us, every one!

Elizabeth Hand
Tooley Cottage, Maine
March 3, 2006